THE SACRED GIFT OF LIFE

Orthodox Christianity and Bioethics

JOHN BRECK

ST VLADIMIR'S SEMINARY PRESS
CRESTWOOD, NEW YORK 10707
1998

The publication of this book has been underwritten through the generosity of
Brian and Marilyn Gerich.

Library of Congress Cataloging-in-Publication Data

Breck, John, 1939-
    The sacred gift of life: Orthodox Christianity and bioethics / John Breck.
    p.   cm.
    Includes bibliographical references and index.
    ISBN 0-88141-183-3 (alk. paper)
    1. Orthodox Eastern Church—Doctrines. 2. Medical ethics. 3. Sex—Religious
aspects—Orthodox Eastern Church. 4. Bioethics. 5. Life and death, Power over—
Religious aspects—Orthodox Eastern Church. I. Title
BX323.B745   1998
241'.697—dc21   98-49629
                                                     CIP

THE SACRED GIFT OF LIFE

St Vladimir's Seminary Press
575 Scarsdale Rd., Crestwood, NY 10707
1-800-204-2665

ISBN 0-88141-183-3

PRINTED IN THE UNITED STATES OF AMERICA

Contents

For Paul and Michael,
with love.

Preface

The discipline of "bioethics" has developed in response to unprecedented advances made during the past three decades in the area of biomedical technology. Many of those advances have an extraordinary potential for good, from reproductive techniques to overcome infertility, to gene therapy to overcome disease. Nevertheless, much of the new technology has placed us as never before on a dramatic slide down the "slippery slope," from partial-birth abortions to physician-assisted suicide, and from surrogate gestation to the cloning of human embryos. How does Orthodox Christianity view these developments? What criteria should be brought to bear on moral issues faced by priests, pastors, medical professionals and the laity, as they seek to discern the will of God and to preserve basic human values in the face of today's increasing pressures to "do it because it can be done"?

This book focuses on questions such as these from the perspective of Scripture and Orthodox patristic tradition. Beginning with a discussion of present-day bioethical dilemmas, it moves in chapter one to an overview of major theological themes that underlie any Orthodox response to issues involving the creation and termination of human life. The following chapters then take up questions concerning the meaning of sexuality and the morality of various forms of sexual behavior; the question "When does human life begin?"; a moral assessment, from an Orthodox perspective, of procedures such as abortion, *in vitro* fertilization, and genetic engineering (including human cloning); and end-of-life issues, including the meaning of suffering, the morality of euthanasia and physician-assisted suicide, and appropriate care for the terminally ill. The conclusion takes the form of a summary statement that attempts to draw together and evaluate the major conclusions reached in the earlier chapters. Three appendices offer a statement of the traditional Orthodox stance regarding abortion, reflections on the problem of suicide based largely on recent findings in the field of neuropsychology, and pastoral considerations relating to burial and cremation.

1

Portions of this material have been previously published and appear
here in revised form. Sections of chapters 1-4 appeared in articles published by St. *Vladimir's Theological Quarterly* in 1988 and 1989, and in
the volumes *Salvation in Christ* (eds. J. Meyendorff and R. Tobias; Minneapolis: Augsburg Press, 1992) and *Ethical Dilemmas: Crises in Faith and
Modern Medicine* (ed. J. Chirban; New York: University Press of America,
1994); an earlier version of part of chapter 5 was published in the journal
Christian Bioethics 1/3, (1995); and portions of the concluding "Synthesis" were excerpted for publication in *Sourozh: A Journal of Orthodox Life
and Thought* (ed. Bishop Basil of Sergievo) 71, (Feb. 1998), and in *St.
Vladimir's Theological* Quarterly (2/1998).

Throughout these chapters I have wanted to stress above all a fundamental element of Orthodox theology that is increasingly neglected, or
outright rejected, by the secularized, pluralistic society we live in today. It
is the biblical witness to *human life as a sacred gift*, bestowed by God,
which is to be received, cherished and offered back to him as an expression of faithful stewardship. Orthodox anthropology places primary emphasis on the transcendent and infinite value of the human person. This
traditional Christian vision of the person, created in the divine image and
destined for eternal participation in divine life, is what gives ultimate
meaning to our life and our death. It provides the lens through which we
need to examine all bioethical issues, in order to make the many "hard
choices" that arise because of modern biomedical technology.

The Sacred Gift of Life has been written especially for pastors, seminarians
and interested lay persons who are members of the traditional Orthodox
churches or who identify with what we can refer to broadly as Orthodox
Christianity. My primary concern is to reflect the theological and spiritual
"mind" of Orthodox Tradition. Nevertheless, there is nothing either definitive or authoritative about the views set forth here. They are the result of personal reflection, sometimes of mere gropings, grounded as far as possible in
dialogue with other ethicists, both Orthodox and non-Orthodox, as well as
in my own pastoral experience. Although I have made every effort to be
faithful to the Orthodox vision in addressing these topics, others—particularly our bishops and theologians —will have to judge whether on any given
subject I have represented the Church's Tradition faithfully and accurately. In
any case, what follows constitutes a very limited approach and will only

serve its purpose insofar as it helps us toward further reflection and dialogue on these urgent yet awesomely difficult moral issues.

Attempts to express appreciation to all those who have contributed in important ways to a study like this one are both difficult and risky. Inevitably we rely on far more people and published sources than we can possibly acknowledge. Some persons, however, have been of special help to me throughout the writing of this book, and to them I feel a great debt of gratitude. They include His Grace Bishop Nathaniel (Popp), episcopal moderator of the Pastoral Life Ministries Unit and Medical Ethics Commission of the Orthodox Church in America, for his suggestions and warm encouragement; Protopresbyter Thomas Hopko and other cherished colleagues of St. Vladimir's Seminary, together with its patient and unfailingly helpful librarians, Eleana Silk and Karen Jermyn; Therese Domanick, R.N., who has kindly supplied me with countless articles and other relevant information over the years; my friends and fellow ethicists Protopresbyter Stanley Harakas and Professor Vigen Guroian, with whom I have shared and enjoyed numerous conversations, retreats and colloquia; Dr. Leon Sheean of Case Western University School of Medicine, for ongoing information and enlightenment via e-mail; Dr. John Chirban and others who have been active in the efforts of the Orthodox Christian Association of Medicine, Psychology and Religion [OCAMPR] to provide an Orthodox forum for serious ethical reflection throughout the United States; and Protopresbyter Boris Bobrinskoy, Dominique Beaufils, MD, and others who have been instrumental in founding the Paris-based Association Orthodoxe d'Études Bio-éthiques [AOEBE] and for their graciousness in electing me président (à distance).

Most especially I want to thank my former students at St. Vladimir's Theological Seminary (Crestwood, NY) and present students at St. Sergius Theological Institute (Paris, France), whose interests, inquiries, agreements and disagreements on various bioethical issues over the past fifteen years have offered me invaluable insight into some of the most difficult and challenging questions we have to face today as Orthodox Christians. Any and all misinterpretations and other shortcomings of this book are to be laid at my doorstep. If it holds interest and value for some readers, that can be attributed to the many contributions made very generously by these friends, colleagues and seminary students.

The Orthodox service of Holy Matrimony includes a petition that God will grant to the newly united couple "the fruit of the womb as is expedient for them...[and] the enjoyment of the blessing of children." That enjoyment and that blessing have been supplied in full measure by our sons Paul and Michael, and to them I gratefully dedicate this book.

—J. B., 15 July 1998
Feast of St. Vladimir

Introduction

The Sacredness and Sanctity of Human Life

Orthodox Christianity affirms that life is a *gift*, freely bestowed by the God of love. Human life, therefore, is to be received and welcomed

5

with an attitude of joy and thanksgiving. It is to be cherished, preserved and protected as the most sublime expression of God's creative activity. God has brought us "from non-being into being" for more than mere biological existence. He has chosen us for Life, of which the ultimate end is participation in the eternal glory of the Risen Christ, "in the inheritance of the saints in light" (Col 1:12; Eph 1:18).

In the language of the Eastern Church Fathers, this transcendent destiny or *telos* of human existence is expressed as *theosis* or "deification." To the patristic mind, God in his innermost being remains forever transcendent, beyond all we can know or experience. An unbridgeable gulf separates the creature from the Creator, human nature from divine nature. The Orthodox teaching on *theosis* nevertheless affirms that our primal vocation or calling is to *participate* in divine life itself, to "ascend to the house of our God," where we shall enjoy eternal communion with the three Persons of the Holy Trinity. How does Orthodox teaching resolve this tension between the absolute transcendence of God and his accessibility in the life of faith? We can answer the question, briefly and schematically, in the following way.

From the inner mystery of his absolute "otherness," the total inaccessibility of his divine nature or being, God reaches out to the created world and to his human creatures, to save, restore and heal all that is sinful and corrupt. By means of what St. Irenaeus called his "two hands"—the Son and the Spirit—God the Father assumes and embraces human life, filling it with his attributes or "energies" of love, power, justice, goodness and beauty. Thereby he opens the way for our ascension into the realm of his holiness, where those who live and die in Christ join with the saints of all ages, to offer their worship of praise and thanksgiving before the divine glory and majesty. Human life, therefore, finds its ultimate fulfillment beyond death, in the boundless communion of "righteousness, peace and joy in the Holy Spirit" that constitutes the Kingdom of God (Rom 14:17).

Yet the apostle Paul, like the evangelist John and other New Testament authors, speaks of the Kingdom as a reality that is presently accessible to us: the Kingdom is "among" us, "in our midst" or even "within" the depths of our being (this is perhaps the meaning of *entos* in Lk 17:21). Although its fullness can only be known after our physical death, our present life within the Church offers us a very real foretaste of the ineffable joy to come. "Righteousness, peace and joy" are qualities St. Paul believes should characterize the ecclesial community on earth as well as life within the eternal "communion of saints." In the Gospel of John, Jesus speaks to those who are tempted by apostasy: tempted to reject their commitment to him and to lapse back into Judaism. He addresses them in the present tense, in the midst of their immediate, present-day experience: "Truly, truly I say to you, he who hears my word and believes him who sent me *has* eternal life and does not come into judgment, but has passed from death to life" (Jn 5:24). From this perspective the Kingdom of God is not merely the object of our future hope. It is a present reality, inaugurated by baptism and nourished by communion in the Body and Blood of the glorified Lord. It is a "sacramental" reality that radically transforms our understanding of the origin and the ultimate destiny of human existence. Life is now experienced as an ongoing pilgrimage marked by inner struggle. It becomes at its heart an *askesis* or spiritual warfare between, on the one hand, sickness, sin and death, and on the other, wholeness, sanctity, and eternal blessedness. It is this struggle, and its ultimate victory, that constitute the "life in Christ."

Created by God as the most sublime expression of his divine love, we are called to enjoy everlasting communion with him in the fellowship of those who reflect through all eternity his radiant sanctity. Yet like those saints who have gone on before us—the myriad of martyrs, "confessors" and other holy people who have "fought the good fight" and emerged victorious—we can only attain to divine sanctity through the exercise of faithful *stewardship*, offering "ourselves and each other and all our life to Christ our God." Admonishing members of the church in Corinth who were tempted to give in to the lure of fornication, the apostle Paul asks rhetorically, "Do you not know that your body is a temple of the Holy Spirit within you, which you have from God?" Then he makes the startling assertion: "*You are not your own*; you were bought with a price. Therefore glorify God in your body!" (1 Cor 6:19-20). Christian stewardship demands that we "render unto God that which is God's." As the parable of the talents makes clear, stewardship of this kind involves not mere caretaking, but the bearing of fruit: rendering to God what is his, with interest, for the glory of God and the salvation of his world.

Created in the divine image and called to assume the divine "likeness" by becoming "perfect" as our heavenly Father is perfect, Christian believers assume, as an inescapable aspect of their life and calling, an arduous, ascetic struggle against demonic powers of sin, death and corruption. Bearing the cross of Christ daily, they embark on an inward pilgrimage that leads, through continual repentance, from death to life and from "glory to glory," to attain at the end everlasting communion with God. This is their God-given vocation, just as it is their unique source of ultimate meaning and personal value.

It is this sublime vocation that confers upon human existence its *sacredness* or *sanctity*. It alone endows human life with eternal value, from conception, through physical death, to resurrected existence in the Kingdom of God. Accordingly, any reflection on the moral issues that shape and influence human life must presuppose an anthropological perspective, faithful to the Church's Tradition, which acknowledges and honors that sanctity.

To speak of the sanctity or sacredness of human life is also to speak of "personhood." One is truly a person only insofar as one reflects the "being-in-communion" of the three Persons of the Holy Trinity. This is a much misunderstood concept in present-day America, where the "person" has been thoroughly confused with the "individual." Individual characteristics distinguish us from one another, whereas authentic personhood *unites* us in a bond of communion with each other and with God. We can truly claim to be persons only insofar as we embody and communicate to others the beauty, truth and love that unite the three Persons—Father, Son and Spirit—in an eternal tri-unity. The Trinitarian God is thus the model, as well as the source and ultimate end, of all that is authentically *personal* in human experience.

It is as personal beings that we bear the ineradicable *image* of God; in fact, that image determines our personhood. Yet we are fulfilled as persons, and thus actualize within ourselves authentic sanctity, through the arduous work of ongoing repentance and ascetic struggle that leads to personal growth in the divine *likeness*. The "sacredness" of life, in other words, is intrinsic to our very nature; yet it is "actualized," made concrete and effective in daily existence, through our ceaseless effort to affirm and preserve an authentic "sanctity" or holiness of life. Acquisition of sanctity, therefore, requires our active participation, a "synergy" or cooperation with divine grace that involves "putting off the old Adam" and "putting on the new." St. Paul expresses the dynamic quality of this ongoing inner conversion in these terms: "Put off your old nature which belongs to your former manner of life and is corrupt through deceitful lusts, and be renewed in the spirit of your minds, and put on the new nature, created after the likeness of God (*ton kata theon*) in true righteousness and holiness" (Eph 4:22-24, *RSV*).

"Sacredness" and "sanctity" are often used synonymously to speak of the divine origin and purpose of human existence. In light of what we have just stressed, however, it might be preferable to speak of our life as "sacred" by virtue of its created *nature* that embodies and gives expression to the divine "image." The life of every person is "sacred," insofar as it is created by God with the purpose of participating in his own holiness, and possesses the capacity to reflect the presence and glory of God from its depths. (However much that capacity may be diminished by sin and willful rejection of God, Orthodox anthropology affirms that the divine image can be obscured but never eradicated; there is no "total depravity," however morally depraved a given individual may in fact be.) "Sanctity," on the other hand, would refer to the *personal* or "hypostatic" qualities that one attains through ascetic struggle against temptation and sin, as well as through the acquisition of virtue. Sacredness would thus be considered as a function of "nature" and sanctity, as a function of "person."

Christian existence is nevertheless paradoxical: although our personal struggle, our "spiritual warfare," is indispensable and unavoidable in the life of faith, its fruits depend entirely on the grace of God. Orthodoxy insists that a "synergy" between God and his human creatures is essential to the work of sanctification, of attaining "sanctity." Still, sanctity remains a gift, wholly unmerited and wholly unattainable by our own efforts. While the quest for sanctity requires a profound sense of responsibility on our part, the fruit of that quest is produced by God alone. As "it is no longer I who live, but Christ who lives in me" (Gal 2:20), so it is not I who achieve holiness, but rather the "Spirit of holiness" (Rom 1:4) who dwells in me and who alone works out my salvation.

Endowed with "sacredness" from its conception, human life thus finds its ultimate sense, its deeply "spiritual" meaning, in the quest for "sanctity" or holiness. This distinction between sacredness and sanctity is useful, and it conforms to Orthodox anthropology. Modern ethical discourse nevertheless tends to confuse the terms. This is especially evident in the impassioned discussions between those who represent either a "sanctity of life" or a "quality of life" perspective in assessing moral issues.

There has been a tendency in recent years to oppose these two perspectives, setting "sanctity" and "quality" over against each other in an unresolvable tension. Proponents of the "sanctity of life" principle, according to a popular caricature, will want to preserve biological existence at all cost, irrespective of the degree of suffering endured by the person concerned. "Quality of life" proponents, according to the same caricature, strive above all to avoid debilitating pain and suffering. Therefore they favor procedures such as "abortion on demand" and "physician-assisted suicide," to assure control over the "quality" of life experienced by a pregnant woman or a terminally ill patient. In reality, the former position represents a philosophical view known as "vitalism." This is a form of bio-idolatry that by its very nature violates the "sanctity" of life, since God-given life is ultimately fulfilled beyond the limits of biological existence. And insofar as the radical "quality of life" position places the avoidance of mental and physical pain above every other value, it deprives human life of its innate God-given value, purpose and destiny.

We shall return to this issue later on in our discussion of euthanasia and the "quality of life" debate that has received so much attention from ethicists during the last decade. For the present we should stress only this point. Rather than set the "sanctity of life" and the "quality of life" in opposition to each other, we need to see the two as complementary. Christian experience knows that pain and suffering are potentially redemptive. While certain levels of physical or emotional anguish can appear to be "dehumanizing," even those who suffer intractable pain are in the hands of God and can experience his loving care and mercy. It is precisely these gifts of divine love and mercy that assure the true *quality* of human life in any condition or circumstance. Similarly, it is the free gift of God's own holiness that suffuses human life with authentic *sanctity*. If both the sanctity and the quality of human life are seen to derive from divine grace, then the opposition reflected in the current debate is simply false. The true "quality" of personal existence is defined by its attainment of "sanctity"; and authentic "sanctity" derives only from a particular "quality" of life, conferred by knowledge of and participation in the loving mercy of an infinitely compassionate God.

This complementarity between the quality of life and the sanctity of life is possible because human life by its very nature is "sacred." Its origin, purpose and ultimate end are given and determined by God alone. Once again, "sacredness" and "sanctity" need to be distinguished, the former referring to the essential goodness and infinite value of human life created in the divine image, and the latter to the arduous yet blessed struggle of the human person to attain and reflect the divine likeness.

Facing Moral Dilemmas

These introductory remarks are intended to provide us with a framework for considering some of the most difficult ethical questions that we as Christian people have to face today. It has often been pointed out that "Christian ethics" is a Western category. "Eastern" Orthodoxy, on the other hand, traditionally focuses on "moral theology," which is basically traditional ascetic theology: exposition of the interior struggle toward sanctification through the grace and transfiguring power of the indwelling Holy Spirit. The new discipline of Orthodox Christian ethics has come into being to help us as pastors and lay people to deal effectively and faithfully, in the light of authentic "living Tradition," with moral dilemmas raised in modern technological societies. Its aim is above all to develop criteria that will enable us to make good, right, just and appropriate moral choices: choices that conform to the will and purpose of God for ourselves and for the world in which we live.

Today's world is one that poses radically new and extraordinarily difficult ethical dilemmas for all of us. This is particularly true in those areas where modern technology has created problems and possibilities that were never envisioned or addressed by either Scripture or patristic tradition. A few examples will suffice to illustrate the problem.

1. Prodigious developments in the area of *biomedical technology* have raised new questions concerning such matters as procreation and the meaning of "parenting," terminal life-support and euthanasia, together with the burning issue of physician-assisted suicide.

Introduction into this country of the French manufactured RU-486 pill is opening the way to do-it-yourself abortions, and other combinations of available chemicals will soon permit a woman to abort an embryo or fetus in the privacy of her own bathroom. Extra-uterine conception has become routine, and its consequences in the realm of sexuality are dramatic. If the pill separated sex from procreation, *in vitro* fertilization

(IVF) has separated procreation from sex. As a result, the covenantal, unitive value of conjugal relations, as a means of participating in God's own creative activity, has been largely obscured. Marriage is no longer perceived as an eternal bond of mutual faithfulness, responsibility and devotion. Prenuptial contracts, live-in experimentation, and quickie divorce are becoming increasingly the norm. We should hardly be surprised, then, at the exponential growth in ersatz homosexual "marriages," teen-pregnancies with single-parenting, and prime-time sexual exploitation.

Then again, respirators, dialysis machines and other routine instruments of modern medicine pose awesome questions regarding the allocation of limited resources and the selection of those who will receive and those who will be denied treatment. Medical advances such as antibiotics, ventilators and vital organ transplants have made it possible to sustain biological existence almost indefinitely, even when the patient is in a deep coma or "persistent vegetative state" (PVS), conditions that in former generations would have allowed the terminally ill to pass quietly into the hands of God. (Only the oldest of us remember when pneumonia was welcomed as "the dying man's friend.") Each of these areas involves us in ethical dilemmas: "hard choices" made necessary by advances in biomedicine. Consequently, it is incumbent upon us as members of the Body of Christ to *reflect together* with medical professionals and theologians, to determine proper uses and limitations of modern medical technology.

2. A second area of grave ethical concern is that of *genetic engineering*, and particularly the "human genome initiative." The ability to identify and restructure genetic material has created the possibility to manipulate life, both human and otherwise, at its most fundamental level. One frightening consequence of these developments is the inevitable reaction of insurance companies, which will refuse to pay for the support of a child that could have been determined *in utero* to be "genetically defective" and therefore subject to legal abortion.

Another potential danger concerns genetic manipulation in the interests of "eugenics," which seeks genetic improvement of the human species. Negative or therapeutic eugenics promises to prevent or cure diseases that up to now were either severely debilitating or lethal. Positive or "innovational" eugenics, which would enhance positive traits and capacities, proved disastrous in the hands of the Nazis and bodes little better for our own day. Some are asking: If we can create new life forms in agriculture and lower animals, why shouldn't we improve the human stock by increasing intelligence, physical strength, and the like? The dilemma, of course, lies in deciding precisely which characteristics will be deemed appropriate to what the eminent Protestant ethicist Paul Ramsey so aptly described as "fabricated man." In the modern world, where competition is a dominant force in motivating human behavior and one's survival often depends on "one-upmanship" while protecting oneself from physical threat and emotional stress, the criteria for determining which "qualities" should be enhanced in the human species are not likely to be determined by reference to the Ten Commandments or the Sermon on the Mount.

3. The Church is faced with equally grave problems created by the *popular media* and the computer-based explosion of *information*. The so-called "information superhighway" offers a remarkable potential for good, making possible interactive education, jobs done at home rather than at a distant workplace, and access to global interconnected resources. But that same superhighway can lead directly to the undermining of social and spiritual values: for example, TV mind-control, which means conformity to the lowest common denominator; or the power of the media concentrated in too few hands, leading to increasingly "managed" news; or the airing of grievances over the Internet, in violation of the most elementary rights of privacy; or the growing interface between universities, the military and business, resulting in a "military-industrial-academic complex" which is highly detrimental to academic and personal freedom.

A consequence of no little significance of this information explosion is that it focuses all of our attention and resources on *technology as such*, as we see so dramatically today in our secondary schools and universities. Together with "computer centeredness" goes a corresponding decrease in appreciation for philosophy, art and literature. To write a program today is vastly more important, and lucrative, than to write a poem. This is a tragic state of affairs that has seriously diminished our capacity for creativity and has led to a severe spiritual crisis, both individual and collective. Consequently, it needs to be treated as a "bioethical" issue of the first importance.

4. *Modern psychology* has also led to developments which must be judged both good and evil. On the one hand, it has provided us with new and important insight into specific behaviors traditionally attributed to

"the will acting in freedom." For example, we now recognize that alcoholism is a disease rather than the product of a "weak will"; that chronic anger is
often an expression of suppressed rage resulting from childhood abuse; and
that certain forms of criminality, and many cases of suicide, result from imbalances in the brain's neurotransmitters. In addition, insights provided by
the study of psychology have led to the production of drug therapies that
have significantly improved the quality of life for people who suffer from
what in former generations were wholly debilitating mental diseases.

The negative consequences of our fascination with modern psychology
are basically spiritual. By stressing the neuro-chemical correlates of various
antisocial behaviors—from alcoholism, through child abuse, to suicide—psychological explanations of our behavior can very well lead to sheer
relativism and to the rejection of personal responsibility. The primary question provoked by much modern psychology is the one raised many years ago
by Dr. Karl Menninger: "Whatever became of sin?" If Orthodox Christians
are to overcome their traditional suspicion of the science of psychology, it
cannot be at the expense of minimizing our awareness of the power of sin
and the importance of responsibility in our personal and social affairs.

Biomedical Ethics as a Theological Discipline

These are just some of the contemporary issues that have led theologians
and philosophers, as well as members of the medical and legal professions,
to create the field of "bioethics." The term itself is unfortunate, since it is so
easily distinguished and divorced in the popular mind from considerations
developed in the traditional discipline of moral theology: considerations
grounded on the premise that human life is indeed a sacred gift, whose
meaning and end can only be described by the vocabulary of asceticism,
sanctification, illumination, perfection and deification.[1]

In the chapters that follow we focus on a number of specific issues in
human life, from conception to death. One of our primary concerns is

---

1   For a highly perceptive analysis of "bioethics in the ruins," resulting from the "content-less
    moral vision" of so many of its current practitioners, see the introduction of H. Tristram Engel-
    hardt's *The Foundation of Bioethics*, 2nd ed. (New York: Oxford University Press, 1996), pp.
    3-31. This is a valuable contribution by a leading medical ethicist whose entry into the Ortho-
    dox Church led to a thoroughgoing revision of the first edition of this work. It is one of those
    rare books whose endnotes are as informative as the text.

with the discipline of medical ethics and its attempts to address problems that have arisen with recent advances in biomedical technology. Before we turn to those issues, however, it is necessary to indicate why, from an Orthodox point of view, medical ethics needs to be understood and developed as a *theological* discipline.

Generally speaking, "ethics" studies human behavior. It is normally regarded as a *descriptive* science that attempts to discern and analyze the underlying principles and values that govern human conduct. "Moral theology," on the other hand, is usually considered to be *prescriptive*: it proposes the "oughts" that shape the moral life in response to God's commandments and purposes as they are revealed in Scripture and other sources of Holy Tradition. To speak of specifically "Christian" ethics, however, complicates the matter, since it suggests that the purpose of the field is not only to analyze our behavior but to propose a cure for our moral illness, our sin. In common usage, then, Christian ethics and Christian moral theology are virtual equivalents, since the act of making ethical judgments involves by its very nature a striving toward sanctity or holiness.

This is true as well with regard to the relatively new discipline of medical or "biomedical" ethics. The expression could refer simply to the way physicians and other health care specialists treat patients. As such it would either be purely descriptive (analyzing the values, motives and intentions of the medical team); or, if it ventures into the realm of prescription (how the team should behave and why), its moral directives would be governed by the ethicist's own philosophical outlook. "Christian medical ethics," on the other hand, if it is in any sense "orthodox," presupposes a value system grounded in certain truths, or rather in "the Truth" that has revealed itself and continues to reveal itself within the Church, meaning the all-embracing reality of God's presence and purpose within creation.

Orthodox ethics, and particularly medical ethics or bioethics that deals specifically with issues of life and death, is based on at least the following presuppositions:

1) God is absolutely sovereign over every aspect of human existence, from conception to the grave and beyond. This conviction is well expressed in a popular morning prayer, attributed variously to St.Philaret of Moscow (d. 1867) or to spiritual fathers of the Optino Monastery: "Teach me to treat all that comes to me throughout the day with peace of

soul and with firm conviction that thy will governs all... In unforeseen events, let me not forget that all are sent by thee." The divine imperative to "Choose life!" is fulfilled by loving the Lord, obeying his voice and cleaving to him (Dt 30:19); that is, by offering ourselves in total surrender to his sovereign authority and purpose. That authority is precisely what requires Orthodox Christians to reject "abortion on demand," active euthanasia, and any procedure that means taking life (and death) into our own hands.

2) The Holy Trinity—characterized by "community and otherness," by essential unity and personal distinctiveness—should serve as the model or icon of every human relationship. Bound together by our shared humanity in the communion of the ecclesial Body, yet serving one another with differing spiritual gifts, we are called to "responsibility": to *respond* to one another with a self-giving love that reflects the boundless love of the three Persons of the Godhead, shared among themselves and "poured into our hearts by the Holy Spirit" (Rom 5:5).

3) Growth in the moral life is only possible insofar as we experience the "eschatological tension" of eternal life present in our midst. "The hour is coming and now is," when the sole meaning and value of human existence is to "worship the Father in Spirit and truth" (Jn 4:23-24). Christian ethics is essentially "teleological"—in the profoundly biblical sense—with its focus on realizing in the here and now the beauty, truth and perfection of life in the Kingdom of God.

What do these three principles or presuppositions imply with regard to medical ethics? Given the climate in which we live today, the following points stand out.

Health and wholeness have ultimate meaning only within the perspective of God's eternal purpose, the divine economy to be fulfilled at "the second and glorious coming" of Jesus Christ. Medical care, therefore, should serve not only the proximate goal of restoring or improving bodily health; it should strive to provide optimal conditions for the patient's spiritual growth at every stage in the life cycle. This means curing disease; but it also means, particularly in terminal cases, easing pain and distress by any appropriate means in order to allow the patient, through prayer, confession and communion, to surrender him/herself into the hands of God. "Medical heroics" result all too often from the prideful attempt on the part of caregivers to avoid "failure," defined as "losing" the patient to death. Such hubris is responsible for a great deal of unnecessary suffering on the part of patients and their families, and it represents idolatry of the worst sort insofar as the medical team assumes the role of God.

Then again, matters of "informed consent" and "patient's rights" need to be evaluated in the light of the Gospel's teaching on freedom and responsibility. Some Christian ethicists today are suggesting that our unity in the Body of Christ implies a mutual commitment that in certain cases transcends the need for informed consent and transforms the self-centered notion of personal "rights" into the self-giving gesture of care offered to others in love. While this raises the specter of the "slippery slope" towards paternalism in a stark and perhaps dangerous way, thus potentially jeopardizing patient autonomy and the very principle of informed consent, the theological vision behind the suggestion is profoundly "evangelical." It recognizes that from the point of view of health care, ultimate meaning and value in life lie not in the mere preservation of biological existence, but in the total surrender of self to the loving sovereignty of God. And it grounds personal relationships—between doctor and patient as between the medical team and the patient's family—in the ultimate relationship of love, trust and mutual devotion shared by the three Persons of the Holy Trinity.

Modern medical technology has performed wonders for which many of us will be forever grateful. But like any human invention, that technology and its application must be subject to constant reevaluation and judgment in the light of Holy Tradition. To paraphrase a well-worn maxim, "ethics is too important to be left to the ethicists." At its core, Christian ethics is a function of the worshiping, serving Church. This means that the work of doing ethics is a communal, ecclesial work for which each of us is responsible. Just as each Christian is called to be a theologian by offering self and the world to God in prayer, each is called to be an ethicist, a "moral theologian" in the proper sense. Informing ourselves of the issues, discussing them in family, parish and on the job, and taking a stand, both public and personal, that reflects our understanding of the Gospel and of God's imperative in our life, we can faithfully and usefully serve the many dedicated health care professionals who live to serve us, while providing them with the guidance and discernment they seek. Thereby "medical ethics" can be restored to its proper place as a *theological discipline* that serves the glory of Christ and the spiritual health of the members of his Body.[2]

Before we consider specific biomedical issues, it should prove useful to spell out in greater detail the *theological presuppositions* that govern our making of moral decisions. With this in mind, chapter one develops several of those Orthodox dogmatic teachings, noted in this introduction, that bear especially on issues of life and death. Its purpose is to offer the reader a particular perspective, a vision of God's presence and purpose in creation and human existence, that provides the rationale for the specific moral judgments reached in the following chapters. Above all, it aims to ground in Holy Tradition the conviction that human life is indeed a sacred gift: one to be received with profound gratitude and offered back to the Author of Life as a "sacrifice of praise."

2   Edward B. Andersen, M.D., raises in a perceptive and provocative way the very question, "Is There an 'Orthodox Medical Ethic'?", *Epiphany Journal* 12/3 (spring 1992), 13-17. He answers the question with a qualified negative, pointing out quite rightly that the Church has never proposed "an overarching system of medical ethics." In a few deft strokes he then offers opinions on a variety of bioethical issues including abortion, reproductive technologies, contraception, organ transplants, sexuality, and euthanasia. In so doing, he is obeying an intuition common to those Orthodox who are interested in ethical issues and feel called to express their views to others: to interpret, insofar as possible, the theological (ascetic, mystical, liturgical) tradition of the Church, in an effort to guide the moral conscience of the faithful. As he well recognizes, such guidance (including that offered in this book) needs to be constantly submitted to the "mind of the Church," beginning with the judgment of our bishops and qualified theologians. If there is indeed "an Orthodox medical ethic," its content can only be provided by Holy Scripture, together with the sacramental and liturgical experience of the believing community: provided, that is, by God himself. Consequently, although it may reach some of the same conclusions as found in a system of religious or secular "ethics," the ethics of Orthodox Christianity is grounded in a very different presupposition. In Dr. Andersen's words, "the answers to the medical ethical problems that each Orthodox Christian may encounter in his lifetime will best be answered in the courses of his own spiritual labors."

1

The Theological Foundation of Orthodox Christian Ethics

*"Everything subsists by the will
of the Father, comes into being
through the action of the Son,
and reaches its perfection through
the action of the Holy Spirit... The
number three therefore comes to
mind: the Lord who commands,
the Word who creates, the Breath
who confirms. And what can it
mean to confirm, if not to make
perfect in holiness?"*

—St. Basil the Great

*"[The] divine beauty is reflected in
and through all the various things
that the Creator has formed, but it
shines out preeminently from God's
living icon, the human person."*

—Bp. Kallistos Ware

The Moral Life: "Freedom in the Spirit"

God is the alpha and the omega of human life, the creator, redeemer and ultimate fulfillment of every personal existence. Every man and woman is created according to God's own "image" and "likeness" (Gen 1:26-27). Everyone, without exception, possesses the capacity for virtue, holiness, and ultimately *theosis* or "deification": a full and eternal participation in the divine energies or attributes. This is why Christian tradition stresses so emphatically that human life is sacred. This sacredness, once again, originates with God and is accorded purely as an expression of his love. As such, it is wholly derivative. It is a gift: the gift of God's own life and holiness, bestowed upon us

19

independently of any merit, value or achievement of our own. Apart from this gift, life is meaningless, absurd. It is the cursed state of consciousness without conscience, the awareness and experience of evil, suffering and death, with no capacity to understand or to hope.

Acknowledgment and celebration of God as Lord of our life is the foundation on which we build both the understanding and the hope that lead to virtuous or holy Christian behavior, behavior that conforms to the divine will and manifests divine attributes of beauty, truth, justice and love. Confession of God as sovereign Lord and celebration of that conviction in the worship of the Church is therefore the ground of Christian moral theology.

The *problematic* of moral theology, which produces ethical dilemmas in our daily life, is caused by the conflict between our confession of faith and our "passions," the "impulses of the flesh" that lead to sin and separation from God, who is the only source and fulfillment of human existence. Were it not for this conflict, we would by our very nature know the will of God and conform our attitudes and actions to it. There would be no "ethical dilemmas," no "hard choices" in the moral life. Sin, however—which is human autonomy (*autexousia*) run amok—has corrupted our created nature, the "natural" capacity of every person, by virtue of the divine image within, to know, to love, and consequently to obey God above all. "All have sinned and fall short of the glory of God," St. Paul declares (Rom 3:23). Each of us suffers the debilitating effects of our own sinfulness. As a result, even the most devoted and most saintly among us have to deal with the conflict between faith and passions.

Attainment of the virtues of goodness, love, mercy and justice requires discipline—an *askesis* or struggle—of continued repentance. The "return" implied by *metanoia* or repentance, however, cannot be to ourselves, to our own fallen and corrupted nature. It can only be a return to God. Christian ethical behavior cannot be predicated on human ideals or goals. Its conditions and aims, like human life itself, must be grounded in God, who alone determines what is good, right and just, and who reveals that determination to us through Scripture, prayer and other aspects of ecclesial experience.

Christian ethics, therefore, must be based on *revelation*. If we are to engage in the struggle to conform our will, desires and actions to the will of God, we need to know what the divine will entails. How, in fact, does God want us to behave? If we look for the answer in the Scriptures and the teaching tradition of the Church, certain indications emerge. One of them stands out above all. "God is love," the apostle John tells us (1 Jn 4:7-12). Accordingly, our attitudes and actions will properly reflect the self-giving, sacrificial love that shone forth especially in the crucifixion of Jesus Christ, the Father's beloved Son.

This revealed love is essentially *trinitarian*, a communion of mutual devotion and self-giving shared equally among the three divine Persons. As such, it is always "other directed"; it consists in a gift of the self, offered freely and joyfully to the other and for the sake of the other. Our human response to that love is also communal. Knowing ourselves to be the objects of God's deep and tender affection, we in turn offer our love to him, through our prayer and our faithfulness to his commandments. At the same time, we reach out in love to the other—to every "other" who, like ourselves, bears in the recesses of the soul the image of divine beauty and life. There is no limit and no qualification to such love. It is to be extended equally and fully to friend and enemy, to Orthodox and non-Orthodox, irrespective of their ethnic identity, social class, race, religion, or gender. God has revealed his love to us in boundless measure; and that love bestows on every human being an infinite worth and dignity. Every "other," therefore, is worthy of our love, indeed requires our love. In the simple but profound words of Olivier Clément, "Tout homme a droit à une compassion infinie." "Every person is worthy of infinite compassion."[1]

This conviction has led Orthodox moral theologians to develop a "love-ethic," as distinct from a narrowly defined ethic of "virtue" or of "natural law."[2] The three, of course, are not mutually exclusive. Orthodox ethics may stress the importance of reflecting divine love through human deeds, but the motivation behind such "works of love" will be the quest for virtue, and its content and application will be specified by God's own "law" revealed in the created order. Orthodox teaching, however, holds that there is no radical distinction between "general" and "special" revela-

---

1   Concluding remarks in a colloquium on bioethics, held at the St. Sergius Theological Institute, Paris, France, 8 May 1997.
2   Vigen Guroian has developed this theme in the first two chapters of *Incarnate Love: Essays in Orthodox Ethics* (Notre Dame, IN: University of Notre Dame Press, 1988), 13-48.

tion, between "natural law" and "the law of Christ" (Gal 6:2). To discern the divine will, we need to draw upon the full range, the depths and riches, of all sources of revelation within the Church: Scripture; the doctrinal, ascetic and mystical writings of the holy fathers and mothers; the Church's liturgy and traditions governing personal worship (for example, "hesychasm" or prayer of the heart); canon law; iconography and other graphic representations of the faith, such as church architecture; and hagiography or the lives and teachings of the saints. Each of these revelatory sources is needed. This is because Jesus Christ, the image or "icon" of God and the reflection of his glory (Col 1:15; Heb 1:3), reveals the "face" of the Father—the divine beauty and the divine will—not only during his incarnate earthly life and not only in the canonical Scriptures, but as the risen and glorified Lord who is present and acting in the whole of the Church's experience through the indwelling Holy Spirit.

Yet as true as this is, revelation of the Father's will in and through the Son and the Spirit is rarely specific with regard to particular actions that must be taken in concrete situations. Especially in this age of awesome advances in biomedical technology, we often face decisions for which there seem to be no reliable guidelines in the sources of revelation, including the Holy Scriptures. The Ten Commandments (Ex 20, Dt 5), the Beatitudes (Mt 5, Lk 6), and similar codes of law (cf. Eph 5, Col 3, 1 Pet 2), together with specific teachings of Jesus, Paul and other apostolic writers (e.g. on marriage and divorce, Mt 19:3-12; 1 Cor 7:10-16; or on resurrection and judgment, Mt 25:31-46; Jn 5:19-29; 1 Cor 15:34-58), provide us with an invaluable if limited number of guidelines for making ethical decisions. They forbid or proscribe certain activities (such as idolatry, murder, theft, adultery) and command or prescribe others (such as purity of heart, reconciliation, works of love, evangelization), sometimes with remarkable specificity: "Whoever divorces his wife except for unchastity, and marries another commits adultery" (Mt 19:9); "Do you not know that whoever is united to a prostitute becomes one body with her?" (1 Cor 6:16); "Do not adorn yourselves outwardly by braiding your hair" (1 Pet 3:3).

In our present day and age, as we noted in the Introduction, there arise major ethical issues about which the Bible and Church tradition appear to be silent: defense policy in an age of nuclear weapons and state-sponsored terrorism, contraception and *in vitro* fertilization, physician-assisted suicide by the terminally ill, and hosts of others. Therefore the question naturally arises as to the *relevance* of the biblical witness. How useful can the Bible be for shaping morality if so many of today's critical ethical issues are not even mentioned in it?

Yet to raise the matter this way is to pose what is basically a false question. The value of Scripture and of all Christian tradition for shaping morality does not lie finally in the various rules and regulations it may prescribe. Christos Yannaras is right when he declares, "If we accept morality simply as man's conformity to an authoritative or conventional code of law, then ethics becomes man's alibi for his existential problem."[3] That existential problem, which touches each of us, concerns ultimately our eternal salvation rather than our conformity to an external code that would govern our behavior. The final goal of Christian morality is not obedience, not even "perfection" defined as faithful imitation of the divine attributes of goodness and love. Its true goal is *life*: eternal, blessed and joyful sharing in the life of the triune God.

Morality relates to our personal destiny as bearers of the divine image who are called, in communion with one another, to attain and to manifest the divine likeness. This implies that morality is essentially communal, ecclesial. There is no "private morality," since the very purpose of our life is to embrace others with the saving, healing power of divine love. The value of Scripture for the moral life lies not so much in the rules it prescribes as the *ethos* it creates within the community of faith. That ethos (from which the word "ethics" is derived) may be described as an ethos of the Spirit, rooted in God's saving act in Christ and nourished by the liturgical-sacramental life of the Church. It is above all an ethos of existential *freedom*, which allows the human person to realize the purpose of life or to reject it, to respond to God and others in sacrificial love or to plunge oneself into the hell that Sartre mordantly characterized as "other people."

From this perspective, morality can be defined as *life lived out in the freedom of the Spirit*. This said, however, it remains true that we need directives in the moral life: clear indications as to what God would have us do in a given situation. Christian existence constantly involves us in a

3   *The Freedom of Morality* (Crestwood, NY: St Vladimir's Seminary Press, 1984), 15.

twofold struggle: on the one hand to *discern* the divine will, and on the other to *conform* our own will and behavior to it. A certain "deontological" or rules-oriented approach to moral judgments is needed if we are to undertake that struggle with any degree of success. Although Scripture and its interpretation throughout the history of the Church will not provide us with explicit answers to many of the ethical dilemmas we face today, it does inform, shape and sustain the Christian ethos in and through which such answers can be found. Within Orthodoxy, this means acquiring a scriptural and patristic "mind," an enlightened perception of certain basic truths that must undergird all appropriate ethical judgments. Those truths concern God, ourselves, and our personal and common destiny. They constitute the vital threads from which the fabric of the Christian moral life is woven.

If there is presently such a great deal of confusion regarding ethical decision-making, it is not only because of the newness and complexity of the issues we have to contend with. It is primarily because *the discipline of ethics has been severed from its theological roots.* If it is to constitute a genuine "moral theology," ethical reflection must proceed from and express the faith of the Church. It must begin and end with the conviction that Jesus Christ alone is the Way, the Truth and the Life, the ground and end of every ethical action, however specific or however trivial it may seem. Ethics is applied theology, theology in action. As such, it finds its most basic and most eloquent summary statement in the familiar liturgical exhortation that concludes many Orthodox litanies: "Let us commend ourselves and each other, and all our life, to Christ our God!"

Before we turn to specific moral issues, we would do well to review some of the fundamental elements of Christian faith that undergird all genuine moral reflection. The remainder of this chapter focuses on certain doctrines or teachings of the Church that basically define Orthodox Christianity: teachings on God as Trinity, on the human person as bearer of the divine image, on the saving work of God in Christ, and on *theosis* or deification as the ultimate goal of human existence. Finally we shall consider the matter of *discernment* in the moral life, and the work of the Holy Spirit in operating that discernment within the human conscience.

By proceeding this way, we should be able to indicate just how biblical and patristic tradition can speak directly and forcefully to the moral issues that appear so troublesome today. The primary question to keep in mind is this: How can abstract theological principles be usefully applied in specific "ethical moments," especially when life and death decisions need to be made? How, in other words, can the principles of our faith help us to discern God's will in concrete situations, and to take actions that conform to that will, for our own well-being and the well-being of those for whom we are responsible?

God as Trinity

The Eastern Church Fathers begin and end their theological reflection with *revelation*: self-disclosure of the divine life and purpose. God reveals himself in the natural order (Rom 1:20), but only as the sovereign Creator, Lord and Judge. Knowledge of God as Savior and Redeemer, who communicates to us the depths of his love and enables us to participate in his divine life, is acquired by the special revelation that finds expression in Scripture, in the doctrinal affirmations of the Ecumenical Councils, and in the experience of the worshiping Church. These complementary elements make up what we call Holy Tradition, which conveys knowledge of God for the salvation of humankind.

All revelation is ultimately soteriological. It is granted, as the Eucharistic Liturgy declares, "for the life of the world and its salvation." To the Greek Fathers, however, this does not mean that we know God only in his acts or saving work. We also have knowledge, limited as it is, of God's inner life and being. Accordingly, they distinguish between *theologia* and *economia*, the former referring to relations within the Godhead, and the latter to God's saving work within creation. True "theology" thus concerns what may be called the "immanent Trinity," whereas the work of salvation is an expression of the "economic Trinity," God *ad extra*. The distinction is somewhat artificial, but it is useful insofar as it allows us to affirm that our knowledge of God is not limited to his "mighty acts" within history but includes as well a perception or vision of God as he is *within himself,* apart from his relationship to creation.

The content of this revealed knowledge of God is most adequately expressed in the language of the first two Ecumenical Councils as the union of three divine Persons (*hypostaseis*) in one divine Nature or Essence (*ou-*

sia). According to the theological synthesis produced by the fourth century Cappadocian Fathers (Basil the Great, Gregory of Nazianzen and
Gregory of Nyssa), the three hypostases are finally distinguishable only in
terms of their *origin*: the Father is eternally "unbegotten," the Son is eternally "begotten" of the Father, and the Spirit eternally "proceeds" from
the Father. Consubstantial (*homoousios*, "of one [divine] nature") and
without beginning, the three share not only a common essence or nature,
but also a common will and a common energy or activity.

In human experience, the divine will is expressed as the "economy,"
the operation or action of God for the salvation of humankind and the
cosmos as a whole. Utterly unknowable in his divine essence, God reveals
himself and effects his will through the divine hypostases or Persons. Byzantine theology describes this "economy" in terms of a "pneumatic christology." It stresses the absolute unity-without-confusion of the concerted
operation of the Son and the Spirit in leading the faithful into knowledge
of and union with the Father. Revelation and saving grace proceed from
the Father, through the Son, and are manifested and made accessible by
the Holy Spirit within the Church. Pneumatic christology discerns a double movement from the Godhead toward the world. On the one hand,
the faithful experience the presence of the saving power of the Word of
God, and the Word or divine Son subsequently sends the Spirit upon the
believing community (Jn 15:26; 16:7; Acts 2:33). On the other hand, the
Spirit "sends" the Son through the incarnation (Lk 1:35) and manifests
him through the resurrection (Rom 1:4; 1 Tim 3:16, the probable meaning of *edikaiôthê en pneumati*). He then continues to reveal the Son or
eternal Word in the eschatological age of the Church. This "double revelation"—of the Son by the Spirit and the Spirit by the Son—serves to
communicate the unique knowledge of God that Jesus equates with "eternal life" (Jn 17:3).[4]

Salvation consists in "knowledge of God," acquired through revelation.
Such knowledge, pertaining to both the "immanent" and the "economic"

4 For an elaboration of this theme, see J. Breck, "The Lord is the Spirit: an Essay in Christological
   Pneumatology," *The Ecumenical Review* 42/2 (1990), 114-121; and B. Bobrinskoy, "Le repos
   de l'Esprit sur le Fils. Christologie pneumatique chez les Pères cappadociens," in *Communion
   du Saint Esprit* (Bellefontaine, Spiritualité Orientale no. 56), 1992, 51-70; original English
   version: "The Indwelling of the Spirit in Christ. 'Pneumatic Christology' in the Cappadocian
   Fathers," *St. Vladimir's Theological Quarterly* 28/1 (1984), 49-65.

Trinity, derives wholly from God's self-disclosure. It is the Spirit himself who manifests the eternal Word of God and inspires interpretation of the scriptural witness to that Word. It is the Spirit who makes of that Word "the power of God for salvation to everyone who has faith" (Rom 1:16).

The self-revelation that leads to knowledge of God and eternal communion with him is an expression of the common will and action of the three divine hypostases. It is a *personal* revelation, that communicates divine life as an act of self-transcending love. That love unites the three Persons within the Godhead (the Spirit remains a distinct hypostasis and is never reduced to a *nexus amoris* or "bridge of love"). In its inexhaustible depth and intensity, that love overflows and surpasses the "boundless limits" of divine being, in order to embrace, save and transfigure the object of its affection.

What, then, is the object of God's saving love? To the Greek Fathers it is not only humanity—men and women made in the image of God—but creation itself.

To Origen († 254), creation is a function of the divine *nature*. Consequently, creation must be co-eternal with that nature, and hence Origen posits the eternity of the created order. Against this view, St. Athanasius († 373) and the Orthodox consensus hold that creation is *ex nihilo*, being from non-being, accomplished as an expression of the divine *will*. God, as it is sometimes expressed, "runs the awesome risk of positing a nature other than his own." Out of nothingness he "calls all things into being," so that creation has both an origin and a *telos*, a beginning and a fulfillment, when death shall be destroyed, and the Son shall subject himself and the cosmos as a whole (*ta panta*) to the Father, that "God might be all in all" (*panta en pasin*—1 Cor 15:28).

This necessary and radical distinction between divine nature and created nature leads the Fathers, from Athanasius to Gregory Palamas († 1359), to make a further distinction within the Godhead. In order to express the mystery of divine intervention into the created order and still preserve the absolute "otherness" of God, they differentiate between the divine *essence* (*ousia*) and the divine *operations* or *energies* (*energeia*). While God remains wholly unknowable and inaccessible in his essence, he reveals himself and effects his will through his energies—that is, his attributes such as love, mercy, wisdom, power and justice—that are often equated with divine grace. This is not, as has been charged, a gnosticizing theory of emanations.

God is wholly present in the energies, drawing persons and the cosmos into communion with himself. Through the energies he transfigures the cosmos, infusing creation as a whole with holiness or sanctity.

Although the initiative behind that saving activity remains entirely God's own, the objects of that initiative—humanity and the cosmos—are neither passive nor static. By virtue of our created nature we possess an inner, dynamic capacity for *response*, one that involves the entire cosmos of which each of us is a "microcosm." It is this God-given capacity—one of "freedom in responsibility"—that makes it possible and necessary for us to engage in continuing repentance and in ascetic struggle against demonic powers within the created order. But this capacity to respond to God's initiative in "the freedom of the Spirit" also offers us the possibility to attain the self-transcending and transfiguring participation in the divine energies that leads to our "deification."

The Human Person: From Image to Likeness

The human person is the most sublime expression of God's creative activity. Adam and Eve, man and woman, are created according to the "image and likeness of God" (Gen 1:26). God is both the origin and the destiny of created human life. His "image" is realized in human beings not so much through particular attributes or capacities (love, reason, etc.) as through the distinctive *personal* quality that sets humans apart from and above every other corporeal being. The "image of God in man" is identified by many Greek Orthodox theologians today (Yannaras, Zizioulas, Nissiotis, Nellas) with human "personhood": the divinely bestowed capacity for relationship with God, self and others, exercised in freedom and in love. We are truly "persons," therefore, only insofar as we reflect the ultimate personhood of God: the divine Personhood characterized by a total mutuality of love shared among Father, Son and Holy Spirit.[5]

If we are indeed obliged, as Yannaras asserts, to deal above all in the moral life with "the existential adventure of our freedom," this is because

---

5   "The God who is essential to my personhood, without whom I cannot be genuinely human, is a God of mutual love: not a simple monad, not one person loving himself alone, but three persons—Father, Son and Holy Spirit—loving one another in reciprocal relationship." Bp. Kallistos Ware, "The Uniqueness of the Human Person," in *Personhood. Orthodox Christianity and the Connection Between Body, Mind, and Soul.* (Westport, CT & London: Bergin & Garvey, 1996), 3.

the Fall (understood both individually and collectively) forces us into a permanent situation of *choice*. Our free decision to rebel against God's will has exiled us from Paradise. The human creature, according to St. Basil, "is an animal who received the command to become God."[6] By succumbing to temptation, however, we have alienated ourselves from God and betrayed our ultimate vocation. In Christ we have the possibility of progressing "from glory to glory" (2 Cor 3:18) toward that full and perfect communion with divine Life that provides the indispensable foundation for authentic humanity or personhood. Yet the constant need to choose light and truth over darkness and deception engages us in an ongoing inner struggle against demonic temptation and our own tendencies toward auto-idolatry. Genuine asceticism, therefore, is essential for our growth toward salvation.

This means that God's initiative must be met by human *response*, by the exercise of human will—through repentance, prayer and works of love—that enables us, as bearers of the divine image, to progress, through a process of inner purification and sanctification, towards attainment of the divine *likeness*. St. Diodochus of Photiki expresses this love-based ascetic response with his customary eloquence:

> All men are made in God's image; but to be in His likeness is granted only to those who through great love have brought their own freedom into subjection to God. For only when we do not belong to ourselves do we become like Him who through love has reconciled us to Himself.[7]

How are we to understand "original sin" from this perspective? Orthodox theology is not as concerned as Protestant theology tends to be with the tension between freedom and responsibility, free will and determinism. Nevertheless, the Orthodox also reject the scholastic dogma of original sin, particularly as it implies the transmission of the sin and guilt of Adam to succeeding generations, like some genetic defect. In fact the Orthodox are loath to speak at all of "original" sin, unless we understand by that expression that the origin of one's sinfulness lies in oneself: in the corrupted, fallen will that retains the capacity for good (once again, there is no "total depravity") yet freely, and at times inevitably, chooses evil. Romans 7 may

---

6 Quoted by St. Gregory of Nazianzen, 43rd Oration.
7 *Philokalia*, vol. I, ed. by G. E. H. Palmer, Philip Sherrard and Kallistos Ware (London & Boston: Faber and Faber, 1979), 253.

depict "man under the law," but it also speaks poignantly of the struggle of faithful Christians.

Western and Orthodox interpretations of "original sin" are based largely on different interpretations of the familiar passage Romans 5:12, "As sin came into the world through one man and death through sin, so death spread to all." The crucial phrase is the one that follows: *eph' hô pantes hêmarton*. To what does the relative clause *eph' hô* refer? Western scholastic theology renders it "in whom," implying that all are subject to death because all sin *in Adam* (*in quo omnes peccaverunt*, in the Vulgate version). Eastern patristic tradition, followed by most Protestant versions, on the other hand, renders *eph' hô* as "because": all die *because* all commit sin. According to this interpretation, what is "inherited" from Adam is not the stain of guilt in consequence of his sin in Paradise. Rather, if we can speak of "inheritance" at all, it must be seen as the inheritance of *mortality*: "death spread to all *because* all sin." We have willfully corrupted our capacity for self-determination (*autexousia*), and this auto-idolatry has alienated us from God and from communion with divine life. Mortality is the direct result of our disobedience: mortality being understood either as the "natural" consequence of a rupture in communion with the source of life, or as the divinely imposed limit placed upon human temporal existence so that our alienation does not last forever (patristic tradition preserves both views). In the latter case, God is seen not only to judge sin, but to exercise mercy toward the sinner by imposing death as a means for ending our exile and introducing us again into communion with the source of eternal life.

Sin and death, therefore, are viewed as corrupting powers that are mutually causative. While death enters because of sin ("The wages of sin is death," Rom 6:23), death is also the source or cause of sin. The rendering of *eph' hô* by "because" implies that death itself is the origin of sin. *Eph' hô*, according to this understanding, refers to *thanatos* ("because of which," namely death), and therefore the phrase can be understood to mean that we commit sin "because of death." The impetus behind sin, in other words, is the desperate attempt to escape death and consequent meaninglessness. *Death, or the dread of death, thus becomes a powerful motivating force within the moral life.*

Although sin and death are conceived, in St. Paul's vision, as enslaving cosmic powers, they are limited in their capacity to corrupt and to destroy

the human person. Orthodox theology holds that sin can never totally ef-
face the divine image in which we are created. Nor can the human will be
totally corrupted by disobedience and rendered incapable of repentance
and the acquisition of virtues. The human creature is created essentially
"good," as is all of God's handiwork (Ps 8). While the divine image may
be badly tarnished and all but obscured, a dimension of the human
will—what St. Maximus the Confessor († 662) refers to as the "gnomic" as
opposed to the "natural" will—possesses an inviolable capacity for freedom
of choice. Understood as a function of the human *person* rather than of being—a hypostatic rather than a natural property—the gnomic will *can* respond to God's will with faith, love and obedience. Repentance remains an
enduring possibility even in the darkest, most corrupt heart. This is because
sin originates with the personal rather than with the natural dimension of
human existence. Yet it is also through this *personal* aspect of one's life—the
aspect, often identified with the *nous*, that transcends nature and permits
communion with God—that freedom operates to produce the fruits of repentance that open the way toward personal deification.

The human will is in bondage, as both Luther and modern psychology
affirm. But that bondage is relative and limited, as Orthodox anthropology would insist. Maximus' distinction between the "natural will" and the
"gnomic will" is useful, therefore, insofar as it holds in proper tension
both the bondage and the freedom of the human will. By so doing, it can
deal realistically with the antinomy of determinism and free will, while re-
solving the problem of freedom and responsibility. It also safeguards human initiative, the performing of "good works" (Eph 2:10), as an
indispensable element in the "divine-human dialogue."

This means that for Orthodox theology, salvation can be accomplished
only through *synergy*: the co-operation or co-action between God and ourselves that culminates in our participation in his very life. Yet Orthodoxy
(with much Reformed thought) rejects the scholastic distinction between
"operating" and "cooperating" grace. Salvation and deification cannot be
expressed by categories of cause and effect. "Synergy" implies a fundamental (and non-Pelagian) paradox: the initiative rests wholly with God; it
originates and finds its fulfillment only within the life of the Holy Trinity.
This does not mean, however, that God is active while we are passive. An
appropriate human response is necessary in order to receive saving grace.

Askesis, the life of disciplined spiritual struggle, involves action, including repentance, prayer and works of love. The initiative, however, remains in the hands of God, from whom we receive the sanctifying grace that transforms us, as bearers of the divine image, "from one degree of glory to another" (2 Cor 3:17f). We respond to that ineffable outpouring of divine love and grace simply by internalizing it within our personal existence. Yet even this work of "internalization" is accomplished not by ourselves but by the Holy Spirit, who dwells and labors within the "temple of the heart."

To Maximus, however, human initiative goes beyond a strictly personal response. It includes a cosmic aspect as well. The human person is a microcosm, whose vocation is to overcome the various divisions introduced into creation through the Fall: divisions between uncreated and created being, the celestial and terrestrial, intelligible and sensible, Paradise and the world of fallen natural phenomena, even between male and female (cf. Gal 3:28). This awesome task is accomplished through the practice of specific *virtues*. Chastity overcomes sexual division, love overcomes cosmic division, and so forth, until the person "in Christ" exercises his or her priestly function of offering both the self and creation back to God. This process, by which the fundamental divisions are healed, results finally in the deification of the person and the transfiguration of the cosmos.

Yet here as well the initiative and the effective power in this process belong to God alone. For the very virtues that permit those divisions to be healed are bestowed by God in the form of *deifying energies*: energies that are actualized ever again in the experience of the Church through the cosmic dimension of the Liturgy, so appropriately termed "Divine."

The Work of Redemption: "God Was In Christ"

The central dogma of Orthodox life and faith is the proclamation that "the Word became flesh" (Jn 1:14). During the third and fourth centuries of the Christian era, trinitarian theology was worked out on the basis of ecclesial reflection concerning the person of Jesus Christ. While the doctrine of the Trinity may be logically prior to every other, the center or wellspring from which it and all other doctrines flow remains the assumption of human nature by the Logos or eternal Son of God. The touchstone of Orthodoxy, therefore, is its christology.

Arian, Nestorian and Monophysite heresies all managed to distort the scriptural witness to the person of the Son of God by throwing into question either his full humanity or his full divinity. The Chalcedonian definition of 451 strove for balance. It recognized the diversity that exists among New Testament christologies, and it tried to reconcile that diversity in a synthesis that reflected ecclesial experience. If Nicea I (A.D. 325) had proclaimed the Son to be *homoousios* ("of the same nature") with the Father, the ecumenical council of Chalcedon affirmed that through the incarnation the Son fully assumed our human nature in the womb of the Virgin, becoming like us in everything but sin (Heb 4:15, 7:26; 1 Pet 2:22; 1 Jn 3:5). In the one Person of the Logos two "natures" or "essences" (*ousiai*), human and divine, are perfectly united "without confusion, without change, indivisibly and inseparably." Since will is a function of nature (rather than of person), the Sixth Ecumenical Council (Constantinople III, 680-81) affirmed the doctrine of "duotheletism": the presence of two wills in the Person of the incarnate Word. Thereby the humanity of Christ is preserved intact against any "monophysite" tendency to absorb humanity into divinity.

Yet the Chalcedonian definition, together with succeeding clarifications accepted as orthodox, insists that the union of humanity and divinity in the incarnate Logos is "asymmetrical."[8] The Person or Subject who becomes incarnate remains the eternal, divine Son of God, since it is God alone—and not a human person—who can work out our salvation. The eternal Son assumes full humanity and is therefore "consubstantial" with us; his Person or Hypostasis, however, remains that of the divine, preexistent Logos. This stress on the asymmetrical character of Christ's incarnate existence may sound "monophysite," as though his human nature were diminished by or subordinated to his divinity. In fact, the equilibrium expressed by the Nicene Creed—fully God and fully man—is preserved completely. Rather than diminish or limit Christ's assumed humanity, *the incarnation renews and restores human nature to its original perfection.* While remaining the eternal divine Word, the Son of God becomes the

---

8 This point has been elaborated particularly by Fr. John Meyendorff in his study of the development of christology from the fifth century, *Christ in Eastern Christian Thought* (Crestwood, NY: St Vladimir's Seminary Press, 1975), especially chapter 4. See also his *Byzantine Theology. Historical Trends and Doctrinal Themes* (NY: Fordham University Press, 1974), esp. ch. 12.

"Last Adam." Yet he is also the archetypal Adam. As the visible image of the invisible Father (Col 1:15) who "bears the very stamp of the nature [*hypostasis*]" of the Father (Heb 1:3), he serves as the model or divine paradigm of personal human existence, the eternal prototype according to which Adam, or all humanity, is created. Consequently, because he is consubstantial both with the Father and with mankind, he is able to mediate salvation and open the way to the hypostatic—the genuinely *personal*—deification of the believer. In the words of the author of Hebrews, "He had to be made like his brethren in every respect [except for sin, understood as a 'lack' rather than as a positive attribute], so that he might become a merciful and faithful High Priest in the service of God, to make expiation for the sins of the people" (Heb 2:17; 4:15; cf. 1 Jn 2:1-2).

The eminent patristics scholar, Father Georges Florovsky, warned repeatedly of a rebirth of ancient heresies in today's pluralistic world: neo-Arianism, neo-Nestorianism, etc. In fact many christological trends current today are far more removed from the biblical and patristic understanding of the person and work of Jesus Christ than were the teachings of ancient heretics. We live in an age in which the humanity of Jesus has been stressed to the point that his "divinity" appears to many to be a mere metaphor. "Incarnational" theology has been replaced by various theories that hold basically to an "adoptionist" christology: Jesus was "adopted" as Son of God at his baptism (Mk 1:1-15), or "established" as Son of God through his resurrection from the dead (Rom 1:1-4). Theologians, even those who identify themselves with the Church's "catholic" faith, are loath to use metaphysical language to speak of the mystery of "God in Christ" (cf. Col 2:9), preferring to use relational language, convinced that it alone preserves Jesus' full identity with God's human creatures. The consequence of this christological reductionism is in effect to do away with both incarnational and trinitarian theology. Some theologians, it is true, will pay lip-service to trinitarian theology, yet they will deny that any *ontological* relationship exists between the eternal Logos or Word of God, and the man Jesus of Nazareth. Or at best they will represent a sort of Nestorian dualism which holds Jesus to be the "man" (a human creature only) in whom the Word of God came to expression, through Jesus' teaching and preaching.

If the work of redemption is limited to a purely forensic matter, in which the sinner is declared "justified" by faith in Christ's death "for us" on the Cross, then indeed there is no necessity for traditional incarnational or trinitarian theology. If salvation consists merely in our "justification"—being pronounced righteous while we remain under the sway of sin (Luther's *simul iustus et peccator*, cf. Rom 7:24-25)—then there is no need to affirm an ontological identity between the eternal Son of God and the man Jesus. "Faith" in such a case, however, is less in the person of Jesus than in God's action through him. And the focus of that action is less on the resurrection than on the crucifixion. However it may be formulated by any given tradition (or by any individual theologian), God's work of redemption from this perspective is expressed as a *theologia crucis*, a "theology of the Cross." At the same time, those who represent such a view tend to reject Orthodox christology, which they believe takes a non-biblical, strictly metaphysical approach to a doctrinal question that would be better dealt with by using existential rather than ontological categories. Why in fact do the Orthodox continue to insist on the need for an ontological rather than an existential approach to the person of Jesus Christ and his saving work?

The answer, in the briefest terms, lies in the truths expressed by two familiar patristic formulas. The first is the affirmation, found in various forms in the early Fathers, that we usually associate with St. Athanasius: "God became man so that man might become god (or 'divine')."[9] This expresses the fundamental Orthodox conviction that our most basic vocation, our ultimate *raison d'être*, is to become *by grace* what God is in his divine existence. Stated in other terms, the end (*telos*) of human life is *participation* (*koinônia, methexis*) in the very life of God—meaning, however, a participation in the divine "energies," rather than in the utterly transcendent and inaccessible divine "essence" or "nature."

This is the original vocation accorded to Adam, the vocation he and every Adam rejects by his free decision to rebel against the divine will. Adam is "fallen." Human nature is corrupted, subject to the demonic forces of sin and death. Bondage to sin and death thus involves human *nature* and not merely personal relationships or forensic judgments. Fallen human nature must be restored to its original glory, a glory derived from its creation in the image of its Creator. That fallen nature, however,

---

9   "Man" is understood here generically, of course, to include both men and women.

cannot save itself from the powers of sin and death, nor can it accomplish the restoration of the divine image through its own efforts. In a word, *only God can work out our salvation.* Therefore we need a "Redeemer," one who not only identifies with the human condition, but who also assumes, liberates and exalts human nature with himself, through his own victory over the corrupting power of death.

The second patristic formula, then, expressed particularly by St. Gregory of Nazianzen, affirms the need for the Creator to assume the fullness of created human nature, in order to restore that nature to its original meaning, wholeness and beauty: "What is not assumed is not healed, but what is united to God is saved" [Ep 101, *ad Cledonium*].

Alternative theologies of redemption that focus rather upon the forensic category of "justification" or the expiatory character of vicarious sacrifice also have their place within an Orthodox perspective. Byzantine theology accepts the Pauline concept of *dikaiosyne*—understanding it, however, more as divine "righteousness" than as "justification"—as it accepts other New Testament images that speak of the atoning value of Christ's sacrifice ("Lamb of God," "expiation," "ransom," etc.). Yet perhaps it is not too much of an exaggeration to say that the Greek Fathers were more concerned with *who* died on the Cross than with the question of *why* that particular form of death was necessary. This particular sacrificial death effects our salvation precisely because it involves the death of *the Son of God.* Again, ontological (rather than forensic or sacrificial) categories are dominant. Therefore, Orthodoxy expresses its understanding of Christ's redemptive death by the doctrine known as "theopaschism." In the words of St. Cyril of Alexandria († 444), this declares that "the Logos suffered in the flesh." For God to save his human creatures, he had to assume—in the person of the eternal divine Son—the fullness of human nature, then die and rise again *in that nature,* so that by his exaltation through the ascension he might glorify us with himself and make possible our participation in divine life.

"What is not assumed is not saved." That affirmation does not simply concern human nature in the abstract, since a "nature" must be "hypostasized," incarnated, as it were, in a specific personal existence. According to Leontius of Byzantium (6th cent.), Christ "enhypostasizes" human existence in his own divine hypostasis or personal mode of being. Although the Subject of the incarnation remains the eternal Son of God, he assumes a *personal* human life, including susceptibility to temptation and the necessity of death. He who dies on the cross, and descends into the realm of death to raise the dead with himself, is none other than the *God-Man*. While "patripassionism" is rigorously excluded (the Son, and not the Father, suffers and dies), "theopaschism" remains the irreducible foundation of any Orthodox theology of redemption.

If Orthodoxy makes little use of theories of "justification," "satisfaction," "vicarious atonement," and the like, to explain the way by which Christ accomplishes our salvation, it is for at least two reasons.

First, such concepts seem to reflect the Roman Catholic-Protestant dispute over the way the guilt of original sin is removed: either by meritorious works, or by the free gift of God's unmerited grace. As we have seen, this question was not an issue in the development of the Orthodox doctrine of (original) sin.

The second reason, and the most important, is the one we noted earlier: the fact that none of the traditional Western theories of justification, atonement, etc., really necessitates personal *divine* involvement in the death that accomplishes our redemption. If many Western theologians today tend to minimize the divinity of Christ (or at least to neglect the conciliar formulations of christology and trinitarian theology), it seems due to the fact that Western theories of redemption and salvation simply do not require that Jesus Christ be ontologically identified with the Godhead. The Chalcedonian definition must be defended as the cornerstone of Christian faith only if Jesus of Nazareth had to be "God in the flesh": that is, only if *God* had to assume humanity "without change,"[10] die upon the cross, descend into hell to break the bonds of death by his resurrection, and ascend into glory "in the flesh" (St. Ignatius), all in order to accomplish our salvation. Yet this is precisely what Orthodoxy affirms. And this is why it has such difficulty with any other approach that seems to limit salvation to a matter of justification or atonement. That, to the Or-

---

10 "Without change" (*atreptôs*): one of the four defining adverbs of the Chalcedonian definition: Christ is one Person in two Natures which are united "unconfusedly, unchangeably (*atreptôs*), indivisibly, and inseparably." The term is also the crucial adverb of the "Monogenês," the second antiphon of the Byzantine eucharistic liturgy, which affirms, following the Christ-hymn of Phil 2:5-11, that the eternal Son of God "became man and was crucified," yet without surrendering his status as *homoousios* or "equal in nature" with God the Father.

thodox, is merely the beginning of a process of eternal duration. Salvation itself is not the end or *telos* of human existence; it is merely the "negative" aspect that achieves liberation from the consequences of sin and death. The true meaning of God's work in Christ can only be seen in the ongoing process that leads from initial salvation, through sanctification, and on to a "deification by grace" of the human person.

"Theosis" or Deification

Divine participation in human existence opens the way for human participation in the life of God. If the *telos* or ultimate end of our existence were less than a total sharing in triune life—if we were called, for example, to mere "fellowship" with God through justification, or even to eternal enjoyment of the "beatific vision"—then it would have been theoretically possible for God to work out our salvation without resorting to a true incarnation which required that the eternal divine Logos accept death in his assumed humanity. Full ontological participation of God in *human* life is necessary if human persons are to know the same quality and degree of participation in *divine* life.

The Cross of Christ ultimately means *liberation*: freedom from anxiety, sin, death and corruption. Yet as our experience amply confirms, each of these remains a reality in daily life, for the Christian as much as for the non-believer. The liberating power of the crucifixion lies in its *ultimate* victory over those experiences so poignantly depicted in the eschatological imagery of the final chapters of the Book of Revelation. According to that vision, God, dwelling in the midst of his people, "will wipe away every tear from their eyes, and death shall be no more...."

Nevertheless, the death of the Son of God within human history effects a liberating transformation of human life already within the scope of that history. This "existential freedom"—a freedom *in the Spirit*—is what enables us to respond to God's saving grace with faith, obedience and love. This freedom therefore serves as the indispensable ground of our sanctification and of the Christian moral life as a whole.

Like salvation itself, sanctification is a process based upon synergy or divine-human cooperation. Here again the initiative belongs wholly to God. It is the Spirit who communicates truth, who bestows gifts, and who fills our hearts with the Father's love, all within the Body of Christ. It is the Spirit who elicits faith, confers grace, and inspires virtues that take the form of "works of love." Without our active receptivity, however, his work would come to nothing. Divine initiative must be met by a moral response on our part if the work of sanctification is to achieve its intended goal.

To avoid any suggestion of "absorption" into the divinity with a consequent loss of individual personality, Orthodox theology bases its teaching about deification on two complementary themes. First, it holds that in Christ the true humanity, including the unique personal identity, of each human being is preserved and restored to its original fullness and beauty. Second, taking up the distinction between essence and energies that goes back at least to St. Gregory of Nyssa (4th cent.), the Greek patristic tradition affirms that deification is achieved by *grace*, through the sanctifying power of the divine energies. There can never be a "participation in the divine *nature*," if by "nature" we understand not "being" (which is the meaning of 2 Pet 1:4) but the divine *essence*. That essence remains utterly transcendent and inaccessible to any form of created reality. "Deification," therefore, does not suggest that we *become* God, despite the somewhat audacious language used by some of the early patristic writers. It means that by the initiative that belongs to the three divine Persons, the human creature is introduced into a personal relationship of *participation* in the uncreated, divine energies or grace. Thereby the bearer of the divine image becomes "by grace" what God is "by nature."

Is such a teaching grounded in the Holy Scriptures? Or does it represent what Harnack referred to as the "acute Hellenization" of early Christian faith, an unhealthy accommodation to the thought forms of pagan antiquity?

Plato spoke of a transformation of human life through *anamnesis* ("remembering" in the sense of reactualizing) that issues in a certain "likeness" of God, and Gnosticism taught that human divinization results from the acquisition of *gnosis* or esoteric knowledge. Hebrew thought knows nothing of this kind of language, nor of the dualistic ideas that lie behind it. This is due in large measure to the Hebrews' instinctive concern to preserve divine transcendence and to avoid any confusion between created and uncreated reality. It is clear that early Christian patristic writers employed verbs such as *theopoiein* ("to deify"), and later the noun *theôsis* ("deification"), to describe the end of human existence. Did they merely adopt and attempt to christianize language and ideas of purely Hellenistic provenance? Or does their language reflect concepts that are authentically biblical? Just how faithful to the apostolic witness are expressions such as *genetai Theos* ("become God," Theophilus of Antioch, *ad Autolycum* 2:27; cf. Basil the Great, *Treatise on the Holy Spirit* IX.23, *Theon genesthai*), or even the assertions of St. Ignatius of Antioch that we are "God-bearers" (*theophoroi*), called to be "partakers of God" (*Theou metexete, ad Eph.* 9:2; 4:2; cf. *Poly.* 6:1)?

Without going into an exegesis of the texts, we can point to a significant variety of New Testament passages that serve to ground and authenticate the patristic teaching on deification.

The classic passage is 2 Peter 1:4, which affirms that through God's great promises "you may escape from the corruption that is in the world because of passion and become partakers of the divine nature (*genêsthe theias koinônoi physeôs*)." This verse is not without difficulties, as we have seen, because it affirms what Orthodoxy adamantly rejects, namely that our participation is in the very *nature* of God. Theological language, of course, was fluid in the late first and early second century, when this letter was written. We may recall that even in the fourth century St. Cyril of Alexandria could speak of "one nature (*physis*) of God incarnate."

More solid ground is provided by several other New Testament witnesses, from the apostle Paul and the evangelist John, to the author of Hebrews. St. Paul's teaching on filial adoption (Gal 3:26, 4:5; cf. Acts 17:28), for example, together with his blessing that invokes the *koinônia* of the Spirit (2 Cor 13:13-14), lead clearly in the direction of participation in divine life. Still more significant is his language that expresses his "Christ-mysticism": phrases such as *en* and *syn Christô* ("in/with Christ"), and the exclamation, "It is no longer I who live, but Christ who lives in me" (Gal 2:20). St. Paul and St. John both offer a Christian reinterpretation of the *merkabah* tradition from Jewish apocalyptic sources by speaking of a transfiguring and assimilating *vision* of God, when at the Parousia we shall behold Christ and ourselves in our true glory: "When he appears, we shall be like him (*homoioi autô*), for we shall see him as he is" (1 Jn 3:2; cf. 1 Cor 13:12; 2 Cor 3:18; Phil 3:21; and the apocalyptic vision of Rev 22:3-5).

The clearest basis for a doctrine of *theôsis* in the Johannine writings is found in the concept of mutual indwelling expressed by the verb *menein*, "to abide," but also "to indwell." As the Spirit descends upon Christ at his baptism and "indwells" him (Jn 1:32), so that same Spirit indwells the believer (Jn 14:17; 1 Jn 3:24; 4:13). The Johannine concept of "eternal life," accessible already within earthly human existence and brought to fulfillment at the eschaton, the "last day" (Jn 5:21-29), similarly attests to the authentic participation of human in divine existence.

Another key concept in this regard is that of "partaking" or participation, expressed by the verb *metechô* and its cognates, or by the phrase *(syn)koinônos ginomai*. St. Paul accepts his apostolic mission in order that he might partake of the blessings of the Gospel (1 Cor 9:23), referred to also as "the inheritance of the saints in light...[in] the kingdom of [God's] beloved Son" (Col 1:12-14). The author of Hebrews takes this a step further when he speaks of our share in or partaking of "a heavenly call" (3:1), which involves our becoming "partakers" of Christ (3:14) and of the Holy Spirit (6:4). Finally, the apostle Paul again affirms that those who rise in Christ will "put on" God's own incorruptible immortality (1 Cor 15:52-57; cf. 2 Cor 4:16-5:8).

We could cite many other passages, all of which seem to reflect two basic themes: Jesus' own teaching concerning the believer's participation in the Kingdom, manifested in Jesus' person; and the living experience of the Church, in which the Pauline Christ-mysticism culminates in personal transfiguration. To be "in Christ," through baptismal grace to which we respond in faithfulness and love, is already to enjoy a foretaste of the coming, total participation in divine life. Like "eternal life" in the perspective of the Fourth Gospel, deification is a *present* possibility for those who dwell in Christ and the Spirit.

Non-Orthodox exegetes, whose own tradition or personal views exclude the notion of "deification," might well insist that these passages admit of very different interpretations than those given here. It is true that a certain extrapolation is needed to move from the New Testament witness to the patristic teaching on *theôsis*, just as it is to move from the biblical image of God dwelling in "unapproachable light" (1 Tim 6:16) to the Athonite hesychast tradition, according to which that light is beheld by the eyes of the flesh. This kind of extrapolation can finally be made only on the basis of *ecclesial experience*, where the living Word of God is encountered not only through Scripture, but also through liturgical celebration and sacramental grace.

There, in the corporate experience of the Body of Christ, "deification" is the fruit of a ceaseless inner quest that begins in the present age and, in the lives of the saints, achieves its fullness in the Kingdom of God. The driving force behind that pilgrimage is "longing" for God, the ardent desire to "know" God and to dwell forever in joyful communion with him. An Orthodox prayer focuses that longing on the person of the divine Son: "You, O Christ, are the true desire and the ineffable joy of those who love you, and all creation sings your praise forever!"[11] The longing (*erôs*) that motivates the pilgrimage toward deification is ultimately longing for participation in the life of the Holy Trinity. That longing, more intense than any other, enables us to accept the tortuous pathway of ascetic labor that leads from *purification*, through *sanctification*, and on to transfiguring *illumination*. Thereby it also serves as the primary motivation behind the Christian moral life. Ethical behavior is never an end in itself. Its only real and final justification is found in the arduous yet blessed pilgrimage that leads toward eternal communion with the God of love.

The moral life, then, is grounded in the unshakable "hope of glory," which St. Paul describes as "Christ in you" (Col 1:27). It is life assumed as a sacred gift, lived out in the freedom of the Spirit and destined for an eternal sharing in the glory of the exalted Christ: "Where the Spirit of the Lord is, there is freedom. And we all...beholding the face of the Lord, are being changed into his likeness from glory to glory" (2 Cor 3:17-18). From this perspective, the pathway of Christian morality is nothing other and nothing less than the pathway to deification.

The Making of Moral Decisions

To this point we have considered some of the basic elements of Orthodox dogmatic theology that undergird the process of moral decision making. Now we have to turn to the question of how such decisions are actually made. What is the process by which we arrive at moral judgments? How do we make decisions concerning what is good, right, just and fitting behavior in any given concrete situation?

11 First prayer of thanksgiving after Holy Communion.

Orthodox patristic teaching approaches the matter of moral decision making by emphasizing the role of *conscience* and the virtue of *diakrisis* (discernment). Conscience is an innate faculty or capacity for making moral judgments. Orthodox moral theologians will distinguish between a "preceding" conscience and a "succeeding" or "judging" conscience. The preceding conscience is either persuasive or dissuasive.[12] As persuasive, it leads us to perform certain actions that are judged by the faculty of "discernment" to be "good," which by definition means in accordance with the will of God. As dissuasive, the preceding conscience leads us to reject or abstain from those actions, behaviors and attitudes perceived by *diakrisis* to be evil, wrong, unjust or inappropriate. What we call the "preceding" conscience, therefore, is a faculty that exercises discernment prior to the carrying out of any specific moral act and serves to direct our behavior toward accomplishing or refraining from that act. The "succeeding" conscience, on the other hand, follows upon the act and, also by the exercise of discernment, judges that act to have been good or evil, right or wrong, in conformity with God's will or opposed to it.

As the God-given faculty by which we make moral judgments, both prior to and following our actions, the conscience is inherently good. When we speak of having a "bad conscience," we are not passing a value judgment upon the faculty itself. We are speaking rather of what is more appropriately called a "guilty" conscience. By this we mean that the judging conscience has deemed a committed action or pattern of behavior to be basically wrong or evil, and that judgment brings about a sense of pain and anguish perceived as either guilt or shame.

Guilt and shame, we should note, have been popularly distinguished in the following way: I feel guilt when I *make* a mistake; I feel shame when I *am* the mistake. Shame, in other words, is an intensified feeling of guilt transferred from the action as committed, to myself and my own sense of personal worth or value. Put another way, we can say that we feel guilt when we have broken specific rules which we accepted as normative guides of appropriate conduct; whereas shame is guilt heightened and internalized to the point that I condemn myself, rather than my action, as being bad or evil.

12　For a fine discussion of the "preceding conscience" and the process of decision making in general, see Stanley Harakas, *Toward Transfigured Life* (Minneapolis, MN: Light & Life Publishing, 1983), ch. 9.

In the Christian moral life, guilt plays a very positive role in helping us discern whether or not we have been obedient to God's will as expressed through the divine commandments. Shame, on the other hand, can be both positive and negative. If I commit some action which I know violates the will of God as expressed through the commandments, and I have done this intentionally of my own free will, then shame is an appropriate response: my action reflects upon my character and calls into question my faithfulness as a "child of God." All too often, however, shame can result from an unhealthy transference of my value judgments from the act I have committed to myself as a person. In this case, it is not so much the act that is perceived as wrong, as it is myself that I perceive as evil, wicked and basically worthless in the eyes of God, others and myself.

This distinction is an important one in the realm of pastoral care. Priests who hear confessions often fail to perceive that the penitent is unable to admit and to surrender guilt because it has been transformed into shame. We can repent of our guilty actions and attitudes. A very different kind of healing process is usually required for us to rid ourselves of "false guilt" or shame, particularly when it results from our internalizing and making our own the negative judgments others have made about us.[13]

The conscience, then, is inherently good because it reflects the divine image in which we are created. It may be considered a function of our nature, which itself is good, even though, as "fallen," it is subject to the corrupting influence of sin. The conscience, nevertheless, is either *developed* or *undeveloped*, that is, it reflects the divine image with greater or lesser degrees of faithfulness and fullness.

Used in a moral sense, the term "conscience" emerged in Greek philosophy during the first century before Christ. The noun *syneidêsis* is derived from a verb form meaning to have common knowledge or "to know with" someone. This became associated with the idea of bearing witness

---

13 On the matter of shame, and its significance as a motivation of human actions, see esp. John Bradshaw, *Healing the Shame That Binds You* (Deerfield Beach, FL: Health Communications, Inc., 1988); Gershen Kaufman, *Shame: The Power of Caring* (Cambridge, MA: Schenkman Books, Inc., 1985), and esp. his more recent work, *The Psychology of Shame: Theory and Treatment of Shame-Based Syndromes* (2nd ed., NY: Springer Publishing Co., 1996). These are psychological approaches that provide useful information on the mechanism of shame. Their conclusions, however, need to be modified in light of a Christian anthropology that acknowledges the healing power of repentance, confession and continued ascetic discipline.

with, for or about someone, and particularly the self. In Hebrew thought there is no true equivalent of the Greek concept of conscience. This is because the Hebrew mind was not introspective and did not dwell upon the inner mechanism by which we render judgments, particularly concerning our own behavior. Nevertheless, the psalms and the prophets bear eloquent witness to the heightened sense of guilt and the strong awareness of sin characteristic of the Hebrew people.

The oldest witness in Judaism to the formal concept of "conscience" appears in a work of Hellenistic Greek origin, the Wisdom of Solomon (17:11): "For wickedness is a cowardly thing, condemned by its own testimony; distressed by conscience, it has always exaggerated the difficulties" (*RSV*). In this context the conscience appears as a moral voice that signals disobedience with regard to the Mosaic Law. Wickedness pronounces its own condemnation by virtue of the conscience. Significantly, the conscience functions here both as preceding the act and as judging and condemning it once it is committed. Conscience not only declares enacted wickedness to be "cowardly" and "condemned." It also serves as a bulwark against the performance of further wicked deeds.

This same double emphasis occurs in the New Testament. In his letter to the Romans, St. Paul, speaking about the natural law perceived by the Gentiles, declares: "They show that what the law requires is written on their hearts, while their conscience also bears witness and their conflicting thoughts accuse or perhaps excuse them on that day when, according to my gospel, God judges the secrets of men by Christ Jesus" (Rom 2:15-16). This notoriously difficult passage suggests that the conscience is indeed an innate faculty that permits even the Gentiles to know the "natural" law or the will of God, and that same faculty also passes judgment on those acts and attitudes that contravene the divine law. The Gentiles, like the Jews, bear responsibility for their moral actions because they, too, are guided in their behavior by the innate God-given capacity to discern good from evil, right from wrong. As St. Paul's anguished reflection in Romans 7 makes clear, however, conscience does not automatically determine our behavior. Even those who are baptized into the Body of Christ, whose lives are filled with the grace and power of the Holy Spirit, experience an on-going conflict between good and evil, right and wrong, between obedience to the will of God and enslavement to one's own will. Conscience

nonetheless remains as an inner voice of discernment that judges our behavior, and little by little it guides us toward a fuller acquisition of *virtues*:
moral qualities that lead us to reflect in our day to day actions and motives the compassion, love and mercy of God.

A further illustration is provided by chapters 8-10 of 1 Corinthians.
Here conscience functions in such a way as to discern between those who
are "weak" and those who are "strong" in the matter of eating meat that
has been sacrificed to idols. Conscience guides the strong toward edifying
behavior that serves to upbuild the Church as community. And it does so
both by directing behavior away from scandalous actions and by condemning such actions once they have been performed.

Finally, St. Paul also speaks of an aspect of conscience that confirms his
judgment and feelings regarding the destiny of his "kinsmen by race"
(Rom 9:1ff). Here he affirms that his conscience witnesses and confirms
to him (and to others) that the anguish and sorrow he feels over the rejection of Christ by his fellow Jews is authentic and unfeigned. Particularly
significant in this passage is the fact that the apostle's conscience bears its
witness *in the Holy Spirit,* and the truth of that witness is grounded *in the
person of Christ.* As one interpreter has expressed it, conscience is "quick-
ened by the Spirit" and "enlightened by Christ."[14]

Moral discourse of the medieval Western Church (St. Thomas Aquinas and others) refers to conscience as that faculty of the mind by which
one makes moral judgments. It is the capacity by which one recognizes
the duty to perform acts deemed moral or in conformity with the divine
will. This capacity is exercised in light of what Aquinas refers to as *syneidêsis,* meaning "the first principles of moral action." Those principles
must be inculcated through a process of *education.* Although conscience is
God-given, it can nevertheless err. One can "in good conscience" perform
acts that are morally reprehensible, including everything from child abuse
through excessive punishment, to the crime of "ethnic cleansing." The
conscience, therefore, must be educated, and this education is acquired in
large measure through immersing ourselves in the ascetic tradition of the
Church: its life of prayer, sacramental and liturgical celebration, Scripture

---

14 W. D. Davies, art. "Conscience," *Interpreter's Dictionary of the Bible,* vol. I, (NY: Abingdon,
1962), 675.

study, and the like. The education of our conscience also depends upon our acquiring wisdom from those who are more advanced than we are in faith, love and knowledge of God. In our day there is a tragic lack of spiritual elders (such as the 19th cent. Russian *startsi*) whose own lives and experiences have brought them to a height of wisdom that is essential for the perfection of the conscience. For the most part, we have to rely upon the written tradition of the Church: the Scriptures, the liturgy, and hagiography or lives of the saints.

In this respect we have a great deal to learn from the writings of St. Maximus the Confessor, who declares:

> Do not treat the conscience with contempt, for it always advises you to do what is best. It sets before you the will of God and the angels; it frees you from the secret defilements of the heart; and when you depart this life, it grants you the gift of intimacy with God.[15]

St. Maximus depicts conscience as an intimate friend, one who advises us "to do what is best," reveals to us the will of God, and protects and liberates us from the corrupting influence of our own reasonings and our own feelings or "passions." More strikingly still, Maximus depicts the conscience as an advocate, which defends and vindicates us before divine judgment. At the same time, it lays the foundation for our eternal communion with God, insofar as it guides us to become "perfect" as our heavenly Father is perfect.

Elsewhere Maximus speaks of the education of our conscience as accomplished by the acquisition of virtues.

> He who has succeeded in attaining the virtues and is enriched with spiritual knowledge sees things clearly in their true nature. Consequently, he both acts and speaks with regard to all things in a manner which is fitting, and he is never deluded. For according to whether we use things rightly or wrongly we become either good or bad.[16]

This remarkably optimistic assessment of the role of virtues in human life is clearly based on St. Maximus' personal experience. It conforms totally to the fundamental Christian conviction that the conscience is educated and the person becomes "good" precisely by performing good actions. Virtue is acquired through the exercise of virtuous deeds. Al-

---

15 *Philokalia*, vol. II, ed. by G. E. H. Palmer, Philip Sherrard and Kallistos Ware (London: Faber and Faber, 1981), 96, no. 80.

16 *Ibid.*, 63, no. 92.

though the conscience is inherently good, and in a sinless world would lead spontaneously and inevitably to righteous acts, in our fallen world conscience—and with it the supreme virtue of discernment—must be acquired through formative experience.

This, however, raises the question as to just *how* we exercise the discernment that leads to virtuous action. In his discussion on the matter, Fr. Stanley Harakas enumerates several elements that go into the process of making moral decisions.[17] He lays important stress on the resources provided by the Church in the form of Scripture, canons, hierarchical teaching authority, and the liturgy. These provide "laws" or "rules" that serve to reveal God's will and to shape our responses to that will. The deontological language will appear rigid to many in this present day of acute egocentrism, with its self-serving relativism and relentless quest for instant gratification. Nevertheless, his point is well taken. America is a society devoid of an Orthodox ethos. Patterns of behavior tend to be shaped less by religious conviction than by economic forces. Consumerism and competition, considered vices by biblical and patristic tradition, have been elevated to virtues in modern Western culture.[18] As a result, Christian people often find themselves adrift, unable to distinguish between genuine values that reflect God's will and those that derive from social custom or convenience ("Don't we really need a new car?"; "Shouldn't old Aunt Harriet be taken off the respirator?"; "Isn't it better for a child to be raised by a 'same--sex couple' than to live in an orphanage?"). Answers to questions like these can only be formulated appropriately if the moral reflection that leads to them is grounded in the "mind of the Church," the living Tradition that offers clear and authoritative guidelines for Christian behavior.

Yet as Fr. Harakas notes, "rules" can contradict one another, and traditional guidelines may not be adequate to help us make particular decisions, especially in the critical situations dealt with by the field of bioethics. Other criteria are needed. Therefore he considers as well the consequences of our actions (their good or evil results), together with our

---

17 *Toward Transfigured Life*, ch. 9.

18 Apart from the many biblical passages that call for an attitude of stewardship over worldly goods, acknowledging that all is given by God and is to be offered back to God, the homilies of St. John Chrysostom focus repeatedly on the Christian's responsibility to live with a minimum of material goods and to share any excess with the poor. See esp. the collection *St. John Chrysostom On Wealth and Poverty*, (New York: St. Vladimir's Seminary Press, 1984).

intentions, motives, and means. Acknowledging the danger of a "contextual" ethic, he nevertheless gives appropriate consideration to the *situation* in which particular decisions must be made. We shall have occasion further on to stress how important such a consideration is, when we attempt to translate abstract moral principles into specific responses to critical moments in human experience. This does not mean that we substitute relativism for principle. It means that we recognize that *the application of moral absolutes must be made by giving full consideration to the specific context or situation at hand.* Placing a teen-aged accident victim on life-support, for example, would presumably be morally required; but the same cannot be said for an anencephalic newborn.

Yet while consideration must be given to the context or situation in which any moral decision is made, this does not mean that we fall into the kind of "situation ethic," popularized several decades ago by Joseph Fletcher, that still governs a great deal of moral reflection today. In a "situation ethic," the criteria for moral judgments are supplied by the situation itself. "Moral absolutes" simply do not exist. In its extreme form, this is an ethic of sheer relativism, which makes decisions on the basis of purely subjective criteria such as the "quality" of the life in question. Later on we shall return to the relation between "quality of life" and "sanctity of life" judgments, an issue raised briefly in our introduction. For the moment, it is enough to say that moral absolutes of the kind provided by Holy Tradition can and must be translated and applied in ways appropriate to any given situation. In addition to the elements of Tradition mentioned above, are there any other resources provided to us within Christian life that can help us in making critical decisions, both for ourselves and for others in our care?

We are in fact making ethical judgments and acting upon them at virtually every waking moment of our life. The questions, "Do I raid the refrigerator?" or "Do I report to the police the gunshots I just heard coming from next door?" are both moral questions, albeit of differing urgency. They concern not only my behavior, but the *consequences of that behavior* for my own spiritual well-being and that of others. In most cases, a moment's quick reflection—practically an instinctual reflex—leads me to act according to what I feel is best or most appropriate. When conflicts arise between what I *want* and what I know to be rather in accordance with God's will, then my "preceding" conscience comes into play. Whether I opt for the former course or the latter, however, depends on the degree to which I have allowed the moral teachings of the Church to shape my own values and the behavioral responses I make based on those values. Again, this is usually a reasonably clear-cut process. Either I obey the dictates of my conscience, or I do not and lapse, knowingly and intentionally, into sin or disobedience to the divine commandments.

Many of the bioethical issues we are dealing with, however, either admit of no specific resolution that covers all cases, or else they have not been given sufficient consideration by theologians and others in authority within the Church to provide the clear and definitive answers we are looking for. Even the most sincere attempts to analyze an issue in terms of the Church's rules, the motives and means of our actions, and the potential consequences, often leave us with a feeling of helpless frustration. A decision, perhaps a critical life or death decision, must be made; and we lack the resources to *decide* in a way that "feels right" or clearly conforms to what we know to be God's will. Often, in fact, God's will is not at all clear, and the temptation can be simply to throw up our hands in despair.

Orthodox moral theologians (including Fr. Harakas) would point out that the reasoning process behind this frustration can only lead to a dead-end. Whether the decisions we make involve trivial matters in the course of a day's activities, or a life-or-death judgment with little or no time to reflect and seek the advice of others, those decisions can be faithful to the divine purpose only insofar as they are essentially *ecclesial* decisions, made on the basis of a conscience that conforms to *the mind of the Church*.

This means as well that the critical decisions we may be called upon to make are in fact made *within the community of the Church*. This is the community of the living and the dead, the "saints" of all ages, who dwell with us in the universal Body of Christ. On the one hand, we turn to them for counsel, through personal dialogue or through the writings they have left behind. (How many of us today have gained fresh and blessed insight from the retrieved notes of persons like Nicholas Motovilov, or Fr. Alexander Eltchaninov, or St. Silouan of Mount Athos!) On the other hand, *we ask for the prayer of the saints,* their intercession on our behalf, that we might be guided appropriately in our ethical reflection. We ask that we might be led, by the inspirational grace and power of the Holy Spirit, to actions that in fact do correspond to the will of God for ourselves and for all others involved.

This is to say that we never make ethical decisions alone. Our moral judgments, and the actions consequent upon them, are always made within the living Body of the Church. Through our baptism we are incorporated into one another, we become "members one of another" (Rom 12:5). The decisions I make affect and influence the Body as a whole. Just as my own sinfulness impacts upon the entire Church community, as it does on my family and circle of friends, so my ethical decisions and their consequences involve and affect, for good or for ill, the entire "communion of saints." The positive aspect, indeed the marvelous promise of that truth, is that I can depend upon the Body as a whole to assist and guide me in critical decisions, through their love, concern, personal involvement (where appropriate), and above all, through their prayer.

Practically speaking, this means that all of us, whether clergy or laity, need to build up personal "support systems" of professional experts and close friends, who can provide us with counsel and advice as we make critical decisions. It means as well that we *as the Church* need to recognize and accept our responsibility toward one another, to provide the support, guidance and intercession that is required. When death threatens, or severe chronic illness plunges one of us into depression and hopelessness, or a couple in the parish is moving toward divorce, all too often we tend to ignore the problem, merely out of embarrassment or fear. We "don't want to get involved." It is the same self-protective attitude, translated into the parish setting, that makes us recoil on the streets of Manhattan when we see someone lying in a doorway or in the gutter. We simply don't want to get involved... Little wonder, then, that Orthodox moral theologians have felt themselves obliged to develop an ethic founded on the imperative of self-giving and self-sacrificing love.

In the final analysis there is only one reason why Christian people accept the narrow way of the moral life. If we choose self-giving love over hedonism, God over Mammon, it is because we are fundamentally convinced—on the basis of our own experience as well as the witness of others—that God himself is love: that he is indeed the Author and End of our life, who alone endows it with meaning, purpose and value. As such, he is intimately involved in every crisis we encounter and every choice we make. Such crises and choices are part of our daily fare. They cannot be avoided, since to refuse to decide, and therefore to act, is a moral commitment in itself. When it happens, as it often does, that we cannot discern God's will in a given situation, then we need to remember that Satan—the Tempter—works most effectively through our confusion, frustration and despair. When we find ourselves obliged to make a decision that has serious consequences, yet the elements needed to discern God's will and purpose seem to be lacking, then we need to step back and remind ourselves of what is really going on. We need to recover the intuition of the Church's great ascetics, that such critical moments in our life are battlegrounds, arenas of the Spirit, in which the most important decision we can make is to *surrender into the merciful hands of God both ourselves and the other persons involved.*

All this suggests a paradoxical yet inescapable conclusion: whether we can know with certainty that any given moral decision conforms to God's will and represents the "right choice" ultimately does not matter. What does matter is that in our often agonizing moral deliberations (concerning, for example, the proper care for a terminally ill parent or an appropriate response to an addict's destructive behavior) we reject the prideful temptation to seize control ourselves, and instead "commend ourselves and each other, and all our life to Christ our God." This does not mean that we renounce our freedom or abdicate our responsibility. It means that we render to God what is God's, namely the whole of our life, which includes our motives and desires together with our choices and actions. And we do so with the unshakable conviction that in any situation where disinterested love governs our behavior, God can bring out of our errors and poor judgments whatever is needed to fulfill his purpose. The faith of the Church is that God's will governs all things. The essence of the Christian moral life, therefore, consists in surrendering our own will to the will of God, with the fervent prayer that his will be done.

This total act of surrender is needed whether or not we feel confident that we share "the mind of Christ" and can conform our decisions and actions to it. It requires a profound act of faith and a large measure of humility to admit our own limits in making moral choices and to deliver over the decision-making process into the proper hands. It also requires both humility and trust to turn to others and beg them to accompany us in that process with their love and intercession. But this is precisely what is asked of us as members of a Body and members one of another. The first and last decision we need to make, then, is the decision to submit our moral deliberations to him who is the Head of that Body, with the single-minded concern that whatever action we may take in any specific situation will be to his glory and for the salvation of those he has entrusted to our care.

In the following chapters we turn our attention to specific ethical issues, many of which have arisen in the wake of recent developments in the area of biomedical technology. In order to provide a foundation for reflection on the morality of newly developed reproductive procedures, together with the matter of abortion, we begin with a consideration of the nature and meaning of human sexuality. Our concern is to offer a perspective on sexuality that is faithful both to Scripture and to patristic tradition, stressing in particular an aspect that is not only neglected but overtly rejected by prevailing attitudes: namely, that sexual activity has as its only good and appropriate context a consecrated marital union.

This will lead us to an evaluation of the recent debate on "the beginning of human life." Our conclusions concerning this question will significantly shape our attitude toward procedures such as abortion, *in vitro* fertilization, and genetic engineering involving human gametes. The question of the beginning of human life, however, concerns as well the ultimate meaning of personal existence, suffering and death. Consequently, the way we answer the question, "when does human life begin?," will also condition our attitude toward end-of-life issues such as pain management, advance directives and, in general, the care and treatment of patients who are terminally ill.

2

Sexuality, Marriage and Covenant Responsibility

"Husband and wife are one body in the same way as Christ and the Father are one."

"If we regulate our households by seeking the things that please God, we will also be fit to oversee the Church, for indeed the household is a little Church. Therefore it is possible for us to surpass all others in virtue by becoming good husbands and wives."

"Whenever you give your wife advice, always begin by telling her how much you love her."

—St. John Chrysostom

How we assess the morality of abortion, assisted reproduction and the manipulation *in vitro* of human gametes depends on our understanding of the place and purpose of sexuality within human experience. Is the primary aim of sexuality procreation, pleasure, or something still more basic, more profound? Is the desire of a couple to bear children a God-given one, or is it merely the expression of some evolutionary instinct that drives us toward preserving our genetic heritage by reproducing offspring from our own DNA? The way we answer questions such as these will determine whether abortion on demand is an option for us, and to what extent we may turn to reproductive technologies to facilitate conception.

The "Sexual Revolution"

Our understanding of the place and purpose of sexuality has changed so radically in recent times that it should prove useful to begin by evoking something of the sexual mood that prevails in American society at the threshold of this new millennium. While sexual experimentation among teenagers is hardly new, the number of teens who are "sexually active" has increased dramatically in the past three decades. Homosexuality, once a taboo subject that evoked reactions from twisted humor to revulsion, is now a common topic of discussion in the media and in school sex-ed. curricula. Partly because of the AIDS crisis, but also because of the pressure to affirm "gay pride" and concomitant "gay rights," serious scientific study is being devoted to the origins of homosexuality, to determine the relationship between "nature" and "nurture" in the phenomenon itself. Is it a matter of conditioning, susceptible to modification, or is sexual orientation inscribed in our genes, suggesting that it is unalterable? In any case, homosexuality has "come out of the closet," and a certain number of pastors and theologians are among those who defend it as God-given and God-willed, and therefore to be protected along with other legally sanctioned rights and privileges.

To many people, including many Christians, this entire transformation in our country's sexual ethos is to be applauded. They consider sexual liberation to be a vital item on our cultural agenda, analogous to the civil rights movement of the 1960s. Just as the churches of that period took the lead in interracial marches and other demonstrations, some churches today are playing a major role in the movement toward sexual liberalization by producing position papers and more formal declarations that treat extramarital (especially premarital) sexual encounters, together with homosexual relations, as normal and even desirable. Many initiatives of this kind, taken by various leaders within the mainline Protestant churches, express nevertheless what is definitely a minority opinion. This is evident from the general hostility that greeted the recent Lutheran and Presbyterian declarations on human sexuality, both of which were withdrawn under withering criticism.[1]

---

1 The most influential figure behind this revamping of traditional Christian sexual ethics is the Episcopal Bishop John Shelby Spong, *Living in Sin? A Bishop Rethinks Human Sexuality* (San Francisco, CA: Harper & Row, 1988). His blessing of divorce, homosexual liaisons and extra-marital sex in general has provoked a great deal of critical reaction, particularly for the way he exegetes Scripture to support his views. For a much more traditional (biblical and patristic) approach, see the articles on Christian marriage in *Lutheran Forum* (winter 1997) by Ronald Bagnall, Robert Jensen, et al.

How do most Orthodox Christians view this entire development? Clearly, with no little misgiving. To make the point, the following represents what might be considered a typical Orthodox assessment.

Since the early 1970s the United States has declared itself to be a "sexually liberated" society. Gone are the Victorian restraints that to the minds of many people produced both sexual repression and patriarchalist sexism. Things have changed and changed swiftly—and often for the good. Women are receiving more equitable treatment in the workplace, sexual abuse of all kinds is being recognized and condemned, and spouses feel less obliged to remain in what are in effect disastrous marriages. Over the years, however, pastoral experience as well as the newspapers have made it clear that the sexual revolution introduced into American society more confusion than freedom, more license than liberty. Once television came into its own and manufacturers began to appreciate just how powerful a tool sex can be in selling products, the way was open for massive social reeducation concerning sexual values, and this led to a significant restructuring of traditional sexual roles. A major consequence was the breakdown of long-standing taboos regarding pornography, extramarital sex, and "illegitimate" children. From the fairly innocent, flirtatious playfulness that characterized (public) male-female relations during the first half of this century, we have moved on to cyberporn, militant "acting out," and an epidemic of teen-age pregnancies.

In balance, it seems that the "revolution" has not brought much in the way of progress. Instead it has created an atmosphere of sexual fixation and exploitation that imposes a requisite licentiousness—a cheap and seductive sleaziness—on everything in all media. "R" and even some "PG-13" rated films now depict sexual acts with a degree of explicitness that would have had them "X" rated just a few years ago. Scatological and sexually explicit language has become mandatory, even in prime time. Condoms are more available to adolescents today than cigarettes, while educators, counselors and pastors encourage our young people, male and female, not to leave home without one. Much of this perverse indoctrination (that in our schools goes by the euphemism of "sex education") is excused and justified by reference to the AIDS epidemic—without acknowledging that there would be no such epidemic if our society had not come to condone what in former generations was regarded as grossly immoral behavior.

In other words, our threshold of tolerance toward sexual explicitness and exploitation has been lowered dramatically. Yet ironically, at the same time that we encourage sexual saturation of the media and of the culture in general, we are coming to recognize and condemn the horrendous abuse so many women and children have endured, from harassment on the job and "acquaintance rape" to pedophilia. On the one hand, we condemn forms of "acting out" that infringe on people's *rights*; yet on the other hand, we encourage an atmosphere of abuse and exploitation because it serves so well the economic bottom line. But a society that lives with this kind of ambivalence, to the point of moral schizophrenia, simply cannot endure. Over a million and a quarter convenience-abortions each year, the appalling frequency of child sexual abuse, the nearly 50% divorce rate coupled with the generally accepted practice of "living together," homosexual "marriages," and the overly hyped but nevertheless factual breakdown of the modern family as our basic social unit: these are consequences of a sexual revolution gone awry, consequences whose impact on the quality of American life is at least as powerful and detrimental as the continuing spread of AIDS.

The spiritual and psychological toll exacted by this situation is incalculable. Young adolescents are experimenting with sex, often against their desires and better judgment, because "it's cool," it's the thing to do to be accepted by their peers. If films and TV depict couples in bed together on their first date, if canned laughter greets sitcom allusions to genitalia and oral sex, if active homosexuality passes under the approving label "gay" and is accepted as "a viable alternative life style," then it is no wonder that an unbridgeable chasm appears to separate biblical morality from the "do your own thing" ethic of our times. As a result, Christian young people seem as vulnerable as any others to bewilderment, despair and suicide. Their elders, at home and in the Church, too often greet their sexual experimentation either with indifference or with outrage. Neither helps, because neither heals. Both reactions tend to push our children ever farther into patterns of behavior that are inherently destructive, to themselves (promiscuity, STDs) and to others (abortions).

Because of the environment in which they have grown up, these young people tend to dismiss biblical morality, especially as it concerns sexuality, as quaint, outmoded, and repressive. Madison Avenue has taught us that this is a "feel-good" age; the legal profession has convinced us of the primacy of rights over responsibilities; and pop therapy has led us on a relentless ego-trip whose destination is "self-realization," meaning usually the fulfillment of our basest desires. Our god is Mammon, our goal is "the good life," and the motor for achieving it is aggressive competition. We're on a junket rather than a pilgrimage, lusting after instant gratification rather than longing for eternal consolation. In such an atmosphere the biblical imperatives of faithfulness, self-sacrifice and struggle against sin could only sound quaint, irrelevant and intrusive—and nowhere more so than in the realm of sexuality, since "sex" is one of the very few pleasures people can still count on in today's turbulent and apparently meaningless world.

While most Orthodox Christians would not express themselves quite so vehemently, this is more or less the way they experience their own and their children's cultural ethos. It is an analysis accompanied by a feeling of frustration and helplessness. The "moral majority," if there ever was one, seems to have been reduced to a silent minority, whose traditional values have been simply overwhelmed by the bumper sticker ethic, "If it feels good, do it!" Yet despite the odds against receiving a serious hearing, the Orthodox Church continues to affirm its traditional teaching on sexuality. It is a teaching that reflects the conservative values of most "traditional" believers, whatever their confessional affiliation. Orthodoxy, however, grounds its understanding of sexuality in its *particular theological vision,* not in Puritan moralism. This is a crucial point that must be understood if we are to grasp the uniqueness of the Orthodox stance.

Sexuality is not an option in our experience. It is a fundamental "drive" which expresses an elementary need that every person knows: a need for affection, understanding, compassion, tenderness, and love. Sexuality embraces far more than genital activity. It touches the whole person, mind, body and soul. Given by the Creator as a defining mark of our humanness (we shall come back to this point), gender distinction and its sexual expression provide us with a capacity for the deepest, most intimate relationships we can know. When sexuality is cheapened and distorted, those relationships, too, are cheapened and distorted. When self-gratification becomes more important than self-sacrifice out of love and respect for another, the very notion of "relationship"—implying willing mutuality—is severely compromised. As a result of the sexual revolution, we are experiencing the results of this compromise to a degree unprecedented in our history. It is therefore more important than ever that we hear and proclaim the "voice of the Church": the revealed wisdom about who we are and how we are to relate appropriately to one another.

Marriage as Covenant

What, then, does the Orthodox Church teach about human sexuality and its attendant responsibilities? To address the question, we need to rely on both Scripture and patristic teachings, since the two are complementary elements in the complex of Holy Tradition.[2]

Most recent Orthodox studies on the subject of sexuality focus either on Christian marriage and its sacramental character, or on the sensitive issue of gender and its implications for the Church's ordained ministry.[3] Al-

---

2   Orthodoxy has always held Scripture to be the normative, canonical Word of God. It reveres the teachings of the Church Fathers, particularly Greek tradition, as offering the most faithful—and thus the most authoritative—interpretation of Scripture, yet it acknowledges that any of the patristic writers can, and at times does, err. Only the Holy Scriptures are "canonical," admitting of no error in essential doctrinal and moral teachings. This is not to say they are "verbally inerrant," only that they preserve the fullness of revealed Truth and convey that Truth when they are accurately interpreted.

3   On marriage as sacrament, see especially J. Meyendorff, *Marriage: An Orthodox Perspective* (Crestwood, NY: St Vladimir's Seminary Press, 1975); Th. Stylianopoulos, "Toward a Theology of Marriage in the Orthodox Church," *Greek Orthodox Theological Review* (*GOTR*) XXII/3 (1977), 249-283; J. Chirban, ed., *Marriage and the Family* (Brookline, MA: Holy Cross Orthodox Press, 1983); C. Yannaras, *The Freedom of Morality* (Crestwood, NY: St Vladimir's Seminary Press, 1984), 152-172; P. Evdokimov, *The Sacrament of Love* (Crestwood, NY: St Vladimir's Seminary Press, 1985); V. Guroian, *Incarnate Love: Essays in Orthodox Ethics* (Notre Dame, IN: University of Notre-Dame Press, 1987), ch. 4; V. Rossi, "Sanctity, Sexuality and Sacrifice," *Epiphany Journal* 7/2 (1987), 29-34; W.B. Zion, *Erôs and Transformation. Sexuality and Marriage. An Eastern Orthodox Perspective* (NY and London: University Press of America, 1992), esp. chs. 1-6; J. Chryssavgis, *Love, Sexuality, and the Sacrament of Marriage* (Brookline, MA: Holy Cross Orthodox Press, 1996); and S. Harakas, "Dynamic Elements of Marriage in the Orthodox Church," in *Personhood: Orthodox Christianity and the Connection Between Body, Mind, and Soul*, ed. J. Chirban (Westport, CT and London: Bergin & Garvey Publishers, 1996), 121-136. For popular treatments, see D. Constantelos, *Marriage, Sexuality and Celibacy. A Greek Orthodox Perspective* (Minneapolis, MN: Light & Life Publishing, 1975); the issue of *AGAIN* magazine on "Marriage in the Orthodox Church" (Mt. Hermon, CA: Conciliar Press), vol. 13, no. 2 (June 1990); and the marriage preparation guide by Fr. John Mack, *Preserve Them, O Lord* (Ben Lomond, CA: Conciliar Press, 1996). For a good selection of hagiographical material, see David and Mary Ford, *Marriage as a Path to Holiness. Lives of Married Saints* (South Canaan, PA: St. Tikhon's Seminary Press, 1994). Of the many recent studies on the question of gender, see esp. T. Hopko, ed., *Women and the Priesthood* (Crestwood, NY: St Vladimir's Seminary Press, 1983); T. Hopko, "Galatians 3:28: An Orthodox Interpretation," *SVTQ* 35/2-3 (1991), 169-186; articles by S.A. Harvey, T. Hopko, V. Harrison, and K.P. Wesche in the issue "God and Gender," *SVTQ* 37/2-3 (1993); P. Evdokimov, *Woman and the Salvation of the World* (Crestwood, NY: St Vladimir's Seminary Press, 1994); D. C. Ford, *Women and Men in the Early Church: The Full Views of St. John*

though a systematic study of sexuality from an Orthodox perspective is very much needed, my purpose here is rather different and much more modest. I want first to demonstrate the essential goodness of sexuality in human life and relationships, then to draw some conclusions regarding specific sexual practices, both within and outside the context of marriage.

Discussions on sexuality usually focus on the relation between its procreative and "unitive" functions. Is the primary purpose of sexuality to beget children? Or is it to deepen the conjugal bond through mutual nurturing, including the delight of shared sexual experience? The debate is an old one. Rather than enter into it directly, however, I would prefer to look at the matter in a somewhat different way by considering it from the point of view of "covenant responsibility." Only when we come to appreciate that the bond between husband and wife is properly one of *mutual commitment based on a covenant relationship,* can we understand the place within that relationship of procreation and sexual pleasure.

The Covenant which the Lord God seals with Israel engages each party in mutual responsibility and mutual commitment. God commissions the first man and woman to "be fruitful and multiply, and fill the earth and subdue it," thereby granting them dominion over God's own creation. As Psalm 8 indicates, this commission confers both blessing and responsibility, the basic components of "covenant."[4] Throughout Israel's history the Lord establishes various covenantal relationships with Noah, Abraham, Moses and David. Each involves his unconditional commitment to fulfill a promise or an obligation that has enduring value. To Noah, and through him to "every living creature," God promises to preserve creation forever from the waters of primeval chaos (Gen 9:1-17). He promises to give Abraham and his descendants the land of Canaan to be their possession for all time (Gen 15), sealing that promise with the command for circumcision by which Israel demonstrates its own commitment to the covenant relationship. Moses is the recipient of the covenant that God forms with his people at Sinai, one which is to be preserved by means of

---

Chrysostom (So. Canaan, PA: St. Tikhon's Seminary Press, 1996); V. Karras, "Patristic Views on the Ontology of Gender," in *Personhood. Orthodox Christianity and the Connection Between Body, Mind, and Soul,* 113-119; and in the same volume, G. Morelli, "The Biopsychology of Sexuality and Orthodoxy: Some Reflections," 107-112.

4   For a technical discussion of covenants in the ancient Near East, Israel and the early Church, see the article "Covenant" by G.E. Mendenhall and G. A. Herion in *The Anchor Bible Dictionary,* vol. I (New York: Doubleday, 1992), 1179-1202.

appropriate ethical behavior and cultic observance. Through the prophet Nathan the Lord declares regarding David, "I will establish the throne of his kingdom forever; I will be his father, and he shall be my son" (2 Sam 7:13-14). Thereby God promises that from David's lineage there will come forth the savior-king of the elect people. The tragic circumstances surrounding the prophet Hosea in his marriage to the harlot Gomer graphically portray the Lord's faithfulness to these covenant commitments and Israel's betrayal of them. Finally, the Church, as the true "Israel of God" (Gal 6:16) that unites Jew and Gentile into the one Body of Christ, is the inheritor of "a new covenant, not in a written code but in the Spirit" (2 Cor 3:6). This is the new covenant or "new testament" in the blood of Christ, which is poured out for the life of the world.[5] In each case, *the two parties of the covenantal bond commit themselves to unconditional faithfulness toward the fulfillment of a pledge or promise that will last forever.*

Thus the Covenant which the Lord establishes with Israel and with the Church engages each party in mutual responsibility and mutual commitment. If Israel "goes a-whoring" and commits adultery by turning to idols or "other gods," the covenant bond can only be reestablished through the people's repentance and God's forgiveness. If members of Christ's Body turn from their Head in sinful abandon, they too can only be restored by repenting and receiving divine forgiveness. Election involves both God and ourselves in an eternal commitment, one in which God remains unconditionally faithful. While we can betray that commitment through acts of sinful rebellion or wanton negligence, and the covenant bond can be broken, it is nonetheless intended by God to endure into eternity.

Within the Church, the clearest and fullest expression of that covenantal commitment is the sacrament of marriage. (It is, of course, implicit in other sacramental actions, particularly baptism and ordination.) The very purpose of marriage is to provide between two parties—two persons—a bond of covenant responsibility and faithfulness that represents and reactualizes the eternal bond established by God with his chosen people. It is this perspective that allows the apostle to declare that marriage is a "great mystery" which refers to Christ and the Church (Eph

---

5   See Mk 14:24; Mt 26:28; Lk 22:20; and 1 Cor 11:25 for the eucharistic setting of the new covenant, together with Heb 8:6f, 13, 9:15; 12:24; 13:20, where Jesus is depicted as the mediator of a "new" and "eternal" covenant.

5:21-33, the Epistle reading for the Orthodox wedding service). The covenantal bond within which God works out our salvation is in essence a nuptial bond. And conversely, the nuptial relationship achieves its true purpose and attains to its true fullness only insofar as it is based upon an eternal covenantal commitment.

Sexual expression properly belongs only within that covenantal bond. Orthodoxy affirms that the only place "genital sexuality" can be exercised to a good and fitting end is in the context of *a monogamous, heterosexual, blessed, conjugal union.* Each of the adjectives is significant. "Monogamous," because God is a jealous God, his commitment to his people is total and uncompromising; therefore marriage itself requires the exclusive and total commitment of two persons to each other as an iconic reflection of the uniqueness and faithfulness of Christ's commitment to the Church. "Heterosexual," because "he created them male and female" with the express purpose of providing for procreation: continuing his work of creation by joining two lives in a loving embrace that will normally, in the words of the marriage ceremony, produce "the fruit of their bodies, fair children." "Blessed," because from the beginning God blessed man and woman with both the capacity and the calling to "be fruitful and multiply" (Gen 1:28), and he alone, by his blessing, can create life in the womb. And "conjugal," because the union to which God calls man and woman represents a "new creation," making of the two "one flesh" by which to bring forth children, fulfill one another in love, and work out their mutual salvation.

The transfiguring, creative dynamic inherent in such a blessed conjugal union is poignantly captured by St. Andrew of Crete in his penitential canon:

> Marriage is to be honored by all, and husbands and wives must be faithful to each other, for Christ blessed them by his presence at the marriage in Cana. There he ate and changed water into wine, performing this, the first of his miracles, that you, my soul, might likewise be transformed. (Ode 9)

For the soul to be transformed from water into wine, for the human person to become what it was created to be as both the image and the likeness of God, it must preserve in its relation to Christ the same quality of faithfulness that Christ's blessing of marriage makes necessary between husband and wife. Nuptial union, once again, images the union between

Christ and the soul, between Christ and the Church. Therefore nuptial union, with its sexual expression, finds its proper place only within the ecclesial community. Blessed within the Church, it exists to serve the Church by continuing God's creative work through procreation, by imaging the eternal love of God for the Church and through the Church for the world, and by creating a loving witness between spouses that can direct and accompany them both toward eternal life.[6]

That love, however, expressed through the entire spectrum of conjugal experience, is in its purest form self-transcending. Ultimately its purpose is to lead beyond the experience of the flesh and to center wholly on God. Erotic love has as its *telos*, its end and fulfillment, the love of genuine *erôs*. This is a love no less passionate, yet no less self-denying and self-transcending, than human conjugal love at its most pure and most perfect. It is a love that responds to God's prior love (cf. 1 Jn 4:10). It is the deepest movement of the soul, impossible for us to produce or sustain. Rather, it is initiated and maintained by the passionate love of God, acting within the human soul or totality of the human person. "God is love," the apostle declares. The Church Fathers understood this to refer to ontology: to God's very being or nature. From the depths of that boundless love God reaches out to embrace his fallen human creatures, to lift them up and free them from the powers of sin, death and corruption. He fills the soul with his saving, redeeming love, granting it the capacity to love in return. His "erotic" love, his profound desire to be eternally reunited with his human creatures, inspires within the soul an "erotic" response, an intense longing for God that tears express better than words. Embracing all that is signified by the term *agapê* (disinterested, self-giving love), *erôs* is the "unitive love" that draws the soul into an eternal communion with God. Beginning with the passion of desire or fervent longing, it ends in

6 Recent Roman Catholic reflection on this issue has produced statements that are quite compatible with an Orthodox perspective. For example: "Man and woman constitute two modes of realizing, on the part of the human creature, a determined participation in the divine being [ref. 2 Pet 1:4]: They are created in the 'image and likeness of God' and they fully accomplish such vocation not only as single persons, but also as couples, which are communities of love. Oriented to unity and fecundity, the married man and woman participate in the creative love of God, living in communion with him through the other..." Vatican Congregation for Catholic Education, "Educational Guidelines in Human Love" (1 November, 1983), *Origins*, 13, n. 27, 15 December, 1983, 451-53; reprinted in *Medical Ethics: Sources of Catholic Teachings* (2nd. ed.), K. D. O'Rourke and P. Boyle eds. (Washington, DC: Georgetown University Press, 1993), 303.

the blissful joy of "dispassion" (*apatheia*). In this state, the soul finds itself in utter surrender, consumed by the object of its deepest longing.[7]

In the words of St. Maximus the Confessor, "The soul is made perfect when its powers of passion have been completely directed toward God."[8]

This sublime quality of passionate/dispassionate love is the subject of a great deal of ascetic literature destined primarily for those in monastic life. But to a limited extent such love can be known as well by married couples. St. Paul's observation that the married man is "anxious about worldly affairs, how to please his wife," (1 Cor 7:33) is of course true. Those concerns, however, should not preclude a quest for authentic *erôs*, any more than they should preclude prayer or acts of charity. To everyone, celibate or married, God offers the possibility to exercise what is known as the "appetitive aspect of the soul" (*to epithymitikon*) in such a way as to transform passion into dispassion, the erotic into erôs.

It is often said that the monk directs his passionate love directly toward God, whereas the married person expresses love for God through love for the spouse. This is misleading. The passionate love of the married person, no less than the dispassionate love of the monk (for self, others, the creation), is only true to its ultimate purpose, and not idolatrous, when it is directed through created beings toward the Creator. To the extent that its end and fulfillment is God himself, conjugal love, together with its sexual aspect, bears the potential to transcend itself, to transform lust into genuine *erôs*. Insofar as it achieves this transformation—all the while preserving the intimacy and joy of conjugal sexual relations—it makes of the marital union an image of "Christ and the Church." Thereby conjugal love assumes a profoundly ecclesial character that makes of the Christian home what St. John Chrysostom calls "a little church."[9]

This transforming movement is captured by St. Maximus in a remarkable passage:

---

7 Abba Isaiah, with the Eastern ascetic tradition in general, sees passionate and dispassionate love as complementary expressions of the same reality: "Blessed is the soul that has reached such love, for it is dispassionate" (Logos 21, 9; quoted in John Chryssavgis, *Ascent to Heaven. The Theology of the Human Person according to Saint John of the Ladder* [Brookline, MA: Holy Cross Orthodox Press, 1989], 188. See also his *Love, Sexuality and the Sacrament of Marriage* [same, 1996] for an excellent discussion of the place of erôs in conjugal life.

8 O. Clément, *The Roots of Christian Mysticism* (London: New City Press, 1993), 177, no. 98.

9 Homily 20 on Eph 5:22-24; *Nicene and Post Nicene Fathers of the Christian Church*, vol. XIII, (Grand Rapids, MI: Eerdmans Publishing Co., 1976; hereafter *NPNF*), 148.

When a man's intellect is constantly with God, his desire grows beyond all measure into an intense longing for God and his incensiveness [passionate feeling, anger] is completely transformed into divine love. For by continual participation in the divine radiance his intellect becomes totally filled with light; and when it has reintegrated its passible aspect, it redirects this aspect towards God, ...filling it with an incomprehensible and intense longing for Him and with unceasing love, thus drawing it entirely away from worldly things to the divine.[10]

It is well known that Maximus, following St. Gregory of Nyssa, rejects the idea that sexual desire is an element of human nature.[11] Much of what he says suggests that all expressions of human sexuality are to be rejected or at least overcome if the soul is to attain perfection. Although he can declare that sensual desire must be "extinguished,"[12] he means rather that desire is to be detached from what is bodily and transformed into "a noetic yearning for heavenly blessings."[13] As the above passage indicates, human desire (passion) is to be "completely transformed into divine love." This is a common theme in the ascetic writings, stemming as they do from monastic sources. When Maximus thinks of marriage, he means primarily "the marriage of the soul with the Logos," which is the only source of true and lasting pleasure.

Yet even he can affirm that "we are not *commanded* to live as virgins (or) to abstain from marriage."[14] Like evangelical poverty and the call to solitude, chastity (and the monastic vocation as such) is a gift, bestowed by God upon those who can bear it. Nevertheless, with much of the ascetic tradition Maximus considers sexual pleasure to be a cause of sin if not inherently sinful. Consequently, sexuality will be properly directed toward procreation alone and not toward the satisfaction of personal desires, which amount to concupiscence or lust. St. Gregory the Great († 604) is a typical representative of this opinion:

> The married must be admonished to bear in mind that they are united in wedlock for the purpose of procreation, and when they abandon themselves to immoderate intercourse, they transfer the occasion of procreation to the service of

10 *Philokalia*, vol. II, 73, no. 48.
11 "Pleasure and distress, desire and fear, and what follows from them, were not originally created as elements of human nature, for in that case they would form part of the definition of that nature. I follow in this matter St. Gregory of Nyssa, who states that these things were introduced as a result of our fall from perfection, being infiltrated into that part of our nature least endowed with intelligence." *Philokalia*, vol. II, 178, no. 65.
12 "On the Lord's Prayer," *Philokalia*, vol. II, 297.
13 *Philokalia*, vol. II, 179, no. 66.
14 *Philokalia*, vol. II, 108, no. 67.

pleasure. Let them realize that though they do not then pass beyond the bounds of wedlock, yet in wedlock they exceed its rights.[15]

Other Orthodox Fathers, however, together with the Church's marriage service, stress the positive, sacramental character of conjugal love. A friend and correspondent of St. Maximus, the Libyan abbot Thalassius, states: "An all-embracing and intense longing for God binds those who experience it both to God and to one another."[16] Here Thalassius is speaking of Christian love in general rather than of conjugal love as such. The point is, however, that every expression of genuine love is rooted in a deep-seated yearning for union with God: human *erôs* which responds to the divine. In his "Homily XX on Ephesians," St. John Chrysostom declares, "There is no relationship between human beings so close as [the love] of husband and wife, if they are united as they ought to be." He continues, "This love (*erôs*) is deeply planted within our inmost being. Unnoticed by us, it attracts the bodies of men and women to each other, because in the beginning woman came forth from man, and from man and woman other men and women proceed."[17]

Here as elsewhere in Chrysostom's writings, the bodily, physical aspect of conjugal love is acknowledged to be essential and affirmed to be inherently good. Sexuality belongs to the procreative process and is therefore blessed by God—but, once again, only when the desire that motivates it is ultimately directed toward another: toward the spouse and toward God. As the above quotation from St. Thalassius suggests, the love that binds husband and wife in "one flesh" is rooted in and reflective of a more profound, "intense longing for God." Yet this "other-directed" love of husband and wife is merely their human response to God's prior, boundless love, that seeks to embrace in an eternal communion with himself all those who bear his divine image.

In his poem "In Praise of Virginity," St. Gregory of Nazianzen allows a married couple to speak of their vocation in these terms: "United in the flesh, one in the spirit, they urge each other on by the goad of their mutual love. For marriage does not remove from God, but brings all the closer to him, for it is God himself who draws us to it."[18] Conjugal love

---

15 Quoted in J. Chryssavgis, *Love, Sexuality, and the Sacrament of Marriage*, 52.
16 *Philokalia*, vol. II, 307.
17 *On Marriage and Family Life*, (Crestwood, NY: St. Vladimir's Seminary Press, 1986), 43-44.
18 Quoted by Stanley Harakas, "Dynamic Elements of Marriage" (*op. cit.*, 134); translation by Boniface Ramsey, O.P.

thus acquires a sacramental quality, and attains to the perfection for which it was created, by pointing beyond sexual gratification to God, who is the object of the soul's deepest longing. Pleasure and sexual desire are not to be eliminated. They are to be "transferred" or redirected from the self to the other.[19] This is, of course, no easy achievement, especially in a culture where conjugal love has been reduced to "having sex," and conjugal commitment has been replaced by no-fault divorces and prenuptial contracts. It requires that marriage be assumed as a genuine vocation, a "calling" to reproduce within conjugal life the same covenant bond of faithfulness and self-sacrifice that the Lord God concluded with his people Israel and the Son of God sealed with the Church.

Christ's love for the members of his Body has both a sacramental and an eschatological dimension. By his personal self-offering Christ seeks to "present the Church to himself in splendor, without spot or wrinkle" (Eph 5:27), that is, in perfect purity and integrity, cleansed of anything that would separate his Beloved from the eternal love of the Father. This sacred intention serves as a model for conjugal love. For man and woman to become "one flesh" in the sense intended by God, they need to assume toward one another the same kind and quality of faithfulness and self-sacrifice that Christ assumed and continues to assume on behalf of his people. This requires that the couple accept an ongoing, *ascetic struggle*, not to eliminate sexual desire or repress it, but to purify and perfect it by directing it toward the other: to accompany, hear, serve and embrace the other with tenderness and devotion. In this way—being faithful in the "little things" of married life—the couple creates of their union a "mystery" of crucified and saving love, whose ultimate end is mutual participation in the life of God's Kingdom.

From this perspective, the ultimate purpose of the conjugal relationship is neither procreation nor personal fulfillment, but the *working out of the spouses' mutual salvation*. This is an aspect of the covenant bond of marriage that has generally been neglected, even by elements of the patristic tradition. St. John Chrysostom can insist that "marriage is a remedy to eliminate fornication,"[20] and St. John of Damascus, taking up a familiar theme of Gregory of Nyssa, will argue that "marriage was devised that the race of men may be preserved

19 Cf. Maximus the Confessor, *Philokalia*, vol. II, 93, no. 64.
20 "Sermon on Marriage," *On Marriage and Family Life*, op. cit., 81, 86.

through the procreation of children."[21] Yet we need to keep in mind that these great teachers were speaking to particular issues that shaped their views in significant ways. In his "Sermon on Marriage," for example, Chrysostom the pastor is concerned with the problem of married men committing adultery; and the purpose of John of Damascus is to praise the superior virtues of virginity. Their observations concerning the power and subtlety of sexual temptation are correct, and their intention to defend chastity, both within and apart from the conjugal state, is laudable. It is true, though, that their focus tends to obscure the biblical witness that identifies the true end and purpose of marriage within God's providence. That purpose is to transfigure fallen sexuality into an act of *worship*—an offering of praise, thanksgiving and intercession—by which the union of husband and wife prefigures and prepares their eternal communion with God.

Addressing the Corinthians' question, whether a woman who has become a Christian may divorce her pagan husband, St. Paul expresses willingness to accept such a divorce if it is initiated by the unbeliever (1 Cor 7:13-15). Yet he ends his reflection with a pair of rhetorical questions: "Wife, how do you know whether you will save your husband? Husband, how do you know whether you will save your wife?" If the apostle admonishes couples to remain united in the bond of marriage, it is because that bond has a profoundly "covenantal" character, in which the believing spouse is to bear witness to the unbeliever, so that both might be saved.

Gender and Sexuality

If biblical and patristic tradition appears to hold sexuality and sexual pleasure in disfavor, it is due to its awesome power and propensity for leading us into sin, not because sexuality as such is inherently sinful or evil. Hebrew law, for example, prescribes harsh punishments for various sorts of sexual activity that were considered aberrant or unnatural. These include adultery, incest, homosexuality and bestiality (cf. Lev 18). Each of these threatens both family and society because each is motivated by self-centered lust. Procreative activity, on the other hand, is understood to be blessed by God, even to the extent that he provides levirate marriage to ensure the preservation of a deceased man's name and lineage (Dt 25:5-6; cf. Gen 38:8; Mt 22:23ff and parallels). Then again, the

---

21 "Exposition of the Orthodox Faith," *NPNF*, vol. IX, 96.

psalmist can cry, "Behold, I was brought forth in iniquity, and in sin my mother conceived me" (Ps 50/51:5).[22] As the plural "sins" (*hamartiais*) of the Septuagint indicates, this does not refer to "original sin"—the guilt of Adam transmitted by the sexual act (St. Augustine). It means rather that every person is born into a fallen world marked by the tragedy of sin and alienation from God. (Thus it follows logically upon what precedes it: "I know my transgression and my sin is ever before me.") Conception and sin are closely linked, but not causally. No judgment is cast on the procreative act itself.

In a similar vein, the Church's liturgical texts warn repeatedly of the temptations and possible corruption associated with sexual behavior, yet it never condemns sexuality per se. Consider these two random examples. In the prayer before the Great Entrance of the eucharistic Liturgy, the priest acknowledges: "No one who is bound with the desires and pleasures of the flesh is worthy to approach or draw near or to serve Thee, O King of Glory...." This concerns any attachment to worldly affairs that might lead to idolatry, the worship of false gods, but it may be interpreted as speaking particularly to sexual temptations. The Compline "Prayer to our Lord" implores God to "preserve us from the gloomy slumber of sin and from the dark passions of the night. Calm the impulses of carnal desires, quench the fiery darts of the evil one which are craftily directed against us. Still the rebellions of the flesh, and put far from us all anxiety and worldly care." The allusion to sexual lust here is clear. The passage is remarkably candid and realistic about the struggle needed to preserve chastity, whether in marriage or in monastic life. Yet just as in the preceding petition, it simply underscores the power of sexual temptation to lead to sinful behavior; it does not condemn sexuality as such.

This raises the question as to whether sexuality and gender are elements of God's original creative act, and therefore reflect the divine image, or whether they are attributable to the Fall and should be relegated to the sphere of passions and bodily needs that eventually pass away.

There is a fascinating debate currently going on among Orthodox theologians that touches directly on this point. It concerns the origins of gender and sexuality: whether they are essential aspects of our humanity and thus reflective of the image of God, or whether they are concessions to our fallen state and thus postlapsarian phenomena that possess no inherent spiritual

---

22 Verse 7 in the Hebrew and Greek versions.

or ontological significance. Because of the importance of this question for our attitude toward the human body, including procreation and health care, it would be worthwhile considering the debate a little more fully.

The most common reply to the question of the origin of gender and sexuality is the one we have represented here: that gender differentiation is an aspect of God's good creation. It interprets Genesis 1:26-27 as meaning that "maleness" and "femaleness" are inscribed in human nature as an expression of God's will. St. Paul's declaration in Galatians 3:28, that in Christ "there is neither male nor female" (literally, "nor is there male and female," placing the accent on the gender distinction itself rather than on the persons) is interpreted to mean that incorporation into the Body of Christ through baptism allows the couple *in the Church* to transcend the culturally conditioned differences—with their sociological and psychological consequences—between Jews and Greeks, slaves and free, men and women.[23]

A similar interpretation is usually given to Jesus' teaching concerning life in the resurrection: when they rise from the dead, men and women are "like angels (*hôs angeloi*) in heaven" (Mk 12:25; Mt 22:30; Luke 20:36 reads "they cannot die any more, because they are equal to angels [*isangeloi*] and sons of God..."). This means that in the resurrection men will not marry and women will not be given in marriage, because the marital bond established in this life is eternal, and because genital functioning will have no place in the Kingdom, since there will be no need for procreation, and all love will be ultimately directed toward God.[24]

According to this view, gender distinction and sexuality are elements of God's good creation and intrinsic to human nature. In the resurrection

23 See Thomas Hopko's article, "Galatians 3:28. An Orthodox Interpretation," 169-186, which demonstrates that the apostle does not suggest that gender distinctions are abolished in Christ ("The letter to the Galatians does not have a theology of gender...", 179), but that "There are now no differences whatsoever within the 'Israel of God' (6:6) in the covenant members' relationship to the Lord, for in the 'new creation' all believers 'are one in Christ Jesus' (3:28)," 176.

24 The Lukan expression "equal to the angels" occurs in Philo (*De sacrif. Abel* 1.5), and similar ideas appear in other Jewish and Jewish-Christian writings. See. J. Fitzmyer, *The Gospel According to Luke X-XXIV* (New York: Anchor Doubleday, 1985), 1305. It is a Greek expression that shifts the meaning somewhat from Mark's more Semitic *hôs angeloi*. The latter is certainly closer to Jesus' own meaning: those who rise from the dead shall be "like angels" in that they do not marry; the levirate marriage law (according to which a man must beget children by his widowed sister-in-law in order to preserve his deceased brother's lineage—Dt 25:5; cf. Gen 38:8) is no longer in effect. This is the meaning of this passage, and not that humans will become "angelic." There is no confusion in Scripture between human beings and what the Church celebrates as "the bodiless powers of heaven."

it is not gender distinction that is abolished, but the various *consequences* of that distinction, including sexual activity and relationships of dominance and submission. To use our modern categories, in Christ and in the Kingdom there is no longer an imbalance of power and consequent domination of Jew over Greek (as within early church communities), of freemen over slaves, or of men over women. Galatians 3:28, in other words, concerns sociology, not ontology. It proclaims equality between the sexes, and not the obliteration of gender.

Other Orthodox theologians give a very different interpretation to these passages. Following St. Maximus, who bases his reflection on St. Gregory of Nyssa's "On the Creation of Man," they deny that either sexuality or gender differentiation is an essential component of human nature, and hold that they arise only in consequence of the Fall. Valerie Karras, for example, has made an interesting and well crafted case for this view. She interprets patristic teaching to mean that the human body in its fallen state does not reflect the image of God. The Fathers, she holds, "distinguish among the physical, emotional, and psychological effects of our fallen bodies, especially our gender, and the ultimate genderless nature of the human soul." She continues: "Beyond physical sex, gender itself is seen by all of the Fathers as an element added to our humanity only because of God's foreknowledge of man's fall." This leads her to conclude: "But if the image of God in humanity does not extend to human sexuality, and if humanity was neither intended to include gender nor will be sexually differentiated in the resurrection, then there is *no spiritual dimension, no ontological significance, to gender.*"[25]

Aside from introducing an intolerable body-soul dualism into Orthodox anthropology, this argument also confuses gender with sexuality and "body" with "flesh." Partial support for her view can be found in Maximus' thesis that all divisions within creation will ultimately be overcome, including the distinction between male and female. To Maximus' mind, however, that distinction is not evil per se, nor is it a consequence of the Fall. Like the four other distinctions (between paradise and the inhabited world, heaven and earth, the intelligible and sensible, the uncreated and created), gender differentiation is a given of the created order. It is susceptible to sin, and that susceptibility expresses itself in fallen sexuality. Sex-

25 "Patristic Views on the Ontology of Gender," 113-119; emphasis added.

ual procreation became necessary as a consequence of human sin and its "wages," which are death or mortality. Commenting on Maximus' *Ambigua* 41, Lars Thunberg states the issue quite succinctly:

> [S]ince Maximus presupposes that God had prepared another form of human multiplication and fertility for man the non-sinner, this negative perspective on sexuality does not carry the implication that the generative force of man is altogether evil. It may be used in a positive and spiritual way. *The masculine and feminine elements are not destined to disappear,* only to be subsumed effectively under the principle (*logos*) of the common human nature.[26]

The point to note here is that the division between man and woman which is healed by the dual mediation of Christ and man concerns sexuality, not gender. Similarly, when Maximus speaks of aspects that "were not originally created as elements of human nature," he names "pleasure and distress, desire and fear, and what follows from them."[27] Again, he is referring to passions, sexual and other, rather than to gender.

Attempting to demonstrate that virtually all of the Fathers (and not merely Gregory of Nyssa and Maximus the Confessor) teach that gender is "an element added to humanity only because of God's foreknowledge of man's fall," Dr. Karras refers to the view of St. John Damascene in his treatment of virginity and the married life: "John of Damascus sums up the whole of patristic tradition by stating that God, in His foreknowledge, created humanity with gender for procreative purposes."[28] St. John does hold that virginity was an original and innate quality of human nature in its prelapsarian state. Only after death had been introduced as a consequence of human sin did sexual procreation become necessary, in order to preserve the human race. It is also true that St. John holds virginity in far higher esteem than he does conjugal life. But once again, this concerns sexuality. It says nothing about gender distinctions which he, with most patristic witnesses, assumes are given with the creation of the first man and woman in their pre-fallen condition. Indeed, in the same chapter the Damascene affirms that marriage is "good" (even though virginity is "better"), citing Jesus' blessing of marriage (at Cana, Jn 2), together with the injunction of Hebrews 13:4, "Let marriage be held in

---

26 *Man and the Cosmos. The Vision of St. Maximus the Confessor* (Crestwood, NY: St. Vladimir's Seminary Press, 1985), 82; emphasis added.
27 *Philokalia*, vol. II, 178, no. 65.
28 *Op. cit.*, 116, re. "On the Orthodox Faith," IV.24.

honor among all, and let the marriage bed be undefiled." Even here the emphasis is on purity and appropriate chastity in conjugal relations. Consequently, St. John can conclude that "marriage is good" insofar as "lawful intercourse" prevents "the madness of desire" from being inflamed into acts that are unnatural or against nature (*anomos*).[29]

Nothing here supports the view that gender appeared only after the Fall or that it is not an inherent element in human nature. Sexuality, on the other hand, in the mind of many patristic writers, is clearly postlapsarian, a point they stress to avoid the notion that concupiscence and other passions are expressions of created nature, which is inherently "good." Yet even this does not mean that sexuality is evil or that sexual activity is inherently sinful. Speaking against "Jewish fables" and Old Testament notions of purity and impurity, St. John Chrysostom declares: "all things are pure. God made nothing unclean, for nothing is unclean, except sin only. For that reaches to the soul and defiles it... You see how many varieties of uncleanness there are [from a human point of view]. Yet God made child-birth, and the seed of copulation."[30] To Chrysostom's mind, *it is not the biological functioning which is sinful, but its misuse.* In the same homily, therefore, he can declare that the fornicator and the adulterer are unclean, "not on account of the intercourse (for according to that reasoning a man cohabiting with his own wife would be unclean), but because of the wickedness of the act, and the injury done to his neighbor in his nearest interest." The intentions of the heart and the circumstances surrounding the act are what render fornication and adultery evil, not intercourse itself.

In any case, no reasonable exegesis of the biblical passages cited earlier (Gal 3:28; Mk 12:25 and parallels) can conclude that gender per se will be eliminated in the resurrection, any more than Genesis 1:26-27 can bear the interpretation that gender was not an essential or "natural" aspect of human creatures before the Fall (what, after all, does it mean to affirm that "he *created* them male and female"?). The same is true with the notion that gender distinction existed before the Fall only because God foreknew that man would sin and bring death upon himself, and there-

29 John of Damascus, "Exposition of the Orthodox Faith," *NPNF* 2nd series vol. IX (Grand Rapids, MI: Eerdmans, 1976), 97.
30 "Homily on Titus III," *NPNF* XIII, 530-531.

fore sexual procreation would be required in order to preserve the human species. This is not simply a non-issue in the biblical texts. It is clearly contradicted by the Genesis creation account, which includes gender identity and differentiation in the "good" creative activity of God, as it is by Jesus' blessing of the marriage at Cana, and by St. Paul's teaching that the body is a "member of Christ" (1 Cor 6:15), which even in its fallen (and gender-specific) state is capable of sanctification (1 Thess 5:23). Still more decisive is Jesus' statement that unequivocally confirms the goodness of gender and its place within the divine economy: "*From the beginning of creation* 'God made them male and female,'" so that in marriage "they are no longer two but one flesh" (Mk 10:6-8).[31]

Gender, then, is not an after-thought, nor is it a concession to human weakness. In the words of Thomas Hopko, "Gender-differentiation for human beings is an essential element in their ability to reflect and participate in God's divine being and life whose content is love... And it is exactly as men and women, and in their intercommunion together, that human beings find and fulfill themselves as creatures made in God's image and likeness..."[32]

A persistent confusion between "flesh" and "body" seems in large measure responsible for the quasi-Gnostic opinion that the body—and with it, gender—has "no spiritual dimension, no ontological significance."[33] This opinion is based on the view that the fallen, physical body

31 To a certain extent, the problem here is one of method. Specifically, it results from a tendency toward "proof-texting": selecting passages of Scripture—or, more commonly, of the Fathers—and reading them out of context. This is a temptation to which all of us are susceptible, one that is virtually built-in to our attempts to extract from the biblical and patristic witnesses *systematic* teachings that are not there. These sources are precisely that, "witnesses": their concerns are pastoral and evangelical rather than formally "dogmatic." Because of the importance of Dr. Karras' argument, and its significance for Orthodox anthropology, it would be worthwhile to take a closer look at a few of the patristic references she marshals in defense of her thesis. Refer to the Extended Note at the end of this section.

32 "God and Gender: Articulating the Orthodox View," 160. Dr. Karras quotes this passage critically, but she focuses her comments only on the question of whether gender images Persons of the Holy Trinity. This is a difficult issue (which Fr. Hopko has treated with great care and caution), but it does not concern his basic argument that gender is an "essential element" in human existence, necessary for establishing communion in love both between spouses and with God.

33 A well-known logion from the Gnostic *Gospel of Thomas* (Log. 22) seems to offer support for the notion that gender difference will disappear in the Kingdom of God. In reply to his disciples' question, "Shall we then, being children, enter the Kingdom?," Jesus said: "When you make the two one, and when you make the inner as the outer and the outer as the inner and the above as the below, and *when you make the male and the female into a single one, so that the male will not be*

does not reflect the image of God, and therefore gender is not an essential aspect of our humanity. I have tried to indicate why I believe this is a non sequitur. It presupposes a body-soul dualism that is foreign both to Scripture and to Orthodox tradition. What Dr. Karras terms "the body in its postlapsarian state" is in reality that fallen *orientation* of the body which St. Paul identifies as "the flesh" (*sarx*) or "the old Adam."[34] "Flesh" refers basically to the superficial aspect of our being, the seat of the passions, which is constantly susceptible to temptation and sin. As such it is contrasted in St. Paul's thought, not with the "body," but with the "spirit." Although biblical and patristic language is fluid, the term "body" (*sôma*) generally denotes the entire being: heart, mind, flesh and spirit (or soul). In the resurrection the body will certainly be changed: transformed from a "physical body" to a "spiritual body" (1 Cor 15:44)—but it will remain a unique "body," a unique hypostasis, in total continuity with its personal earthly existence. (Consider, for example, Jesus' resurrectional appearances to Mary Magdalene and to his disciples: John 20, Luke 24, etc. Although at first he is not recognized, once he reveals himself by word or "in the breaking of bread," he is perceived and welcomed as precisely who he is in his unique personal identity: the risen Lord is one with Jesus of Nazareth.)

It is true that the ascetic literature often speaks of the body in very negative terms. It addresses, after all, the struggle monks must assume in maintaining chastity and purity of thought. Yet when the Fathers use the expression "body" in this context they are usually referring to the Pauline notion of "flesh," the locus of spiritual warfare. "Flesh" and "body" are not separate components of the human person that oppose or stand in tension with the "soul," any more than "flesh" and "spirit" denote different parts or

male and the female (not) a female, when you make eyes in the place of an eye, and a hand in the place of a hand, and a foot in the place of a foot, (and) an image (*eikôn*) in the place of an image (*eikôn*), then shall you enter the Kingdom." (*The Gospel According to Thomas,* A. Guillaumont et al., eds., Leiden: Brill/New York: Harper, 1959, 17-18). Feminists have seized on this apocryphal saying to bolster the notion that gender distinction (and particularly male domination) will not persist into the Kingdom. The irony is that the Gnostic theology of the "single one" (*monachos*), despite the surface impression given by this logion, in fact assumes that the female will be absorbed into the male. The new "image" is neither of androgyny nor of "sexlessness," but of perpetuated "male domination." This is only one reason why the Church—*pace* the "Jesus Seminar"—never accepted this Gnostic writing as "the fifth Gospel."

34 *Sarx* can refer to human nature as such (e.g., Jn 1:14; see references in J. Chryssavgis, *The Ascent to Heaven,* 66, n. 110), but normally it signifies "the carnal mind": "to set the mind on the flesh is death" (Rom 8:3-8).

aspects of our being that constantly wage war against each other. This is the popular view, and it arises in part from the fact that neither Scripture nor the patristic writings use the terms in a wholly consistent and systematic way. "*Sarx*" (flesh) and "*sōma*" (body) properly signify the *totality* of the person, but viewed from different perspectives. Similarly, when the terms "flesh" and "spirit" are used together in the context of St. Paul's ethical dualism, each refers to the whole person: "flesh" to man as fallen, "spirit" to man as redeemed. The Pauline expressions "mind of the spirit" and "mind of the flesh" thus refer to a specific orientation of the *whole being*: toward life and peace, or toward death (Rom 8:5-6).[35]

"Flesh," then, refers to the orientation of the human person that leads to sin and death, since the "mind of the flesh" is set on things of this world rather than on God. The term "body," on the other hand, can be used in several ways. It can refer to the physical or psychological aspect of our being, and in this sense it is nearly synonymous with "the flesh." Or it can signify the whole person, capable by grace of transfiguration and resurrection in the image of Christ. The former usage occurs in St. Paul's anguished reflection on the "body of death," where the self is "carnal, sold under sin" (Rom 7:14-25). The latter, more normative usage is found in his appeal to "present your bodies as a living sacrifice, holy and acceptable to God" (Rom 12:1) and in his admonition to the Corinthians: "Shun immorality!... Do you not know that your body is a temple of the Holy Spirit within you, which you have from God? You are not your own, you were bought with a price. Therefore glorify God in your body" (1 Cor 6:18-20). A combination of the two meanings appears in 1 Cor 15: 38-39, where *sarx* appears to be the equivalent of *sōma*. Finally, the normative usage recurs unambiguously in the following passage (15:44): in the resurrection, the earthly physical body (*sōma psychikon*) will be transformed into a celestial spiritual body (*sōma pneumatikon*). Here the apostle refers not only to the flesh, but to the total person, one's whole being.

These reflections lead to the conclusion that humanity (that is, the "body" in its prelapsarian state) was indeed intended to include gender,

---

35 John Chryssavgis expresses this clearly in *The Ascent to Heaven*, p. 52: "'Flesh' in Paul's epistles denotes the *whole* man *qua* fallen, while 'spirit' denotes the *whole* man *qua* redeemed. *Sarx* is the 'old man' which must be laid aside in order to put on the 'new man' (Eph 4:22 and Col 3:9)." The same must be said for the term "soul" (Heb *nephesh*; Gk. *psychē*): one does not "possess" a soul, one *is* a living soul (cf. Gen 2:7, *nephesh hayyah, psychēn zōsan*).

and that gender distinction, as an essential aspect of bodily existence, will be preserved in the resurrection.[36] Gender specificity is innate in human nature, having been bestowed by the Creator "from the beginning." Consequently, we cannot accept the thesis that gender possesses "no spiritual dimension, no ontological significance."

As an essential function of human nature, gender permits procreation which "from the beginning," and not merely as a consequence of the Fall, is blessed by God as the means whereby persons bearing his image can participate in his creative activity (Gen 1:28; 2:23-24, both of which are "prelapsarian"). If we avoid confusing gender with (fallen) sexuality, then it is evident that gender does indeed possesses both "ontological significance" and a profoundly "spiritual dimension." It enables man and woman to fulfill the divine command to "multiply and fill the earth," and to fulfill each other through their complementary expressions of love.

Quite apart from the question whether it images in any way particular qualities or characteristics of the Persons of the Holy Trinity, gender as a function of bodily existence is given by God and blessed by him in his original act of creation. Thus its significance properly extends beyond physical

36 This insistence, Dr. Karras argues, inevitably—and heretically—introduces "an intermediate level of ontological existence between that of essence or nature…and its concrete manifestation in a person or hypostasis." And this in turn leads to the "denial of complete freedom to the person in his or her relationship with God and with other human persons" (*ibid.*, 118). If gender or sexual differentiation is understood—as it must be—as a "function" or "essential element" of human nature, then this conclusion does not follow. To be sure, nature must be transcended: the person, in the exercise of human freedom, must pass beyond the limits of (fallen) natural necessity in order to attain God-likeness or deification. Yet nature and person are not opposed to one another. Rather, in the language of Leontius of Byzantium, the nature is "enhypostasized." It is "contained in" or "proper to" the person. In Vladimir Lossky's words, "The nature is the content of the person, the person the existence of the nature" (*The Mystical Theology of the Eastern Church*, Crestwood, NY: St Vladimir's Seminary Press, 1976, 123). As nature is "overcome" or transcended in the dynamic growth toward God-likeness, it is not destroyed or eliminated; it is transformed instead into what it was originally intended to be. What is eliminated is the *fragmentation* of nature into individual identities. *Theôsis* involves the transformation of the individual into a *person* who gives full and perfect expression to the one human nature, common to mankind, that was created to reflect the likeness of the divine nature. Thus Lossky can affirm (against Gregory of Nyssa and Maximus the Confessor) that "Eve taken from Adam's nature, 'bone of his bone and flesh of his flesh', the new human person, completed the nature of Adam, was one nature, 'one flesh' with him." Therefore, he concludes, "The person becomes the perfect image of God by acquiring that likeness which is the perfection of the nature common to all men" (*ibid.*, 123-124). Since that common nature is shared equally by Adam and Eve in their prelapsarian state, one can only conclude that it embraces gender distinctions, that gender is therefore an essential element of human nature, and that it will remain such in the resurrected life.

pleasure and even beyond procreation. For ultimately, gender which expresses itself in human sexual love is intended to serve as an image or icon
of the nuptial bond that unites Christ with all those who adhere to him in
faith. Yet it can do so only *within the context of Christian marriage,* what we
have qualified as "a monogamous, heterosexual, blessed, conjugal union."
This is the only context that allows gender and its sexual expression to assume an authentic *sacramental* quality. The uniting of man and woman to
create "one flesh" is a profound mystery (*mystêrion, sacramentum*), the
apostle declares, and it refers to the mystical, sacramental union of self-
giving love between Christ and his Body, the Church. Christos Yannaras
expresses this sacramental aspect in these terms:

> In the mystery of marriage, the Church intervenes to give sexual love its full
> dimensions, to free the loving power in man from its subjection to natural neces-
> sity, and to manifest in the unity of man and wife an image of the Church and the
> gift of true life.[37]

Accordingly, Orthodox Christianity views marriage as essentially a
Christian vocation, *a union in and with Christ.*[38] The ultimate end of that
vocation is the same as that of monasticism: *theôsis* or eternal participation in the life of God. Like monasticism, Christian marriage requires a
continual *askêsis*: a spiritual struggle, grounded in ongoing repentance. In
Yannaras's words, "True virginity and true marriage are reached by a common road: the self-denial of the cross, and ascetic self-offering."[39] This
Way of the Cross is symbolized in the Orthodox marriage ceremony by
the nuptial crowns, which are crowns of victory but also crowns of martyrdom, of saving witness one to the other and to the world. "O Holy
Martyrs," the Church sings during the nuptial procession, "who have
fought the good fight and have received your crowns, entreat ye the Lord
that he will have mercy on our souls!"

Christian marriage engages the couple in ceaseless spiritual warfare at
every level of their common life. Through continual repentance and the

---

37 *The Freedom of Morality,* 160f.
38 This implies that "marriages" made apart from the sacramental blessing of the Church are
merely social arrangements, sanctioned for legal purposes (protection of children, transfer of
property, etc.), but with no intrinsic spiritual value or meaning. The fact that most Christians,
like the general population, see little more to marriage than a practical convention explains
why even among them the divorce rate is so high. This is a pastoral issue of major importance
that needs to be addressed in every parish community.
39 *Ibid.,* 168.

seeking of forgiveness, obstinate pride resolves into tender affection, and self-centered lust into self-sacrificing devotion. Beyond that, however, the couple's struggle unites them in a common "priestly" ministry, as they offer themselves and each other to God as a "sacrifice of praise." The *telos* or ultimate end of conjugal union, then, is the salvation of the other, the beloved, with whom one is eternally united in a covenant bond of faithfulness and self-giving love.[40]

Given the trivialization of marriage today, even among Christian couples, this is certainly a "hard teaching." Many people, without doubt, would greet it with ridicule. But it needs to be affirmed in our churches if it is to be confirmed in our experience. And with it there need to be affirmed as well the consequences of this teaching for all aspects of sexual behavior, including premarital, extra-marital and homosexual relations, together with masturbation and the use of pornography. In the following section I would like to consider briefly the moral implications of each of these.

Extended Note

Regarding Dr. Karras' argument that gender distinction will not exist in the resurrected life of the Kingdom, it is necessary to examine the context in which various supporting quotations are found. She cites several passages from St. Basil the Great and St. Gregory of Nazianzus to defend the view that "the Fathers deny that the physical body reflects the image of God." "Basil," she states, "is adamant in distinguishing between the outer person and the inner one. The *real* man is the inner one; the outer is not the true man, but simply *belongs* to the inner man." [*Op. cit.*, p. 115; emphasis hers.] Then she adds a quotation from St. Gregory: "O nature of woman overcoming that of man in the common struggle for salvation, and demonstrating that the distinction between male and female is one of body not of soul!" [*Oration* 8,14; *PG* 35:805B, quoted from an article by V. Harrison.]

Her concern is to demonstrate that ontologically—on the level of the soul—men and women are created equal. This is a point well taken, one that is beyond dispute both in the Scriptures and in the Church Fathers. But an illicit jump occurs in this reasoning, from the essential, ontological equality of men and women to the double conclusion that the *body* does not reflect the image of God and that *therefore* gender distinction will disappear in resurrected existence. The argument presupposes a dualism between the

---

40 Vigen Guroian expresses this well: "Marriage is a form of martyrdom...an image and a proleptic experience of the New Creation in which *erôs*, purified by chastity and freed from lust, is sublimated into a selfless desire and active concern for the well-being of the other (i.e., compassion). Likewise, self-sacrifice is translated into a free communion unconstrained by sin or natural necessity. Marriage is made an entrance into the Kingdom by crucifixion (*askêsis*)." *Incarnate Love*, 105.

"outer man" (the body) and the "inner man" (the soul), that tends to distort both biblical and patristic thought.

In drawing a sharp distinction between the "outer" man and the "inner" man (literally, the "manifest" man, *anthrôpos phainomenon*, and the "inward" or "interior" man, *anthrôpos esô*) ["On the Origin of Man," *Homily* 1,7; *Sources chrétiennes* (SC) 160 (Paris: Cerf, 1970), p. 182.], St. Basil is referring to the apostle Paul's distinction in 2 Cor 4:16, "Though our 'outward' or 'external self' (*exô anthrôpos*) is wasting away, our 'inward' or 'internal self' (*esô hêmôn*) is being renewed day by day." These images of "outer" and "inner" man do not refer to "body" as contrasted with "soul." The apostle (taking up into a Christian context a theme familiar from Platonic, Neo-Platonic and Stoic philosophy) draws a contrast rather between the inner life of the person—filled and guided by the Spirit—and the dimension of the "flesh," which is subject to sin and temptation, but in the context of 2 Cor 4 alludes to physical deterioration due to persecution and the wear and tear imposed by Paul's apostolic ministry.

The "inner man," in other words, is the "new creation" in Christ, the human person as filled with the Spirit and strengthened through faith (cf. Eph 3:14-19; Col 3:10!). The "outer man," on the other hand, is the "old Adam": the visible, vulnerable aspect of human existence, subject to sin and "wasting away." The tension here is not dualistic (soul-body), but *eschatological.* It concerns the ongoing transformation of the whole person from old creation to new (2 Cor 5:17) and from "glory to glory" (2 Cor 3:18), which will culminate in the resurrection. It is through this Spirit-bestowed transformation, Paul declares, that the coming Savior, Jesus Christ, "will change our lowly body (*sôma*) into the likeness of his glorious body" (Phil 3:21). This eschatological metamorphosis, as he makes clear, involves the "body," meaning the total person in its original "hypostatic," gender-specific identity.

St. Basil follows St. Paul by distinguishing "two men" (*duo gnôrizô anthrôpous*): one who is manifest, and the other hidden, invisible. In some respects, he maintains, we are "double" or "dual" (*diploi*), but in fact we are (essentially, we might say) an "inward" being (*endon esmen*). The duality concerns what is essential: the "inner" life of the "new creation in Christ," as contrasted with what passes away: the hand, the (physical) body, the passions. What abides is the "soul" (*psychê*), he adds, meaning the human reason that is included as an aspect of the image of God. [Homily 1,7-8.]

Confusion is introduced because St. Basil, like most of the Greek Fathers, shifts back and forth between biblical and philosophical language and images. Taken in isolation, this passage can well be read as Dr. Karras proposes, suggesting a fundamental dualism in Basil's thought between the body and the soul. The expression "body" can indeed be used to refer to the corruptible aspect of human existence (although this would be more precisely termed the "flesh"). Farther on in this same homily (1,6), for example, Basil reverts to a usage—familiar from Plato, Philo and Origen—that limits *sôma* (body) to the transitory, changing aspect of man that, he says explicitly, does not reflect the image of God: "we do not possess the image (of God) in bodily form. For the form of the body is subject to corruption." The subject here is "form" (*morphê*), and the "bodily form" indeed passes away insofar as Basil identifies it with that which is corruptible (e.g., growth, aging, good or bad health, as well as the passions). In this sense, once again, "body" approximates "flesh." Elsewhere Basil uses the term *sôma* with its broader, more normative meaning to refer to the *person* in his or her totality. [Cf. I:2, where the "body" is equivalent to "myself," which, as I:2,20 indicates, reveals the greatness of the Creator and implies that in some sense the *sôma-egô* does reflect the divine image. Contrast further I: 6,1-5; I: 7,15; and II: 3; II: 5; with II: 2,20f, where body refers to the whole person, created in the divine image. Even in the former references, where Basil seems to present a body-soul dualism, the context is *moral*, not ontological. In I: 7:15, for example, the virtues of the soul in its growth toward perfection are manifested in and through the body, which is the "instrument" of the soul, not its ontological antithesis.]

Dr. Karras also quotes St. Gregory the Theologian (who lauds the spiritual feats of his sister Gorgonia) to affirm that "the distinction between male and female is one of body not of soul" [*art. cit.,* 115]. Her aim is to point out Gregory's conviction that women's moral virtues are equal to or greater than those of men. The soul is the seat of the virtues, which men and women share alike, women being in some respects superior. Again, however, this says nothing that would imply that gender is strictly physical and disappears in resurrected existence. Her laudable concern to stress the "ontological equality" between men and women nevertheless leads her to the unfounded reasoning that *because* a woman can surpass a man in spiritual exploits, and *because* the verb *andrizô* ("to be manly") can be used to describe women saints, *therefore* gender differences are obliterated in the resurrection.

In fact, all that can be said here is what she herself affirms, that *andrizô* in patristic usage "is meant specifically to transcend traditional gender distinctions." This is true if we mean by "traditional gender distinctions" not ontology, but stereotypes of women as morally or spiritually (or even physically) inferior to men. If we understand by this, however, that gender per se will not be a distinguishing characteristic of the resurrectional body (the *sôma pneumatikon* of 1 Cor 15:44), then we have lapsed into a non sequitur. The conclusion simply does not follow from the premises.

The same must be said for another quotation drawn from a funeral oration pronounced by St. Gregory upon the death of his brother, St. Caesarius. [*Or.* 7,23; *PG* 35:785C.] Combining Gal 3:28 and Col 3:11, St. Gregory states that we are one in Christ, "that we might no longer be male and female, barbarian, Scythian, slave or free (which are identifying marks of the flesh, *ta tês sarkos gnôrismata*), but might bear in ourselves only the form of God" (*ton theion charaktêra*: the "divine stamp"—as Christ himself is the very "stamp" of the Father's nature or being, Heb 1:3). We should note that this is a funeral sermon, in which Gregory speaks of the mystery of death and the glorious hope of resurrection. In this life, he declares, we are connected with both the flesh (*sarkos*) and the spirit (*pneumatos*). "I must be buried with Christ, be raised with Christ, be a co-heir with Christ, to become a son of God, even God himself" (*huion genesthai theou, theon auton*).

It is in this *eschatological* perspective, once again, that we need to understand what follows, including the reference to Gal 3:28. Gregory is distinguishing between what is earthly and heavenly, mortal and immortal, lowly and exalted (VII: 23,6). In this specific funerary context he laments the transitory character of earthly existence. Yet he also expresses gratitude that the calamity of Caesarius' death has led him to recall the essence of his faith, since it has made him "all the more eager to depart from this life." His focus is on unity in Christ, where all earthly distinctions will be overcome, including those that separate or divide the sexes, ethnic groups and social classes. That is, *the emphasis is on the elimination of what divides, not on the ontological particularity of the persons involved.* Given this focus and this context, it is misleading to use this passage (and the same must be said for the quotations from St. Basil) to affirm either that "the body" does not bear or reflect the image of God or that gender will not characterize personal existence in the Kingdom of God. [Similar criticisms of Dr. Karras' position have been made by David Ford, *Women and Men in the Early Church.* See esp. p. 148, n. 2, reflecting on another Karras article that puts forth the argument that according to St. John Chrysostom gender will not exist in resurrected existence. Prof. Ford refers to Chrysostom's "firm conviction that marriages forged on earth will continue in some way in Heaven," and concludes on the basis of his own research into Chrysostom's thought that "for him gender distinctions will also somehow continue in the heavenly realm. (And surely, we could add, the Theotokos will never cease being the mother of the Son of God.)" In ch. 2 of this study, he offers a detailed overview of Chrysostom's theology of marriage.]

This point is substantiated by a factor that may seem trivial but is not: the fact that Gregory Nazianzus continues to refer to Caesarius as "he"! In the Theologian's mind, his deceased brother is no less "male" than when he was alive in the flesh; and nothing suggests that such "maleness" will disappear in the resurrection. Those who grow in *theôsis,* in God-likeness, to the point that they "become God," bear the same personal—and gender-specific—identity that characterized them from conception. They do not become androgynous, nor are they "neutered." This point is not contradicted by Gregory's affirmation that in God we shall "bear in ourselves only the divine stamp" and be so formed and shaped by God that we shall be known or recognized by it alone. For it is the *person* who attains God-likeness in the growth toward *theôsis,* and gender is an essential mark of personal identity.

Covenant Responsibility and Sexual Behavior

"All sins are attempts to fill voids."

— Simone Weil

Equality of the Sexes.

Within ancient Israel and throughout most of the life of the Church there has been a striking and, to most people's minds, an unjust imbalance with regard to requirements for sexual fidelity and responsibility. The burden has weighed far more heavily on women than on men. This is due in part to a legacy of disproportion that we can call in today's jargon "sexist patriarchalism." Where the wife is considered to be her husband's property

(her "ownership" having been transferred from her father), she is expected, under severe penalty, to remain a virgin until marriage, then to remain "faithful" to her husband. With few exceptions, no such restraints
are laid upon the man.

In theory, if not in practice, this condition has been done away with by
the "great reversal" brought about by Jesus Christ. St. Paul's declaration,
"in Christ there is neither male nor female," means that the socially and
culturally conditioned inequality between the sexes is abolished: it does
not exist in the mind of God and has no place within the church communities. It also means that in Christ men bear equal responsibility with
women for upholding a moral ethos which is conducive to preserving the
integrity of family life. Consequently, the husband is no less responsible
than his wife for preserving familial structure, stability and nurture necessary for the proper raising of their children. The husband is also as responsible as the wife for fulfilling the prescriptions of Ephesians 5. If the
wife "submits" herself to her husband as to the Lord, her submission mir-
rors that of the Church in relation to Christ. Conversely, if the husband
exercises headship, he does so by reflecting the actions and attitudes of
Christ toward his Body, the Church. (The verb *hypotasso* is correctly rendered "submit" in this context, not "subject," as in so many English trans-
lations. It denotes a voluntary act of love rather than subjection to
constraints imposed by the husband or social convention.) The husband
is to love his wife "as Christ loved the Church and gave himself up for
her" in a sacrificial self-offering of disinterested love. The key to this mutual relationship is provided in Ephesians 5:21, a verse that introduces the
entire passage: "*Submit yourselves to one another* out of reverence for
Christ." The submission, in other words, is reciprocal. It involves both
parties equally yet in different ways: the wife through acceptance of the
husband's responsibility for "headship," and the husband through loving
service offered to his spouse.[41]

The responsibilities and obligations of the conjugal relationship are
mutual and fully equal. Husband and wife exercise different *functions*

---

41 The concept of "headship" is one that needs a great deal more exploration than it has received
to date. To what degree is it inherent in the conjugal relationship, and to what degree is it culturally conditioned? And in modern society, where both spouses are often the breadwinners,
or where the husband assumes domestic chores while the wife pursues a career, how is the husband's "headship" to be exercised?

within the family, just as the priest and laity do in the "family" of the parish community. Those functions, however, are complementary. They are effective only to the extent they are based on the full and unconditional equality of each party with regard to ontological status and spiritual value.

Authentic hierarchy, in the Holy Trinity or in the Church, presupposes just such equality. Order within the Trinity depends on the origin and function of each Hypostasis: the Father is the unbegotten source, cause or wellspring of the Son and the Spirit, as he is of all created existence; the Son is eternally generated by the Father and serves within the divine economy as Revealer, Redeemer and Savior; the Spirit eternally proceeds from the Father and, again within the economy, is sent forth by the Father through the Son, to create, inspire, sanctify and sustain the Church. Yet this complementary work is possible only because the Three share a common essence and a common will.

Within the Church, hierarchical relations are also established both by origin: divinely conferred baptism and ordination, and by function: the specific ministry to be assumed respectively by the fourfold hierarchy of bishop, priest, deacon and layperson. The bishop is the chief pastor and guardian of unity, who is called "rightly to define the word of truth"; the presbyter/priest is the immediate "father" of the community and celebrant of the sacramental mysteries; and the laity is "sent forth" to bear life-giving witness in and to the world. While we may speak of ordination as conferring "the grace divine," we also proclaim that such grace "heals what is infirm and supplies what is lacking." It does not confer special ontological status or value. Hierarchy presupposes and in fact requires the essential equality of its constituent members, an equality that derives from the fact that each member is created in the image of God and each one is called in equal measure to attain to the divine likeness.

The same is true within the family. If we can speak of a hierarchical order among husband, wife and children, it can only be with regard to their origin (in this instance, the divine calling addressed to each within the covenantal bond of marriage) which is expressed functionally in terms of the specific roles of father, mother and offspring. As the "house tables" of Eph 5:21-6:4 and Col 3:18-22 indicate, those roles concern duties and responsibilities of those who share *equally* the new life in Jesus Christ. They in no way suggest that any one role is ontologically or spiritually superior to any other.

Yet those roles are *gender specific*. Whether or not the husband today is the breadwinner, and whether or not the wife occupies herself with typical domestic chores, they can fulfill their covenantal possibilities and responsibilities only to the degree that they assume respectively *paternal* and *maternal* roles within the family. Granted, we are less clear today than ever before about the specific content of those roles. But this is not due to any ambiguity in the divinely ordained functions themselves. It is due rather to the devaluation of gender specificity that has occurred in Western society over the past few decades. If the Church casts a critical eye on "unisexism," it is because it promotes this devaluation and results in a confusion of sexual roles. If our monasteries insist that women wear skirts rather than slacks to services, and if some of our parishes still encourage women to wear a head-covering, it is primarily in the interests of acknowledging and respecting gender specificity and avoiding gender confusion.[42] Within the family as well, the Church calls the couple to fulfill gender-specific roles that have been recognized in all cultures to be "paternal" and "maternal," however difficult it may be to give a precise definition to those terms.

It has been rightly said that the major theological issue of our day concerns gender and sexuality. A great deal of current debate focuses in this regard on the meaning of paternity and maternity, fatherhood and motherhood. Descriptive terms used respectively of the two roles include "active/passive," "self-giving/receptive," "protective/nurturing," and "in the image of Christ/in the image of the Spirit." None of these is really adequate, because it can easily be demonstrated that each expression describes both husband and wife, man and woman. The debate, with its quest for an adequate theological language, is nevertheless necessary and useful. Rather like Justice Potter Stewart's remark concerning pornography, when it comes to gender specificity, we may not be able to define it, but we know it when we see it. This, too, confirms an intuition as old as the Genesis narratives: that gender is an essential and enduring element in our human constitution. It is a function of our "personalized" human nature.

---

42 This is the meaning of St. Paul's remarks in 1 Cor 11:2-16. If the woman wears a head-covering "because of the angels," it is due to the fact that in the mind of Jews and Christians of that age angels were responsible for *taxis* or *order* within the house of worship (cf. 1 Cor 14:40, "let all things be done according to order"). Although it may serve to curb a lustful wandering of male eyes, the covering is prohibited for men and mandatory for women, primarily to avoid gender confusion.

If we have insisted so adamantly on this point, it is because of its implications for the realm of sexual behavior. Most basically, if gender and its sexual expression have neither ontological nor spiritual significance, then sexual behavior is limited to earthly life, with no eternal consequences. In such a case, sexual morality would be a psychological or sociological issue, not a theological one. On the other hand, if the sexes are ontologically equal and complementary, sharing a common nature yet reflecting in ways appropriate to their specific gender the beauty and perfection of the divine nature, then sexual conduct impacts directly on the person's growth toward the likeness of God. Orthodox Tradition unquestionably holds the latter to be the case. In addition to stressing the eternal significance of gender, therefore, we have stressed as well the ontological equality that exists between the sexes. This is necessary in order to combat "sexism" and sexual exploitation. But it is just as necessary in order to situate sexual behavior within the framework of the eschatological and sacramental covenant bond that confers upon husband and wife equal responsibility with an equal potential for achieving by grace the deification of their personal existence. Nothing we can say about extra-marital sex or homosexuality—or, for that matter, about abortion and *in vitro* fertilization—has any *theological* significance if we cannot affirm from the outset that in the eyes of God men and women are ontologically (by nature) equal and that each gender possesses its own eternal value and meaning.

The Virtue of Chastity.

What, then, is the theological significance of sexual behavior within and outside the union of marriage? In a word, sexuality is the touchstone that determines and reveals our commitment to the covenantal bond God has established with his people. It is in large measure through sexuality that our commitment and faithfulness to that covenantal relationship can be measured. Notice that Jesus' words concerning the unbreakable commitment of marriage are followed by the saying about voluntary celibacy: "there are eunuchs who have made themselves eunuchs for the sake of the Kingdom of Heaven" (Mt 19:8-12). Two fundamental vocations exist within the Church: not "clerical" and "lay," but consecrated celibacy and blessed conjugal union. Despite the preference for virginity expressed by many patristic writers, Orthodoxy has generally held that these two vocations are equal in spiritual value and in the potential for guiding the person, monk or spouse, to salvation. The Church will call single people to a commitment of celibacy for the same reason it calls some to monastic life: that by the grace of the indwelling Spirit they may transform lust into love, the erotic into *erôs*. Yet the Church teaches that marriage has precisely that same end, when purified and sanctified love is freely offered to the spouse and children.

Sexuality, then, has profound spiritual and theological significance as the crucible in which ascetic struggle leads toward the transcendence of fallen human nature. If apostolic tradition condemns "sins of the flesh," it is because the pathway to the Kingdom is marked out by self-transcending *chastity*, whether in marriage or in celibate life. Genuine chastity is self-transcending rather than self-denying. As a spiritual discipline, it promotes the wholeness and stability of the person by focusing sexual energy away from the self and its perceived needs, and toward God.

Although it is fully compatible with conjugal sexuality, chastity in marriage will impose limits upon sexual expression (against the hedonistic notion that "anything goes"), while directing the couple's love in such a way as to enfold them both in mutual attentiveness, devotion and joy. Chastity in the form of virginity, on the other hand, is a special vocation that in the first instance reflects the personal purity, self-abandonment and faithfulness to God of the Theotokos, the Ever-Virgin Mary. It is an ecclesial vocation in that it reflects in and to the Church the uncompromising faithfulness demanded of every Christian to the covenant relationship God has sealed with his people. Yet the end of both vocations, married and celibate, is the same: to welcome into the life of the married couple or the solitary monk the love which God expresses as *nuptial love*.

This explains why the Church's ascetic literature abounds with apparently contradictory images of the spouse whose conjugal commitment and communion with God are deepened through chastity, and of the monk (male or female) who relates to God in what is virtually a nuptial union. The primary image that describes both vocations—conjugal and monastic—is that of *marriage*: marriage understood as an eternal, covenantal commitment of loving faithfulness between Christ and his Church. Accordingly, the *telos* or fulfillment of both vocations lies in their eternal participation in the marriage feast of him who is both sacrificial Lamb and Bridegroom (Rev 19:9, 21:2, 22:17).

Premarital Sexuality.

This kind of reflection provides us with a basis for drawing some specific conclusions concerning premarital and extramarital sexual activity, as well as "acted out" homosexuality.

The primary blessing of sexuality lies in procreation, which until very recently was universally recognized as having its proper place within the family unit created by husband and wife. Current pressures to create ersatz families headed by homosexual lovers or single parents violate the Church's most basic understanding of what God calls "family" to be: a man and a woman who join as "one flesh" for the deepening of their mutual love by bringing forth "the fruit of their bodies." The unitive value of marriage, therefore, is inextricably linked to its procreative potential. [43] If a husband and wife are unable to conceive for any reason, their conjugal union as such is not diminished. But as the anguish of the typical sterile couple makes clear, marriage and sexuality find their true fulfillment and achieve their true purpose by bringing forth new life.

This is why Orthodoxy, like Roman Catholicism, insists that in every act of sexual intercourse the couple should willingly accept the possibility that conception might occur. In cases where measures are taken to avoid pregnancy, yet conception does occur, then the couple will receive that

43 This view is shared by traditional Roman Catholic teaching. Cf. *Humanae Vitae*, no. 12: "There is an unbreakable connection between the unitive meaning and the procreative meaning [of the conjugal act], and both are inherent in the conjugal act. This connection was established by God, and man is not permitted to break it through his own volition." Quoted in John F. Harvey, *The Truth About Homosexuality* (San Francisco, CA: Ignatius Press, 1996), 124, n. 1. This argument is used in Catholic tradition (or in any case, by the Magisterium) to reject contraception as inherently immoral, since every coital act must be open to procreation. Most Orthodox ethicists would not agree that the close connection between the unitive and procreative aspects of sexual intercourse excludes all use of contraceptives, provided they are not abortifacients and there is good cause for temporarily avoiding pregnancy. See in this regard the remarks of Stanley Harakas on "the transmission of life," in *Living the Faith* (Minneapolis, MN: Light & Life Publishing, 1993), 130-136. Referring to Orthodox ethicists who accept certain forms of contraception, he states: "Most of these authors...emphasize the sacramental nature of marriage, seeing the sexual relationships of spouses as an aspect of the mutual growth of the couple in love and unity. This approach not only permits, but also encourages the sexual relationships of husband and wife for their own sake as expressions of mutual love. This view clearly supports the use of contraception for the purpose of spacing and limiting children and as an expression of their mutual love" (132). Fr. Harakas discusses this issue in greater detail in *Contemporary Moral Issues*, 78-82. He concludes: "What we are saying is that if a married couple has children, or is spacing the birth of their children, and wishes to continue sexual relations in the subsequent years as an expression of their continuing love for each other, and for the deepening of their personal and marital unity, the Orthodoxy of contraception is affirmed."

new life with gratitude and joy. They will embrace it as a gift of God's bounty, to be cherished, protected and nurtured through the entire gestation period. And they will remain aware that any decision to abort that life for reasons of expediency can only be regarded by the Church as the gravest sin, tantamount to murder.

Unlike their Catholic counterparts, Orthodox bishops and priests today usually acknowledge that married couples may need to practice a form of family planning that includes some method of birth control (more properly: conception control). Not all Orthodox agree with this, however. This very disagreement over the issue of contraception testifies to the fact that within Orthodoxy procreation is understood to be the primary aim of and justification for sexual activity. The *unitive* aspect of sexual love, therefore, is a blessed and joyful corollary to procreation. It is a gift for which we can rejoice and give thanks. It is so, however, only inasmuch as it derives from the more fundamental purpose of Christian marriage, which is to participate directly in God's creative work through the bearing and raising of children.

Premarital and extramarital (adulterous) sexual relations violate the covenantal commitment that marriage is intended to establish. Apart from violent criminal activities such as rape and incest, premarital sex takes the two forms of casual encounters between acquaintances, and deeper, more committed relations between two people who plan to marry. In the former instance the sole purpose of engaging in sex is for pleasure—for fun or gratification—with the focus on the self and one's own needs and desires. Because it is void of personal commitment, and therefore of personal responsibility, it amounts to exploitation of another person, even when the desire is mutual. Therefore it can only be considered, in Catholic parlance, a "moral evil." To the mind of the Church, in other words, sex without commitment is sin.

The case of two intended spouses who engage in sexual relations is more difficult to address. This is not because the Church's attitude toward it is ambivalent, but because there is such a high incidence in contemporary society of unmarried couples "living together," whether or not they consider the arrangement to be a trial marriage. In the wake of this phenomenon, an engaged couple very understandably want to express their love and their commitment sexually. Why should they be obliged to wait, especially if financial or other considerations do not permit them to be married immediately? Why can they share virtually everything as an en-gaged couple, but may not enjoy the pleasures of sex, particularly in this day and age when contraception is so easy and effective?

The question answers itself. There where openness to procreation is systematically rejected, sexuality cannot fulfill its God-given purpose. The same is true within a marriage where the couple refuses to have any children at all. We are not talking about situations where a couple may delay child bearing for a certain period of time, or even where, following the birth of several children, the parents may decide to use contraception indefinitely in order to hold their family to a manageable size. It is where procreation is rejected in principle, whether within or outside the conju-gal union, that the true purpose of sexuality is frustrated. By its very na-ture that rejection is sinful. Its intentionality makes of it a moral and not merely an "ontic" evil.

With regard to intended spouses, there is a basic theological issue that needs to be addressed. In 1 Corinthians 7, St. Paul advises couples who cannot assume the struggle of abstinence to marry, "since it is better to marry than to burn [with lust]." The reluctant tone of this concession can only be understood in light of the apostle's conviction that the *parousia*, the second coming of Christ in glory, is at hand. Thus it is better for eve-ryone to remain in his or her present state, whether married or single, slave or free. Today, tragically, we have all but lost that eschatological hope. Consequently, the period of engagement can seem intolerably bur-densome when it is accompanied by a decision on the couple's part to ab-stain from sexual relations.

Nevertheless, the whole of Christian existence, including sexuality, needs to be held in this eschatological perspective. This is why St. Paul links his various admonitions concerning sexual purity—the rejection of fornication, adultery, homosexuality and all else implied by *por-neia*—with the appeal to assume the new life in Christ and in the Spirit.

Let us conduct ourselves becomingly as in the day, not in reveling and drunken-ness, not in debauchery and licentiousness (*koitas kai aselgeiais,* referring to sex-ual depravity), not in quarreling and jealousy. But put on the Lord Jesus Christ, and make no provision for the flesh, to gratify its desires (or lust, *epithymias*). (Rom 13:13-14)

But I say, walk by the Spirit and do not gratify the desires (*epithymian*) of the flesh. For the desires of the flesh are against the Spirit, and the desires of the Spirit are against the flesh... Now the works of the flesh are plain: fornication (*porneia*), impurity (*akatharsia*), licentiousness (*aselgeia*)... (Gal 5:16-19)

Within this eschatological framework, marriage has theological import as a witness to the new creation wrought by Christ and sustained by the Holy Spirit. There can be only one answer to the question, "Why wait until marriage to enjoy sexual relations?" It is because sexuality is the way in which the sacramental, covenantal bond of "one flesh" is constituted. It is the unique sign of that bond and the unique mode by which it is sealed, just as eucharistic celebration is the sign and primary expression of priesthood. As a sacrament of the Church, marriage must be publicly and communally performed. It must be *celebrated* as a witness to the grace bestowed both on the couple and on the community of faith. For the sacrament of marriage, like that of priesthood, initiates committed persons into a life of loving commitment and sacrificial service; and it does so both in and for the life and ministry of the Church as a whole.

Contractual language, typical of Western wedding services, has done a great deal to obscure the essentially sacramental character of marriage.[44] It has also turned attention away from the covenantal dimension of the conjugal vocation. As sacrament and covenant, marriage must be realized by means of the Church's liturgical ritual, since it is through the service itself that the couple's mutual commitment is publicly expressed and their union is sealed by the blessing of God.

---

44 The Roman Catholic Congregation for the Doctrine of the Faith published in Dec., 1975, a "Declaration on Certain Problems of Sexual Ethics," in *Vatican Council II*, Vol. 2, 1982, 486-96; reprinted in *Medical Ethics. Sources of Catholic Teaching*, 2nd ed., (Washington, DC: Georgetown University Press, 1993), 294-301. While the document treats in a very positive way the problems it addresses, its legal, contractual language separates its understanding of the very nature of marriage from that of Orthodoxy. To quote from para. 7: "Experience teaches that love must be protected by the stability of marriage if sexual intercourse is really to meet the demands of its own finality and of human dignity. For this to be achieved there is need of a *contract* sanctioned and protected by society... Those who wish to be united in matrimony should, therefore, manifest their consent externally and in a manner which the community accepts as *valid*. The faithful, for their part, should *declare their consent* to marry in the way prescribed by the *laws of the Church*. This makes their marriage one of Christ's sacraments..." (italics added). To the contrary, marriage is not a "contract," it is a covenant. In addition, marriage becomes genuinely sacramental by divine grace, not by human declarations, "valid" performance of the rite, and conformity to the laws of the Church, however important those may be to performing the wedding ceremony itself. The ceremony, however, like baptism, is merely the "initiation" into a life of committed response to sacramental grace.

This blessing alone creates a true marital union, which provides the only context in which genital sexuality can be exercised in accordance with the will of God. Unmarried people who engage in sexual relations are analogous to our children who delight in "playing priest." The children can read through the service book, perform every gesture, and consume bread and wine. Yet they are not priests and their game is not a sacrament, since they are not ordained and the ecclesial dimension is missing. For the priestly ministry to be not just "valid" but *real*, the Church must receive and sanction the one called to be ordained, and provide the sacramental context within which God has chosen to bestow his saving grace. The same is true for those called to a life of conjugal union. Apart from that context and that sacramental blessing, there is neither priesthood nor marriage. There is at best play-acting, and at worst, blasphemy.

The parallel often drawn between sexual intercourse and eucharistic celebration is neither overly romantic nor frivolous. Both actions presuppose sacramental *consecration* and culminate in *consummation*, which achieves *communion* with the beloved. In addition, both actions are predicated on *sacrifice* which seals the covenant relationship: the sacrifice of Jesus Christ made accessible in the Eucharist, and the sacrifice of the couple, symbolized by the nuptial crowns, as they offer themselves in loving service to each other and to God. Just as one can not authentically participate in Holy Communion without being baptized, and the priest can not celebrate a true Liturgy without being ordained, so a couple can not enjoy the grace God offers through sexual union unless their relationship is blessed by him in the way prescribed and traditionally practiced by the Church. Their love may be deep and their commitment to one another genuine. But without the grace conferred through the sacrament of marriage, there can be no true *communion* between the two. Their sexual relations simply feed "the desires and pleasures of the flesh," and they are unable to attain to the eternal communion and ineffable joy of divinely bestowed, self-transcending *erôs* that unites them with God as well as with one another.

If the priest must be ordained, thereby receiving the "grace divine" to accomplish his ministry, a man and a woman who desire to live as "one flesh" must be married in order to fulfill their specific calling. Otherwise they live a lie, in which pregnancy is a regrettable accident and the divinely inspired commitment that works out mutual salvation is nonexistent. It is only within the context of a blessed conjugal union, then, that sexuality itself can be blessed as a primary means of fulfilling God's will for the life and salvation of the couple.[45]

How, then, are young people to deal with the normal tensions associated with adolescent sexuality? This is an especially difficult question, since marriage is so often delayed today until the couple has reached their late twenties or early thirties. On the other hand, the capacity to procreate, like the sexual drive itself, exists from puberty. This raises the question concerning acceptable expressions of sexuality while dating or during the period of engagement.

Certain cultures attempt to avoid the problem by prohibiting dating and imposing "arranged marriages." Depending on the cultural ethos, this can be more or less successful. Some Orthodox Christians in the United States, understandably troubled by sexual pressures and promiscuity, have also attempted to keep their children from "getting mixed up in the dating game." Occasionally, this too has had a positive outcome. The danger, though, is that it may isolate the young people from their peers and from the culture as a whole. Rather than prohibiting dating altogether or attempting to control its every aspect by adult supervision, a more effective approach would be to teach our children from childhood the real meaning of sexuality, while inculcating in them a sense of respect and responsibility in *all* their personal relationships. In any case, attempts by adults to *control* their teenagers' dating habits and sexual behavior—as opposed to directing and guiding them—are doomed to failure, except in the rare cases where the children really want such control. The motivation for responsible conduct needs to come from within the young person. It cannot be artificially imposed by others, including parents, without creating resentment and alienation.

One of the most difficult decisions a dating or engaged couple needs to make is "where to draw the line?" When young people begin to think about the question, they usually have a number of specific behaviors in mind that can extend from holding hands, through kissing and petting, to intercourse. Their concern might be to determine in advance just what

---

45 Accordingly, St. Basil asserts, "Fornication is neither marriage, nor the beginning of marriage..." (Second Canonical Epistle, Canon XXVI; *NPNF* XIV, 606); and St. Gregory of Nyssa imposes on fornicators a penance of nine years, the first three "wholly ejected from prayer." The penalty is doubled in cases of adultery. (Canonical Epistle to St. Letoius, Bishop of Melitene; *NPNF* XIV, 611).

level of sexual involvement they will allow themselves. In light of what we have said about the nature and purpose of sexuality, however, this is a very inadequate approach. In the first place, precise limits can rarely be established beforehand, other than to determine certain "off limits." The couple, for example, may decide that they do not want to engage in intercourse, and that sexual play that causes arousal should therefore be avoided. Emotions tend to be so volatile, though, that very quickly the passions dominate reason, and the proposed boundary is crossed. This simply "ups the ante" until one of the two persuades the other to stop, or else capitulates to internal desires and external pressures. It is in just such circumstances that there occurs the all-too-frequent abuse—and crime—known as "date rape."[46]

It sounds quaint today, but the only moral guideline that conforms to the Church's teaching on premarital sexuality is that of *abstinence*. Virginity possesses an emotional and spiritual value that has always been recognized and treasured among Christians, as among Jews and others of strong religious commitment.[47] Many young people today, it seems, are rediscovering that value. Their struggle definitely needs to be acknowledged and supported by the parish as well as by their families. (Unfortunately, with few exceptions the public schools cannot be expected to offer any encouragement or assistance in this area. It is easier to distribute condoms than to deal with the moral and psychological issues that arise over adolescent fascination with sex. In any case, concerned teachers are confronting the awesome fact that well over half of all boys and girls in this country have engaged in intercourse by the time they are eighteen.)

---

46 It is because of this inevitable progression, built in to the peculiarly American style of dating, that many Orthodox Christians are looking for alternative ways to foster relationships between their children and other young people. One solution would be to organize "group dating," as suggested by Fr. Terry Somerville in a perceptive and well-balanced article, "The American Dating Game. Its Dangers for Teenagers," *Epiphany Journal* (spring-summer, 1987), 27-31. This, as he notes, would ensure that virtually all young people in a given social milieu (the church, school, neighborhood) could participate, and that sexual pressures would be kept to a minimum. It is overly optimistic to expect that such an arrangement would be accepted by all, to the point that it prevents teen pregnancy and abortions. Nevertheless, it offers a reasonable alternative to the pairing off that is today's basically unhealthy norm.

47 The Council of Gangra (ca. 345-360) was particularly concerned to stress the value and sanctity of marriage, yet in Canon IX the Fathers assert, "If any one shall remain virgin, or observe continence, abstaining from marriage because he abhors it, *and not on account of the beauty and holiness of virginity itself,* let him be anathema" (*NPNF* XIV, 95).

The only hope, then, for helping our children to preserve their virginity, or even to protect themselves effectively against AIDS, is to encourage them to abstain from sexual relations until they marry. This kind of encouragement can be reasonably effective when it takes the form of educational programs sponsored by the parish community, programs for which the priest is ultimately responsible. Such programs should involve parents to the fullest extent possible, by teaching them the deeper meaning of sexuality and urging them to transmit that teaching to their children, beginning in the earliest school years.

Part of that training will include sensitizing young people to the importance of redirecting sexual energy from the self to others and particularly to God. Transforming the erotic into *erôs* is not simply a monastic exercise. It involves the proper use of sexuality by every Christian, man or woman, married or single. Therefore, a rule of thumb both for dating and for the period of engagement would be to refrain from activity that might produce a level of sexual arousal that can lead to orgasm. As two people come to know, enjoy and cherish each other, it is quite natural that they move from timid gestures of affection to kissing and caressing. They should always keep in mind, however, that the "natural" is fallen, and—particularly in the realm of sexuality—it is constantly open to the demonic. Rationalization, or "rationalized" passions, can very easily lead from one degree of intimacy to another, until the best of intentions are left in the dust and the couple has given in to fornication. As many young people admit in confession: when this happens, they feel dirty and cheapened, not because of the sex itself, but because an ideal has been shattered and, all too often, someone has been irreparably hurt. Needless to say, pastoral sensitivity at such moments is indispensable. It should include firmness, but it should also convey forgiveness and compassion.

It is all but impossible to impose limits—concrete answers to the question, "Where do we draw the line?"—simply because it is so difficult to observe those limits when they appear to be legalistic and arbitrary. Rather than urge our young people to draw a line and swear they won't cross it, another approach would be more fruitful. That is to encourage them, from preadolescence onward, to think and talk about the meaning of their life as children of God, as bearers of his image, and as persons whose only true value and meaning come from faithfulness to God and responsible stewardship offered in his Name to other people. It is within this framework that sexuality can be approached, frankly and openly, with full respect for its power as well as for its beauty and creative potential.

Adultery.

These conclusions regarding premarital sexual relations hold *a fortiori* for extra-marital relations, which constitute adultery. The term "adultery" generally refers to sexual intercourse between a married person and a partner of the opposite sex who is not his or her spouse. The concept needs to be broadened, however, to include *any genital sexuality shared with someone other than one's marriage partner*, including homosexual relations. A married man, for example, who engages in homosexuality is no less an adulterer than one who has sex with a woman other than his wife.

Scripture is unambiguous about the matter of adultery, from the seventh commandment to Jesus' own teachings. One of the great "antitheses" of the Sermon on the Mount makes the point that sexual lust involves the mind and heart as much as it does the flesh.

> "You have heard that it was said, 'You shall not commit adultery' [Ex 20:14; Deut 5:18]. But I say to you that everyone who looks at a woman lustfully has already committed adultery with her in his heart." (Mt 5:27-28)

This is in essence a call to refrain from *idolatry*. By its very nature lust is obsessive. It focuses the attention in an unhealthy (today we would say "dysfunctional") way on a person who is thereby reduced to an object. The obsessive or compulsive element creates an "idol" of that object. Like every idol, it is unreal, the imaginary product of fantasizing. Yet its hold on the mind and heart is such that it turns both from the true God and his unique claim on human life and thought (cf. 1 Cor 8:4-5).

Lust that leads to adultery violates to the core the covenantal bond created between spouses by the sacrament of marriage. Therefore Jesus follows his word about adulterous lust with the rigorous advice that it is better to "cut off" an offending member than to have the whole body go into Gehenna or hell (Mt 5:29-30). The conjugal bond can only endure if it is built on trust, commitment and faithfulness. Because adultery so thoroughly undermines those values, Jesus (according to Matthew's tradition) allows the famous "exception" to his absolute prohibition of divorce: "I say to you that everyone who divorces his wife, except on the ground of unchastity (*porneia*), makes her an adulteress; and whoever marries a divorced woman commits adultery" (5:31; 19:9).

Whether *porneia* in this context is to be understood as referring explicitly
to adultery, or whether it signifies a broad range of sexual offenses, the
point is clear. When it is misused—that is, exercised apart from the conjugal union itself—sexual activity destroys the intimate bond of trust,
commitment and faithfulness that is the *sine qua non* of marriage. It irreparably violates the covenant relationship between spouses and alienates
the offender from God. And it does so because God is the ultimate source
and end of that relationship. Therefore the Lord of the Old Covenant
condemns idolatry as a form of adultery, just as Jesus condemns adultery
as the ultimate rejection of God's purpose in making of man and woman
"one flesh" (cf. Mk 10:4-9).

The canons of the Church often prescribe periods of excommunication for adultery, both as punishment and as a way of leading the penitent
to become cognizant of the gravity of the act. The Council of Ancyra
(A.D. 314), for example, prescribes a penalty of seven years' penance for
the adulterous husband or wife.[48] Even living with an adulterous wife is
sufficient to bar a layman from the priesthood and to cause a cleric to be
deposed.[49] For his part, St. Basil includes adulterers with murderers and
sodomites (homosexuals), and proposes for them a similar punishment.
His Canon 58 (Third Canonical Epistle) stipulates, "The adulterer shall
be four years a mourner, five a hearer, four a prostrator, two a co-stander,"
before being allowed to receive Holy Communion.

The lure of extramarital sex is especially strong where there is loneliness and frustration, particularly in connection with the "midlife crisis."
Apart from divorced and separated men, the typical client of a prostitute
is a middle-aged white male who is "happily married" and reasonably af-
fluent. If he pays for sex, it is usually to compensate for the perception
that his wife can no longer satisfy his desires, or that his career has become
either unbearably humdrum or dog-eat-dog. The clergy, of course, are
not immune to these feelings and disappointments. Insofar as they allow
themselves to fall into fornication, particularly with a married woman,
they undermine the trust of the souls for whom they are responsible, and

48 Canon 20: "If the wife of anyone has committed adultery or if any man commit adultery, it
    seems fit that he shall be restored to full communion after seven years passed in the prescribed
    degrees [of penance]" (*NPNF* XIV, 73).
49 Synod of Neocaesarea, Canon 8 (*NPNF* XIV, 83).

thereby they betray their very vocation. Therefore Apostolic Canon 25 declares: "If a bishop, presbyter or deacon be found guilty of fornication, perjury, or theft, let him be deposed."[50] And the first canon of the Synod of Neocaesarea (early fourth century) states flatly, "If a presbyter marries, let him be removed from his order; but if he commits fornication or adultery, let him be altogether cast out [excommunicated] and put under penance."[51] There is something particularly heinous about members of the clergy destroying marital relationships by committing adultery, and the canons reflect that fact.

What of the pastoral issue involved? Does this mean that a woman who comes to her priest with the claim that her husband has committed adultery should be encouraged to seek a divorce? Does it mean that any sexual misconduct (*porneia*) on the part of one of the spouses irretrievably destroys the covenant bond between them?

On the scale of moral values, adultery is obviously more serious than premarital sexual activity, precisely because it violates an existing marital covenant: the bond of love, trust and commitment between two persons. Nevertheless, neither premarital nor extramarital sex amounts to an unforgivable sin. In the case of adultery, a couple is left with only one means for reconciliation: *repentance* on the part of the offender, with *forgiveness* offered by the spouse. There may be no other situation that challenges the emotional and spiritual resources of a couple more than when one of them engages in an adulterous relationship. The offended spouse, wife or husband, tends to feel betrayed, rejected, humiliated and shamed. Those are powerful emotions that need to be faced, expressed and worked through—often with appropriate third-party counseling—if healing is to occur.

But adultery, like any other sin, concerns not only the persons most immediately involved. It also concerns the Church community. We are "members one of another," bound together in a Body, of which Christ is the Head. We have a responsibility toward each member, to bring about reconciliation and peace whenever possible. To preserve confidentiality, the priest may have to represent the parish community by himself, as he tries to move the couple toward reconciliation and healing. But all those

50 *NPNF* vol. XIV, 595.
51 *Ibid.*, 79.

who are aware of the situation—the spouse and friends, as well as the priest—can and should participate in that process by means of *unceasing prayer* offered on behalf of everyone concerned.

In cases of sexual misconduct, it is crucial that the priest, and any others who are aware of the circumstances, preserve confidentiality to the fullest extent possible, particularly when it involves a penitent's confession. There are rare cases, nevertheless, which may require that confidentiality be broken, primarily those that involve pedophilia, incest or rape. Whether the priest is obliged to divulge his knowledge to legal authorities, or to confront the perpetrator while he comforts the victim and his or her family, he must take every precaution to preserve confessional confidentiality. Apart from situations where the confessed sin places other lives in jeopardy—as with pedophilia, serial rape or intended homicide—that confidentiality must remain absolute. (Fr. John of Kronstadt and other holy priests may have elicited healthy public confessions, but such exceptions are extremely rare, and in today's psychological climate, practically nonexistent. Besides, in such cases the penitent voluntarily confesses within the church body; the priest does not divulge what was spoken to him in secret.) The priest may find that he has to deal with the matter alone. If counseling seems necessary, then he should be prepared to make appropriate referrals. It may also be possible for him to network with others within or outside the parish who know the couple and can be trusted to provide sensitive and confidential support. In any case, the aim should be to seek genuine repentance on the part of the offending spouse and to elicit willing forgiveness from the marriage partner. Insofar as the third party is accessible and open to such a process, the priest is to offer him or her appropriate pastoral care as well.

Although the priest's main concern may be with the offender (particularly if the offender is a friend or another priest), he needs to be especially sensitive to the needs and feelings of the injured party. Too often the temptation is to recuperate the offender while neglecting the spouse, to bring back the prodigal while ignoring the older brother. Both of them require pastoral care, one no less than the other. And the issue is all the more complex, demanding all the more pastoral discernment and sensitivity, when the third party is also a member of the parish community. Priority should be given to preserving and strengthening the family unit as a whole, especially when it includes children. Usually that means the priest must encourage the adulterous spouse to "share the secret" with the other—to open the wound so that it can be treated—and to take whatever steps are necessary to ensure that he or she receives healing through repentance and appropriate counseling.

In addition to pastoral counseling once the offense has occurred, the priest should make clear the Church's traditional stance regarding sexuality in general and sexual sins in particular, through his sermons and other teaching opportunities. It is important, however, to avoid moralizing by emphasizing the theological and spiritual values that sexuality properly embodies. This will include a focus on the importance of *askesis* or ascetic struggle in the life of faith. The objective, after all, is not merely to avoid committing sexual sins. It is to engage in the spiritual warfare that leads to transfigured life.

The struggle against lustful thoughts, like that against sexual "acting out," has to be understood as a profoundly spiritual one. If Jesus and the Scriptures in general condemn sexual misconduct so vehemently, it is because of its potential to destroy human relationships and to reduce the person to a caricature of authentic humanity. Sexuality, once again, must be held in an *eschatological* perspective. For ultimately, sexual morality is only justified—in our overcharged sexual atmosphere it only makes sense—insofar as it charts the pathway that leads through covenant fidelity toward the Kingdom of God.[52]

Pornography.
From this perspective it is clear where the Church stands on the question of pornography. The phenomenon is big business in the United States, and efforts to control it as detrimental to the public welfare have had little success. Part of the problem is that it is so difficult to define. Sexual imagery reflects different values in different cultures. The French, for example, are quite accepting of partial or even total nudity on television and on their beaches; but most would be offended by the cheap salaciousness—sexual gags and innuendo—that is standard fare on American prime time. Nevertheless, there are certain universal intuitions about the

52 For an interesting approach in the same vein from an Evangelical Protestant perspective, see Lewis Smedes, "Respect for Covenant," in *From Christ to the World* (Boulton, Kennedy and Verhey, eds.), (Minneapolis, MN: Eerdmans, 1994), 347-353.

subject ("we know it when we see it") that enable us to make some distinctions and suggest some guidelines.

The first distinction is between "hard-core" and "soft-core" pornography. The former, including sadomasochistic images and "kiddie-porn," amounts to exploitation and abuse of the worst kind. Because it is inherently destructive, every effort should be made by concerned parents, educators and the public in general to eradicate it altogether. This includes boycotting and, where possible, bringing legal action against the perpetrators, as well as those who profit from their activities. Hard-core porn is a scourge that no civilized society should tolerate. Its widespread presence and enormous economic influence in this country tend unfortunately to confirm Georges Clémenceau's mordant observation, that the United States is the only nation in history to go from barbarity to decadence without passing through a period of civilization....

For a quick review of the prevalence and impact of hard-core pornography on the American ethos, it is enough to glance through the February 10, 1997, issue of *U.S. News & World Report.* Against the image of a popular porn film star, the cover announces that "America is by far the world's leading producer of porn, churning out hard-core videos at the astonishing rate of about 150 new titles per week." The cover story offers statistics: "A well-run strip club makes $5 million a year"; "Top porn stars earn $20,000 a week dancing"; "Some $8 billion was spent on porn last year"; the number of hard-core-video rentals rose from 75 million in 1985 to 665 million in 1996, at a cost of over $8 billion; "dial-a-porn" is called up nearly 200 million times each year; and so forth. The report begins by featuring the top porn-film producer in the country, whose company, appropriately enough, is named "Evil Angel Videos." Its basic point is that the industry has reduced women to dehumanized objects of other people's obsessive desires. It is a remarkable chronicle of depravity that most readers, presumably, scanned with a smile and a shrug. And the exploitation goes on relentlessly.

Soft-core pornography is so rampant that we hardly recognize its presence anymore. From the rather benign *Victoria's Secret* catalogs to the more explicit sex magazines and videos, soft-core porn fills our homes and workplaces as well as our schools. Here, too, there is a problem of definition. Is explicit intercourse in an "R" rated shower scene "hard" core or "soft"? And does it really matter? The question is, what are the effects of the media's saturation and the public's obsession with sex? What becomes of the minds and sensibilities of those who watch soap operas every day, or sex-oriented talk shows? What is the impression made on our children when sex and violence are systematically linked in their Saturday morning cartoons?

According to most researchers, there is still no conclusive evidence that pornography leads to an increase in sex crimes. Yet its prevalence in the homes of those who perpetrate rape, child abuse and other violent sexual acts gives strong support to the theory that it stimulates and reinforces deviant behavior. What is beyond doubt is the fact that pornography violates and degrades those it depicts, whether men, women or children. It detaches the most intimate human behavior from any sense of love, faithfulness or responsibility, and it objectifies and cheapens sex by focusing on an image—a fantasy—that by definition has no substance, no reality. (Those sex manuals that encourage the couple to fantasize that their partner is a more alluring someone else are doing nothing other than inciting to adultery.) Thereby it degrades and depersonalizes sexuality in a way that can only be described as abusive. Given this influence, it is difficult to see how reasonable, morally healthy people can claim that pornography, particularly hard-core, should be protected under the First Amendment.

The German atheistic philosopher Ludwig Feuerbach declared, "Man ist was man ißt!": "We are what we eat!" Fr. Alexander Schmemann turned this phrase brilliantly, demonstrating that our true purpose in life is to consume the Holy Eucharist and thereby to "become eucharistic." Iconography exists in the Church precisely to feed the mind and soul with heavenly food, the food of purity, blessedness and sanctity. Pornography is demonic iconography. It infests the mind with corrupt images that produce corruption in the depths of the soul. Pornography is addictive. Those who rely on it—whether to relieve tension and anxiety, or to increase a self-induced sexual "high"—inevitably need to increase the dosage to maintain the same effect. Finally, pornography is abusive. As an industry it exploits and manipulates those who depend on it for their livelihood, and it leads to the self-abuse of those who use it for sexual stimulation. However much it may contribute to the GNP, there is little that can be said to justify it and no way to redeem it. If indeed "we are what we eat," then pornography is clearly poison to the system. As the perverse antithesis of authentic iconography, it invites the treatment Jesus recommended for any offense involving sight: "If your right eye causes you to sin, pluck it out and throw it away" (Mt 5:29). A less radical course of action, but one that is perhaps as effective, is simply to take the pornographic material and get rid of it. "Out of sight, out of mind," is a worn maxim, but it expresses an important truth.

A Church canon, promulgated at the Synod *in Trullo* ("Quinisext," A.D. 692), speaks directly to this issue:

> "Let your eyes behold what is right," Wisdom orders, "and keep your heart with all care." For the bodily senses easily bring their own impressions into the soul. Therefore, we order that henceforth there shall be made no pictures, whether in paintings or any other medium, which attract the eye and corrupt the mind, and incite it to the enkindling of base pleasures.[53]

If Orthodox tradition and the intuitions of Christian people condemn pornography, it is precisely because "the bodily senses easily bring their own impressions into the soul." Pornography debases and corrupts those who produce it and those who use it. Therefore it is a social and a moral problem of major proportions. And because it "dehumanizes" by deforming the image of God in the human person, it is a profoundly spiritual one as well.

Masturbation.
Closely connected to pornography is the practice of masturbation. In recent decades we have moved from myth to myth regarding this issue. From the groundless fear that masturbation causes mental illness and physical deformity, we have come to the point where many medical professionals, as well as clergy and other counselors, are presenting it as a wholly benign activity that is to be encouraged as a means of dealing with sexual tensions, within marriage as well as outside.

In infants, certain forms of self-exploration, often referred to as masturbation, are perfectly normal. As a child grows and approaches puberty, hormonal changes create urges that are also part of normal biological growth. Some self-exploration and stimulation at this age is inevitable and not particularly harmful. The major harm in early adolescence, in

53 Canon 100, *NPNF* XIV, 407, translation slightly modified.

fact, seems to occur when the behavior is surrounded by intense feelings of guilt or shame. These feelings are almost always due to the disapproval expressed by parents or other authority figures in the child's life. It is important, then, that attitudes transmitted to our children be informed both by the Tradition of the Church and by biological reality. Parents who have difficulties with their own sexuality, or who practice masturbation yet do so with shame, are likely to transfer those difficulties and feelings to their children. Sexuality, like most human behavior, is strongly influenced by pressures and attitudes common to the "family system." If those attitudes are healthy and realistic, and compassionate guidance replaces the pressures, then conditions exist for a child to preserve sexual health and to grow toward sexual maturity.

If the urge that leads to masturbation is basically biological and is only reinforced by external influences, then why do the great majority of Orthodox moral theologians, together with our bishops and parish pastors, find the practice to be wrong, or at least unhealthy? The answer is complex, but it includes the same factors we mentioned in connection with premarital relations and pornography.

In the first place, masturbation is usually accompanied by images that are essentially pornographic. Whether the images are internal (fantasies) or external (erotica), they involve the exploitation and devaluation of other persons. Then again, masturbation is a caricature of what should be appropriate conjugal sexual expression. It focuses entirely on the self and on personal gratification. The basic elements of love and commitment characteristic of blessed conjugal relations are obviously lacking. For this reason, Roman Catholic responses to the question, grounded in natural law theology, usually consider masturbation to be contrary to the "natural" purpose for which God created sexuality in the first place. It frustrates the end of procreation, it lacks mutual self-giving, and it violates the command to lead a life of chastity. To fulfill its true purpose, sexuality must promote communion between two persons, a lasting union of "one flesh."

In addition to these spiritual and theological objections, we need to consider as well the fact that masturbation easily becomes addictive. Ever increasing doses of stimulation, whatever its form, must be found in order to produce the same sexual "high." Once the behavior becomes compulsive, it is extremely difficult to curb. National self-help groups such as

"Sexaholics Anonymous" (SA) can be very supportive to those afflicted with sexual obsessions and compulsive masturbation. (There are similar groups that in fact encourage sexual acting out, and they should be avoided altogether.)

If a penitent repeatedly confesses to masturbating, this should alert the priest that the person is struggling with an addictive pattern of behavior. Simply admonishing that he or she stop or change the behavior usually will not work. Occasionally it is possible to devise with the person some form of recovery program. But again, that is most effective when it is undertaken in the framework of SA (with an accompanying sponsor) or with the support of a trained therapist. If the penitent is willing to pray about the matter with the priest, and then to accept brief and renewable periods of total abstinence, healing often comes and the addictive pattern is broken.

It is important, however, that the person in question be treated as someone afflicted with an illness, not as a moral reprobate. Those who struggle with sexual addiction will usually admit that it is a painful, shameful and often unbearable cross. However much he or she may act out, a sex addict gains no more pleasure or satisfaction from the behavior than a porn-film star does from going through multiple retakes of an erotic scene. Compulsive masturbation, in fact, is very often accompanied by feelings of shame, anger and self-loathing. To the degree these feelings are the cause rather than the result of the autoerotic behavior, some form of appropriate therapy is called for.

Pastoral care toward a person involved in compulsory masturbation will express personal concern, forgiveness and support, rather than judgment and condemnation. As he would with any ill parishioner, the priest who recommends someone to therapy will accompany the person, with love, understanding and prayer, through the long journey toward recovery.[54]

---

54 See Wm. Basil Zion's discussion of masturbation in *Erôs and Transformation*, 263-288. This is a compassionate, well-balanced approach that many Orthodox will criticize as too "liberal." The author nevertheless offers useful insight into the psychological issues underlying masturbation, while he stresses unequivocally that such acts are sinful. I would agree fully with his pastoral intuition: "It is, I believe, wrong to castigate those who fall into masturbation to relieve their anxiety, isolation, or depression. The act remains reparative, symptomatic, and usually dysfunctional" (282). He also notes that masturbation is "often compulsive" and "sometimes pathological" (*ibid.*). More consideration needs to be given to the addictive or compulsory aspect of masturbation, but again, with compassion and sympathy for those so afflicted.

Nocturnal Emissions.

A further word needs to be said here about nocturnal emissions and the misunderstanding often associated with them. Frequently young men will come to confession, bearing a certain burden of guilt because the emissions occurred. If it happens on a Saturday or before a feast day, the question arises as to whether they may receive Holy Communion.

Often the man is concerned that he has "committed the sin of Onan" (Gen 38:9) and is responsible for having "wasted his seed." Although "onanism" in today's language refers to male masturbation, its original meaning had more to do with coitus interruptus. (Onan's sin is not that he masturbates, but that he refuses to fulfill the responsibilities of the *levir*, whose duty it is to impregnate his brother's widow in order to preserve his brother's lineage. His offense, in other words, lies not so much in "spilling his semen on the ground," as in refusing to comply with levirate law.) If sperm is wasted through masturbation, then it is clearly the result of a sinful act. The same cannot be said, however, for nocturnal emissions.

We need to understand that nocturnal emissions are a normal and healthy aspect of bodily functioning. As with many things, they can be the cause of sin if the surrounding feelings and images are dwelt upon, and particularly if they lead to masturbation. But the phenomenon itself is not inherently sinful. Even the lustful feelings that often accompany and provoke the emissions are products of our biology and as such can hardly qualify as a moral evil.

The Epistle of St. Athanasius to the monk Ammus is worth quoting in this regard.[55]

Involuntary nocturnal pollutions [sic] are not sinful: "For what sin or uncleanness can any natural excrement have in itself? Think of the absurdity of making a sin of the wax which comes from the ears or of the spittle from the mouth. Moreover we might add many things and explain how the excretions from the belly are necessary to animal life. But if we believe that man is the work of God's hand, as we are taught in holy Scripture, how can it be supposed necessary that we perform anything impure?"

Here Athanasius refers to Acts 10:15, "What God has cleansed, you must not call common," meaning unclean or impure. Although the pejorative term "pollutions" is used, in its context it means simply "emissions."

---

55 From the Canons of Athanasius, *NPNF* XIV, 602-603.

The point is clear: nocturnal emissions, like other bodily wastes, are products of natural functions created and blessed by God. In themselves they are not an impediment to one's receiving Holy Communion. In a similar vein, the Canonical Epistle of Dionysius of Alexandria to the Bishop Basilides (ca. 247), Canon 4, advises: "They who have had involuntary nocturnal pollutions be at their own discretion [whether to communicate or not]."[56] The Canonical Answer of Timothy of Alexandria, Question 12, makes an important distinction in this regard between human lust and demonic temptation: "If a layman ask a clergyman whether he may communicate after a nocturnal pollution?" *Answer*. "If it proceed from the desire of a woman, he ought not, but if it be a temptation from Satan, he ought; for the tempter will ply him when he is to communicate."[57]

As with "thoughts," which the desert fathers knew to be so dangerous, the feelings and emotions that accompany emissions can easily lead to sin, although in and of themselves they represent only "temptation." Everything depends on what we do with them. Like all "thoughts," they should be recognized for what they are, then discarded. In a word, deliver them over into the hands of God, then go back to sleep.

Homosexuality.
Finally, we need to consider the delicate and difficult issue of homosexuality. The subject is delicate because it involves behaviors that have been historically condemned by society as well as by biblical authority, yet specialists maintain that at least ten percent of the population has engaged in some form of homosexual activity or has desired to do so, and three to four percent are of exclusively homosexual orientation. The subject is difficult because it involves so much controversy. In recent years we have witnessed a polarization between those who confuse a homosexual "orientation" with specific behaviors, giving rise to a condemnation of the person, and those who hold that homosexuality is morally neutral and therefore "a viable alternative lifestyle." Those who associate themselves with the "gay-lesbian" movement are involved in a deep-seated conflict with those who defend "traditional values" (exclusively heterosexual unions within the framework of marriage). The conflict has spilled over into

56 *NPNF* XIV, 600.
57 *Ibid.*, 613.

the public sphere with militant gays and lesbians demanding special legislation that would allow same-sex unions (homosexual "marriages"), adoptions by homosexual couples, and unrestricted access to housing and employment. Within the churches, the major point of contention is over access of active homosexuals to the ordained ministry. The entire conflict is exacerbated by the language employed by "homophobes" (epithets that demean homosexuals and vilify homoerotic behavior) and "homophiles" (accusations of "homophobia" and "patriarchalist heterosexism" hurled indiscriminately against those who disagree with them).

The usual definition of homosexuality holds it to be a "predominant and persistent psychosexual attraction toward members of the same sex."[58] The term generally designates both sexual desire for a person of the same sex, and the behavior expressive of that desire. Recent clinical studies have shown that homosexuality is conditioned by multiple factors: physiological, genetic, psychological and social. The precise relationship between "nature" and "nurture"—between the genetic and environmental influences that determine a homosexual orientation—is still unclear. Militant gays tend to stress the genetic component, in defense of the theory that homosexuality is inborn and irreversible, in an effort to establish themselves as a legally protected minority group. Others, such as the Orthodox psychotherapist Elisabeth Moberly, stress the role of environmental factors, particularly relational deficits within the family of origin.

In 1991, neurobiologist Simon LeVay discovered that a small bundle of neurons in the hypothalamus of the brain of homosexual men was only a third to a half the size of that in heterosexual men and about the same size as that of heterosexual women. Since both homosexual men and heterosexual women are erotically attracted to men, this suggested that the size of the hypothalamic nucleus is linked to sexual orientation.[59] (The hypothalamus regulates body temperature, sleep, hunger, heart rate and other autonomic activities including the sex drive.) The question remained, however, whether the diminished size of the nucleus was the cause or the result of the homosexual condition. In 1992, psychologist J. M. Bailey and psychiatrist R. C. Pillard reported further evidence that genetic factors are significant in

58 *Westminster Dictionary of Christian Ethics* (Philadelphia: Westminster, 1986), 271.
59 "A Difference in Hypothalamic Structure Between Heterosexual and Homosexual Men," *Science* no. 253 (1991), 1034-1037.

shaping sexual orientation.[60] Further research has supported but not fully established the claim that genes play a role in sexual preference. Virtually all specialists insist, however, that social and psychological factors need to be considered as well. As John F. Harvey points out, the fact that nearly half of identical twins do not share their identical sibling's homosexual orientation reinforces the argument that psychosexual development is shaped at least in part by a child's environment.[61]

The distinction between homosexual *acts* and homosexual *orientation* is a recent one, based on the work of Freud and other researchers in the area of human sexuality. It is a distinction that was unknown in biblical times, when it was assumed that homosexual behavior was a fully willed, sinful perversion of the God-given sexual capacity. The question is, in what way does that judgment need to be revised now that sexual "orientation" is an established fact? And does the reality of "orientation" mean that homosexual acts resulting from it are to be accepted as morally good or right?

The position of the Orthodox Church on the matter holds that *all homosexual acts are morally wrong:* they distort the natural purpose and functioning of bodily organs, they have no procreative value, and they represent a parody of "one flesh" union. The wildly promiscuous character of much homosexual behavior reinforces the perception that it is inherently sinful, while the specific acts—including anal intercourse as well as oral-genital and oral-anal stimulation—provoke among many people a sense of revulsion and disgust. These feelings are reflected in several of the biblical passages and patristic writings that condemn homosexual activity.

The main scriptural passages in question are Gen 19:4-11, the men of Sodom attempt to rape Lot's male (angelic) visitors; Lev 18:22, "You shall not lie with a male as with a woman; it is an abomination," and 20:13, the death penalty is prescribed for this particular sexual offense; Rom 1:26-27, men gave up natural relations with women, "committing shameless acts with men"; 1 Cor 6:9-11, among those who will not inherit the Kingdom of God

60 *Science News*, vol. 141 (Jan. 4, 1992), 6.
61 *The Truth About Homosexuality*, 45. See also his brief article, "Homosexual Orientation and Genetics," in *Ethics & Medics* 21/5 (May 1996), 1-2, in which he concludes: "We really do not know how genetic and hormonal factors interact with environmental influences to bring about a homosexual orientation in a given individual. At most, one can say that genetic and hormonal factors may *predispose* toward a homosexual orientation, but not *predetermine* it. Predispositive genetic factors alone do not lead to homosexual orientation."

are idolaters, adulterers and "sexual perverts" (as the *RSV* translates *arsenokoitai*, which refers specifically to male homosexuality); 1 Tim 1:8-11, the law is laid down for the ungodly and sinners as well as for *pornois, arsenokoitais* and *andrapodistais* (the sexually immoral, homosexuals, kidnappers); and Jude 7, which refers to the sexual immorality and unnatural lust (*ekporneusasai...sarkos heteras*) of Sodom and Gomorrah. To these must be added Dt 23:17, a prohibition of male as well as female cult prostitution in Israel; and 1 Kg 14:24 and 22:46, which include male cult prostitution among "abominations" in God's sight.

Considerable effort has been expended by certain biblical scholars and others to show that these passages cannot be read as a wholesale condemnation of homosexuality. Some of that effort has been fruitful, but much of it has been motivated by a "political correctness" agenda that has produced a good deal of specious exegesis. According to this kind of reading, the men of Sodom are guilty not of "sodomy," but of a breach in Oriental hospitality.[62] The Levitical prescriptions are held to concern only "cultic purity." In Romans, it is argued, St. Paul inveighs against idolatry, with lust as its consequence. And the Corinthians and Timothy references are understood as directed only against Greco-Roman pederasty, rather than against homosexuality as such. (As far as I know, no one has built a reasonable argument against the *prima facie* meaning of Jude 7.) When these verses are read in context—and especially when they are taken in light of Jesus' teachings concerning marriage and the biblical understanding of conjugal union—there can be little question that they basically condemn homosexual *acts*.

Similar condemnations appear throughout the patristic literature. Didachê 2:2 reads: "you shall not commit murder, adultery, pederasty (*paidophthoreseis*),[63] fornication..." Theophilus of Antioch, Clement and Athanasius of Alexandria, John of Damascus, and many other patristic witnesses condemn *paidophthoria*, but this may be limited to what we would term pedophilia or child sexual abuse.[64]

---

62 Reference is often made in this regard to Ezek 16:49-50, where Sodom is described as guilty of pride, gluttony, luxury, and a failure to aid the poor and needy. The entire context, (16:35-63), however, concerns deviant sex.

63 This is a neologism that replaces the usual *paiderastia*. See *La Doctrine des Douze Apôtres*, Sources chrétiennes, no. 248 (Paris: Cerf, 1978), 148-149 and note 4, 149, for other intertestamental and Jewish references condemning pederasty.

64 See G. W. H. Lampe, *A Patristic Greek Lexicon* (Oxford: Clarendon Press, 1961), 997, *ad loc.*

Less ambiguous are the writings of St. Basil the Great and particularly St. John Chrysostom. Basil's Canon 7 of his First Canonical Epistle states: "They who have committed sodomy with men or brutes, murderers, wizards, adulterers, and idolaters, have been thought worthy of the same punishment....We ought not to make any doubt of receiving those who have repented thirty years [sic] for the uncleanness which they committed through ignorance..."[65] His Canon 62 of the Third Canonical Epistle declares: "He that abuses himself with mankind, shall do the penance of an adulterer" (i.e., fifteen years of excommunication, Can. 58); and Canon 63 adds: "And so shall he who abuses himself with beasts..."[66] The Apostolic Canon 61 prohibits fornicators, adulterers and homosexuals from acceding to the rank of cleric: "If any accusation be brought against a believer of fornication or adultery, or any forbidden action [implying homosexual acts], and he be convicted, let him not be promoted to the clergy."[67]

Most rigorous of all is St. John Chrysostom, particularly in his homilies on Romans 1 and 4. Homosexual behavior is declared to be a "monstrous insaneness," an unnatural passion performed by those who have "deserted God." "This madness, which is so much worse than fornication as cannot even be expressed," degrades a man to a level lower than the animals.[68] Chrysostom's emotional rhetoric is to be explained, at least in part, by the fact that he believed homosexual activity to be purely voluntary, a willful perversion of the heterosexuality common to all men. This view is no longer tenable, since there is definitely a psychologically as well as genetically conditioned sexual "orientation" that in many if not most cases is irreversible. It is this clinically established fact that has led moral theologians to reassess the relationship between orientation and behavior, as well as the moral significance of homosexual acts themselves.

The Roman Catholic Magisterium, expressed through the Sacred Congregation for the Doctrine of the Faith (CDF), has urged that pastoral support and understanding be extended to those of homosexual orientation, while it considers the condition itself to be fundamentally

65 NPNF XIV, 604.
66 For the full text, see NPNF second series, vol. 8, 257.
67 NPNF XIV, 598. Stanley Harakas adds in this connection Canon 19 of John the Faster and Canon 4 of Cyril of Alexandria. Contemporary Moral Issues, 95.
68 Hom. 4 on Rom 1:26-27; NPNF first series, vol. 11, 355-359.

"disordered," flawed, or at the very least incomplete.[69] Several Catholic moral theologians (McCormick, Curran, and Cahill, among others) have questioned the appropriateness of the expression "objectively disordered" to describe the homosexual condition, claiming that it reflects negatively on the person and not only on the behavior. Defenders of the term reply that it does not mean "that the homosexual person as such is evil or bad."[70] While they adamantly condemn as morally wrong all homosexual genital activity ("acting out"), they call for recognition that the homosexual condition itself, even though disordered (we might say "dysfunctional"), is not inherently sinful. The distinction, as well as the terminology, is defended on grounds of Catholic natural theology.

From fundamentalist Protestant churches on the right to the New York Metropolitan Community Church on the left, Christian responses to the phenomenon of homosexuality have been identified as follows: (1) "rejecting-punitive," with blanket condemnation of both acts and orientation as "abhorrent," "deviant," "perverted," etc.; (2) "rejecting-non-punitive," which regards homosexuality as disordered and deficient, yet condemns the sin rather than the sinner; (3) "qualified acceptance," acknowledging that homosexuality and its acts constitute an "ontic" evil, yet in irreversible cases stable, loving relationships are acceptable and homosexual acts in such relationships can be judged permissible and even responsible; and (4) "full acceptance," which considers homosexual orientation as God-given and its behavior as morally appropriate and even desirable.[71]

Several prominent Roman Catholic ethicists support various readings of the third approach (although they are labeled "revisionist" by more conservative Catholics, who represent a "rejecting-non-punitive" attitude). Their position is grounded in an important reflection on the nature of acts themselves. The basic question is, do particular circumstances modify not only one's relation to a specific act, but *the moral quality of the act itself*?

---

69 See esp. the "Declaration on Certain Questions Concerning Sexual Ethics" (29 December, 1975) and the "Letter to the Bishops of the Catholic Church on the Pastoral Care of Homosexual Persons" (1 October, 1986).

70 Cf. *Human Sexuality* (Washington, DC: United States Catholic Conference, 1991), 54-55 and n. 49.

71 James B. Nelson, *Embodiment* (Minneapolis, MN: Augsburg, 1978), 188ff.

In his 1977 study entitled *Sexual Morality. A Catholic Perspective,*[72] Philip S. Keane answers that question affirmatively. He states that "there is a priority or normativity to heterosexual acts and relationships that cannot be dismissed in any theology of homosexuality." Yet he relies on a methodology that views certain acts marked by ontic evil as "objectively grave" but "subjectively not culpable." He asserts: "there are cases in which the ontic evil in homosexual acts does not become an objective moral evil because in the circumstances germane to these cases it is truly proportionate for the homosexual acts to be posited." Accordingly, he concludes, "the persons remain members of the Church in good standing and are free to receive the sacraments." [73]

This position is similar to those represented by Lisa Cahill and Richard McCormick. To Cahill, homosexual acts can be judged "nonnormative but objectively justifiable in the exceptional situation" in which two persons of the same sex form a permanent and exclusive relationship. McCormick concludes that two criteria should determine whether homosexual relations can be considered permissible (not "justifiable," since heterosexual orientation and acts remain normative): "(1) *If* the person is irreversibly homosexual and (2) *if* the person is not called to celibacy for the Kingdom."[74] These judgments, he insists, are the responsibility of the person before God and, in the interests of an appropriate *pastoral* approach, they should be respected by the Church.

Once again, the basic question raised by this serious and sensitive web of reflection is that of Philip Keane: do "the circumstances bearing on an act...change not only the person's moral relationship to the act but also the substantive moral character of the act itself"?[75] Using Fr. McCormick's criteria, can we say that homosexual acts can be considered permissible, or at any rate free of moral evil, when and if the persons who engage in them are irreversibly homosexual and not called to celibacy? Put another way, does the moral significance of an act change depending on circumstances, or do acts possess intrinsic, even absolute moral value?

72 New York: Paulist Press.
73 See esp. 85-87. If I am not mistaken, the *Imprimatur* was subsequently removed from Keane's book.
74 See his study, "Homosexuality as a Moral and Pastoral Problem," in *The Critical Calling. Reflections on Moral Dilemmas Since Vatican II* (Washington, DC: Georgetown University Press, 1989), 289-314.
75 *Op. cit.,* 86.

The Orthodox, with other Christians, recognize that circumstances can mitigate the evil or wrongness of certain proscribed actions, as when killing occurs in war or an ectopic pregnancy necessitates an abortion. Where do we draw the line? Do pastoral concerns justify our accepting stable homosexual relationships to the point that the couple is received to Communion? Or that they are granted the tax breaks accorded to a husband and wife? Or that they be allowed to adopt children and teach in Junior High Schools? In short, do there exist circumstances that warrant the judgment that homosexual acts, while remaining non-normative, are nevertheless "acceptable"? And can it be reasonably held that circumstances change not only one's relation to the act, but the very nature of the act itself so as to render it "objectively grave" but "subjectively not culpable"?

To the contrary, a normative Orthodox response would insist that *acts possess intrinsic moral value, irrespective of circumstances.* It would regard the argument put forth by Fr. Keane as an example of extreme proportionalism that can easily fall into the relativism of situation or contextual ethics. Acts themselves—and not just intentions, attitudes, ends and consequences—have moral significance as good or evil, right or wrong.

The conservative—and today, very unpopular—approach taken by Orthodox Christians to this matter is, or should be, based on theologically grounded moral principle rather than on emotional reactions to the phenomenon of homosexuality itself. That principle, which undergirds all Orthodox anthropology, holds that *the single purpose of human life, including bodily existence, is to glorify God.* That principle also underlies Jesus' command, "You must be perfect, as your heavenly Father is perfect" (Mt 5:48), as it does St. Paul's admonition, "glorify God in your body!" (1 Cor 6:20).

Homosexual (genital) acts by their very nature violate that principle, for reasons we have already mentioned. They misuse the sexual organs in an attempt to satisfy self-centered lust. They are devoid of procreative capacity. They parody the covenantal bond of "one flesh" that only a husband and wife can assume. And, some would argue, because of their "reparative" character, seeking pathologically to compensate for a childhood lack of identity (with the same-sex parent, according to Elisabeth Moberly),[76] they are inherently promiscuous.

---

76 See esp. her early studies, *Psychogenesis. The Early Development of Gender Identity* (London: Kegan Paul, 1982) and *Homosexuality: A New Christian Ethic* (Cambridge: James Clarke, 1983).

More important from a pastoral perspective is an aspect that is seldom
mentioned in the literature on the subject: that *homosexual acts are intrinsically harmful* to those who engage in them. Rather than "repair" or heal
the brokenness in personal relationships that to some degree underlies
them (in addition to any possible genetic component), those acts simply
perpetuate the illness or dysfunction. Where serious attempts are made to
preserve a stable relationship with a "beloved friend," the affection between homosexual lovers is often deep and genuine. Yet it is inevitably
flawed by a narcissistic eroticism, the product of what Basil Zion terms
the "bondage of the narcissistic double."[77] The power of that bondage appears to lie in the compulsive or addictive aspect of homosexuality, which
prevents the person from relating to another precisely as a "person," to
whom one offers oneself in self-giving, disinterested love. There are surely
exceptions to this, where the relationship between homosexual lovers reflects such love more faithfully than many marriages. But these are exceptions that prove the rule. More typically, homosexual behavior is of the
highly promiscuous kind that has been so tragically instrumental in the
spread of HIV infection.

This said, however, it is of the utmost importance that we maintain a
clear distinction between acts and orientation. Whether the cause is genetic, environmental or (more likely) a combination of the two, the homosexual *orientation* is neither sinful nor evil (except insofar as any
disability can be said to be the result of evil in a fallen world). Persons
with that orientation are in the fullest sense "persons," bearers of the image of God and called, with all others, to grow toward the divine likeness.
Especially where they attempt to change to a heterosexual orientation—or simply in their ongoing struggle to remain chaste—they need
the support, encouragement and love of the Church, including its bishops, pastors and lay members. To this end, their participation in self-help
groups such as SA, and particularly in organizations such as Exodus International and Courage, can be of invaluable help. (The Roman Catholic
organization "Courage" was founded by Fr. John Harvey and has active
chapters throughout the United States. Fr. Harvey's experience has led
him to the conviction that a very significant proportion of persons of ho-

77 *Erôs and Transformation*, 321.

mosexual orientation can in fact become heterosexual, even if in many cases homoerotic feelings and fantasies persist.)[78]

It is clear, however, that the homosexual condition is often irreversible: the orientation is permanent. Despite this fact, the Orthodox Church cannot condone homosexual "acting out," even within the framework of a stable and exclusive relationship. Because of the inherent sinfulness—and personal destructiveness—of such relationships, Orthodox moral theology is fundamentally opposed to gay or lesbian "marriages." Out of a pastoral concern for the spiritual, psychological and physical welfare of all its members, both "straight" and "gay," the Church must reject such liaisons, just as it must reject adoptions by homosexual couples. The fact that a homosexual orientation may be irreversible does not justify institutionalizing it and granting it social sanction by assimilating it to authentic marriage as God intended it (Mk 10:6-9) and as Christ blessed it (Jn 2:1-11). Nor does it justify exposing children to a "homosexual lifestyle" under the pretense that, all other things being equal, a child can thrive as well with "two Mommies" or "two Daddies" as with its biological parents. The issue is not even whether a child is "better off" being raised by a homosexual couple than by a single parent or in an orphanage. The real issue concerns the nature of homosexual acts themselves and their effect upon those who engage in them. If it is true, as we believe, that such acts are inherently sinful and detrimental to the persons involved, then the only way a homosexual couple can raise a child in a healthy and responsible way is for them to remain celibate.

78 See his book, *The Truth About Homosexuality,* esp. chs. 4-5 and the appendices. He offers further evidence, based on a number of recent studies, in his article, "Developing into Heterosexuality," *Ethics & Medics* vol. 22, no. 7 (July 1997), 3-4. Here he states his view that "one does not change his sexual orientation. My theory is that each person naturally develops into heterosexuality, however, various impediments may block normal psychosexual development over the years, particularly during the teenage period. With prayer, self-help, group spiritual support, and some professional therapy, many people, perhaps 30% of those who make the effort, can release their natural heterosexual inclinations." With regard to the argument from genetics, he adds: "Empirical evidence substantiating that the homosexual orientation is a result of genes or prenatal hormones is simply lacking" (4). Fr. Thomas Hopko, from an Orthodox perspective and on the basis of his own pastoral experience, also expresses the view that homosexual orientation can often be transformed. In a popular brochure published by the Dept. of Religious Education of the Orthodox Church in America (1989), he states: "Like all temptations, passions and sins, including those deeply and oftentimes seemingly indelibly embedded in our nature by our sorrowful inheritance, homosexual orientation can be cured and homosexual actions can cease. With God all things are possible. When homosexual Christians are willing to struggle, and when they receive patient, compassionate and authentically loving assistance from their families and friends...the Lord guarantees victory in ways known to Himself."

To "glorify God in the body" means that genital sexual activity must be restricted to the blessed, heterosexual conjugal union. The Church can no more bless homosexuals who want to live and express their sexuality together than it can bless adulterers or fornicators. Even where promiscuity is not a problem and the relationship seems to be based on genuine care and love, the homosexual lifestyle remains antithetical to what the Gospel calls people to be. Homosexuals must make a choice: either to abstain altogether from genital sexual activity or, by virtue of their refusal, to cut themselves off from full communion with the Body of Christ.

This means that persons of homosexual orientation who assume the cross of sexual abstinence may receive Holy Communion just like any other faithful member of the Church. It also means that there is no impediment in this regard to their acceding to the ordained ministry. Morally speaking, a man or a woman with a homosexual orientation who accepts a life of celibacy is no different from a heterosexual person who is celibate or who confines his or her sexual experience to the sphere of marriage. If, however, homosexuals elect to "act out" in a persistent and willful fashion, they render themselves as morally culpable as if they persisted in fornication or adultery.

From the point of view of pastoral care, their giving in to temptation should be treated as with any other sexual sin: with a firm call to repentance, coupled with the assurance of loving forgiveness when that repentance comes. If the priest becomes aware of active homosexuality on the part of a parishioner, and that person refuses to repent—to stop the acting out and seek healing—the priest should, with the counsel and support of his bishop, have recourse to the ancient penalty of (temporary) excommunication. This sounds particularly harsh in our day and age. Yet it is crucial that the person(s) concerned be made aware of the seriousness and potential harmfulness of their behavior. Excommunication should always be applied with a genuinely pastoral concern in mind: as a temporary measure, designed to lead the person into an attitude of repentance. Once that has been accomplished, then the person should be immediately restored to full communion, "for the healing of soul and body." Occasional lapses, as with any other sins, are to be confessed and forgiven, if need be, seventy times seven. The priest will have as his primary concern the spiritual well-being of the penitent. He will accompany him or her with his prayer and loving support, being attentive as well to the needs of any former lover, close friend or family member whose life has been adversely affected by the penitent's "conversion." This is particularly necessary in those many cases where HIV infection has occurred.

With regard to Fr. McCormick's criteria noted earlier, there is only one thing to say: from the perspective of Orthodox Christianity, *every person not called to conjugal union is called to celibacy for the Kingdom.* This is a difficult ideal, but the myriad saints throughout the history of the Church are proof that it is not an impossible one. Many of them, in secret and before the eyes of God alone, achieved sanctity precisely through their arduous struggle against sexual temptation. Their motivation should, in fact, be shared by all Christian believers, without exception. It is the simple and basic truth that our every thought and every gesture, sexual and otherwise, reflects our degree of faith and commitment to God, and demonstrates the extent to which we honor his sacrificial gift of love offered on our behalf.

In asking anyone to assume the cross of chastity, we should not overlook the fact that *married life often imposes its own rigorous limits on sexual expression, at times to the point of total abstinence.* That cross also has to be accepted, if the person and the couple are to fulfill their vocation faithfully. For the goal of both vocations—conjugal and celibate—is to assume our life and its particular conditions with gratitude, and to surrender them as an offering of praise to the glory of God.

A Note on Active Homosexuality and AIDS ("Acquired Immunodeficiency Syndrome"):

Considering our present uncertainty concerning the underlying causes of homosexuality—whether genetic, environmental or a combination of the two—what should the Church's attitude be toward those persons who continue to "act out," especially in light of the AIDS crisis? AIDS has been referred to as "the needless epidemic." With today's passion for "political correctness," there have been highly vocal campaigns, both within and outside the churches, defending homosexual behavior and claims to special gay and lesbian rights. Is it morally appropriate for Orthodox Christians to declare openly and firmly what seems to be fact: that were it not for active male homosexuality (and bisexuality), there would be no

AIDS epidemic? AIDS, yes, but not in epidemic proportions. Intrave-
nous drug usage with shared needles, for example, affects a relatively limited population and is proving far more containable than homosexual
transmission of HIV (Human Immunodeficiency Virus)—assuming that
the retrovirus HIV is in fact the cause of AIDS.[79]

It is true that throughout Africa the disease has spread primarily
among heterosexuals; and some militant gays express a morbid delight in
the fact that HIV infection is increasingly prevalent among heterosexuals
here and in Europe. Reaction against such attitudes has taken the form of
persecution of homosexuals by extremist groups such as the "skinheads"
and Neo-Nazis. Yet the average American finds himself or herself caught
in a painful dilemma: either defend the civil rights of those whose behavior they see as sinful or abhorrent, and thereby appear to condone homosexual activity; or speak out against such behavior and risk either reprisals
from gay activists or the appearance of giving support to "gay-bashing,"
the so-called (if grossly mislabeled) "homophobia."

Given the political climate surrounding the gay movement today, coupled with the very real AIDS crisis, how can the Orthodox Church most
effectively and faithfully affirm its traditional attitude toward sexuality? A
partial answer (but it is only that) would be for Orthodox and other

---

79 A number of reputable researchers have questioned the assumed link between HIV and AIDS.
   An article in *Reason* magazine (June 1994), authored by Nobel Prize winner Kary B. Mullis,
   together with biochemist Charles A. Thomas, Jr. and the U. of California at Berkeley Professor of Law Phillip E. Johnson, points to a statistically significant number of AIDS cases without HIV, and to HIV positive cases where no AIDS symptoms have appeared in a period
   longer than ten years. They question the HIV paradigm for three reasons: (1) AIDS is not a
   "disease" as such, but rather a syndrome defined by the presence of some 30 previously recognized diseases *together with HIV positive*—in other words, the very definition of AIDS depends on the presupposition (not clinically verified) that it is correlated with HIV. (2) Factors
   other than HIV seem to cause such diseases as Karposi's sarcoma and to create the blood im-
   purities responsible for the deaths of hemophiliacs. Yet government funding is structured so as
   to support research on the supposed HIV-AIDS correlation—to the point that some diseases
   are being redefined as AIDS to insure coverage under the Ryan White Act. For example, "Tuberculosis with a positive [HIV] antibody test is AIDS; tuberculosis with a negative test is just
   TB." (3) The apparently massive outbreak of AIDS throughout Africa has been linked to HIV
   but without accurate or adequate HIV testing. As reported in the *Sunday Times of London*
   (Oct. 1993), medical relief workers in Tanzania declared that AIDS statistics in Africa have
   been seriously manipulated and exaggerated. "There is no AIDS," they said. "It is something
   that has been invented. There are no epidemiological grounds for it; it doesn't exist for us."
   The authors therefore call for controlled studies to confirm or disprove the supposed link between HIV and AIDS, and they level sharp criticism at the scientific community for refusing
   to publicize the evidence against the HIV paradigm. Subsequent research, however, has consistently verified the HIV-AIDS link.

Christian medical professionals to gather and publicize scientific evidence that confirms the health benefits of the traditional Christian view. This is being done in some areas, but often by conservative evangelical groups who inject into the debate a tone of frantic or angry condemnation. This tends simply to polarize everyone concerned. Sober medical evidence, worked appropriately into statements made by the churches and other organisms of authority in our society, might prove more effective. In any case, Orthodox church-school teachers and catechists, together with our priests, need to inform themselves of the issue and speak to it forcefully and directly, to our children as well as to adults. Clearly, we can no longer trust the public schools to provide anything like full and truthful information on such an inflammatory subject.

One element in that discussion needs to be the often heard charge that AIDS is God's punishment for deviant behavior. This, to my mind, is quite simply false. Certainly God allows us to suffer the consequences of our sinful behavior; and the AIDS phenomenon may be today's most visible consequence of that fact. Yet we cannot hold, as many do, that God inflicts the disease on particular individuals as divine retaliation for the committing of that specific sin. We in America are particularly sensitive to what we regard as "sexual sins." But however immoral, sinful or just plain distasteful homosexual activity may be, it is no more worthy or susceptible of direct retribution in the form of lethal illness than any other willful violation of God' commandments. In fact it may be far less reprehensible than other sinful behaviors, such as abortion, child abuse or theft. The Scriptures declare that we shall be called to answer for our deeds at the Last Judgment. Yet if it is true, as we affirm, that "everything good will be saved," then it would seem presumptuous, if not blasphemous, for us to conclude that HIV infection represents a kind of premature "final judgment," pronounced on the victim by a God of wrath. Were that the case, then in light of St. Paul's teachings (1 Cor 6:9f) we would expect not only homosexuals, but idolaters, adulterers, thieves, drunkards, robbers, and even the greedy, to be similarly afflicted with hopelessly debilitating terminal diseases.

Finally, more study needs to be given to the possible communication of HIV by means of the communion spoon. This, too, is a highly sensitive issue, since many Orthodox Christians recoil from the notion with the feeling that "God would not allow it." Yet some medical professionals have expressed shock and grave concern at our method of distributing the holy elements. It may be argued that the conviction, "God would not allow it," is based on a defective theology of the Incarnation. The Cross is evidence enough that God might indeed "allow it"...certainly not out of vindictiveness, but because of his respect for human freedom in a fallen world. The eucharist is indeed the Body and Blood of the glorified Lord. Yet it is conveyed to us through the earthly elements of bread and wine. The fact that those elements are consecrated means that they are "changed": filled and transfigured by the presence and power of the Holy Spirit. It does not mean that they are thereby removed from the sphere of human life or that they are transformed magically into a transcendent substance which is intrinsically incapable of harboring infectious disease.

Yet the other side of the argument needs to he heard as well. It has often been pointed out that even during periods when the plague ravaged medieval Europe, there is no evidence that priests and deacons who consumed the Holy Eucharist after communion were afflicted with the disease in higher proportion than the general population. And as of this writing, not a single case of AIDS has been traced to transmission via the chalice. There is much evidence indeed that "God would not allow it," given the truth that objectively and ontologically—and not merely in response to the communicant's faith—the eucharistic elements *are* the Body and Blood of the glorified Lord. The faith of the Orthodox Church, and the experience grounded in that faith, are unequivocal in affirming this point. In the words of St. John of Damascus, "The bread and the wine are not merely figures of the body and blood of Christ (God forbid!) but the deified body of the Lord itself."[80]

Some Orthodox ethicists have suggested that we consider alternative means for giving communion, perhaps on individual, disposable plastic spoons. Such an innovation would meet with deep resistance among our faithful. Nevertheless, in recent years many of us have received phone calls and letters from parents who refuse communion for themselves and their children, because they are aware that some members of their parish are homosexual and/or HIV positive. In cases such as these, it is an easy

80 *Exposition of the Orthodox Faith, NPNF* vol. IX, Ch. 13, p. 83.

matter to take the steps necessary to minimize any perceived danger of HIV transmission through communion. This can be done simply enough by having parishioners open their mouths so that the priest can turn the spoon upside down, drop in the elements, and thereby avoid contact with saliva. The priest might also request that those with a history of homosexuality or who are known to be HIV positive receive communion after all others in the congregation have done so.

Above all, the priest needs to affirm, through his teaching and preaching, that Holy Communion is offered by God "for the healing of soul and body." It is to be received with faith and love, as what St. Ignatius termed "the medicine of immortality." As Dr. Paul Meyendorff pointed out some years ago,[81] recent Roman Catholic studies have also confirmed that there is neither theological nor scientific reason for concern over potential transmission of AIDS through the chalice. Yet ironically this most unlikely of possibilities receives more attention in some quarters than the statistically proven transmission through promiscuous sexual conduct, both homo- and heterosexual. In the current atmosphere of "safe sex" we seem to have more faith in the condom than in communion.

An article published in the *Journal of the American Medical Association* back in 1988, concluded that "the risk of infection after exposure to saliva in more casual settings (such as oral contact with items contaminated with microscopic amounts of saliva) should be negligible."[82] This opinion appears to have been well substantiated by more recent clinical investigations. On May 27, 1995, an item appeared in *The New York Times* entitled, "Wafer Reduces Germ Risk in Communion." It described research which measured bacteria on communion wafers and in the communion cup. While in 28% of the 45 cases in question microbes were transferred from one person to another via the wafer, the study concluded that the "potential disease-causing microbes are thought to survive for only a short time in the wine and were not recovered from the wine in any sample." In fact the only risk for infection seems to be to persons who are HIV positive and others with impaired immune systems. Although the study did

81 In an oral communication at the 1994 St. Vladimir's Summer Institute.
82 Alan R. Lifson, MD, MPH, "Do Alternate Modes for Transmission of Human Immunodeficiency Virus Exist?," *JAMA* (March 4, 1988), vol. 259, no. 9, 1353-1356, at 1354. (This study was kindly supplied to me by Charles A. Haile, MD).

not raise the issue of a common spoon, it tended to confirm what researchers have been maintaining for the past decade: that the possibility of HIV transmission by means of the communion cup—including by use of a common spoon—is virtually nonexistent.[83]

We should say one thing further on this issue. As members of the Body of Christ we cannot simply condemn the homosexual person along with his or her sexual behavior. We must distinguish between the two, honoring the sinner while naming the sin: the spiritually as well as physically detrimental character of homosexual relations. Those who are found to be HIV positive, therefore, ought not to be treated as pariahs, whatever the origin of the infection. Whether contracted in the mother's womb, through blood transfusions, or through inappropriate sexual conduct, AIDS victims tend to be shunned today as lepers were in biblical times. Our responsibility towards them is to offer the same kind of care and concern that Jesus offered to all those whom the society of his day rejected and condemned. Jesus, after all, came to forgive the sinful and to heal the sick: prostitutes and lepers, tax-collectors and the blind.

Many Christian people, from nurses to monks, have been ministering to AIDS victims over the past years with acceptance and compassion, in an effort to help them redeem and transfigure the remaining time of their earthly life. It is the responsibility of each of us to do the same. Leaving judgment in the hands of God, we are morally bound to respond to the crisis of AIDS with forgiveness, love and unceasing prayer, for the millions who have already suffered its ravaging effects, and for the multitudes of victims yet to come.[84]

With this overview of various issues concerning marriage and sexuality, we turn now to the question of the origin of human life. Curiously, although specialists are in full agreement as to the process by which life begins—the "how" of human conception—for both medical and political reasons today there is an intense debate being waged concerning the

83 See in this regard the letter by George Demetrakopoulos, MD, MPH, that appeared in *The Orthodox Observer*, 23 September, 1987, 20.

84 For perceptive insights regarding the pastoral care to be offered to homosexual persons, and particularly victims of AIDS, see Fr. Basil Zion, "The Orthodox Church and the AIDS Crisis," *St Vladimir's Theological Quarterly* 36/1-2, 152-158; and Protodeacon Cyprian Hutcheson, MD, "How Our Parish Dealt With AIDS," from the *Resource Handbook of the Orthodox Church in America*, V.II, no. 1 (1993), available through the Chancery of the OCA, P.O. Box 675, Syosset, NY 11791.

"when" of human existence. In the next chapter we enter the debate with some reflections on life's beginnings. This will lead, finally, to a consideration of the other end of the spectrum: the terminal or end stage of human life.

3

Procreation and the Beginning of Life

*"As for man, it was necessary for
him to be created; then having been
created, to grow; and having
grown, to become an adult; and
having become an adult, to multiply;
and having multiplied, to become
strong; and having become strong,
to be glorified; and having been
glorified, to behold the Lord."*

—St. Irenaeus

*"God created man, bringing forth
his body from the preexisting matter
which He animated with His own Spirit."*

—St. Gregory Nazianzen

*"The beginning of existence is one and
the same for body and soul."*

—St. Gregory of Nyssa

Rethinking the Meaning of "Conception" [1]

"When does human life begin?"

The various answers that have been proposed to this long-debated
question often express a political or social agenda as much as they do cur-

---

1   I wish to express my sincere thanks to Robert C. Cefalo, M.D., Ph.D., Professor and Acting
Chair of Obstetrics and Gynecology, Director of Maternal-Fetal Medicine at the School of
Medicine, The University of North Carolina at Chapel Hill; to Germain Grisez, Professor
and holder of the Flynn Chair in Christian Ethics, Mount Saint Mary's College, Emmitsburg,
MD; and to Paul Kymissis, M.D., Associate Professor of Psychology and Pediatrics, New
York Medical College, and Director of Child and Adolescent Psychology, Westchester
County Medical Center, Valhalla, NY, for offering me materials and insights relevant to this
chapter. Of course, any errors of fact or interpretation are entirely my own.

rent knowledge of embryo development. Suggestions include at "quickening," when the mother first feels the infant move within her womb; at viability, the earliest point at which the fetus can survive outside the womb (usually around 24 weeks); at birth, when the child begins to breathe on its own; or several days after birth, once the newborn has demonstrated its "right to live," including, among other things, the absence of any debilitating diseases or disabilities. The more we can separate "the beginning of human life" from the time of fertilization, the greater becomes the "window" for abortion, infanticide and embryo experimentation.

The Church, on the other hand, has traditionally held that human life begins with conception, which it understands to be coterminous with fertilization. Long before medical specialists were aware of germ cells and chromosomes, Christian writers were condemning abortion at any stage in the pregnancy, precisely on grounds that the fetus "formed or unformed" is fully human and bears the "image of God."[2]

The issue is raised anew today from a different standpoint, one with no other concern than to base sound theological reflection on biological fact. Taking their lead from British embryologists, a number of Christian ethicists make a distinction between the embryo and the so-called "pre-embryo." This latter entity is described as a mass of undifferentiated cells, beginning with the single-cell zygote and continuing until development of the "primitive streak" or primitive body axis during the third week of pregnancy. At this point, following implantation in the wall of the uterus, it undergoes a radical transformation known as "singularity," and henceforth it can be said to possess a human soul or human individuality. According to this schema, which we describe in more detail further on, "conception" is to be understood not as a "moment" (e.g., at the completion of fertilization) but as a *process*. The change from a "pre-embryo" to an "embryo," that is from potential to actual human existence, occurs only with the completion of that process. Human life is still recognized as "beginning with conception." But the definition of "conception" is modified, on the basis of recent findings in the science of embryology, to signify "singularity" with implantation of the conceptus in the uterine

<hr>

2   See esp. *Didachê* 2:2, 5:2; Basil the Great, *Canonical Letters* 2 and 8 (*PG* 32: 672, 677; *NPNF* VIII, 225, 227). The Hippocratic oath foreshadowed these writings with its prohibition against giving poisons and procuring abortions.

membrane, which occurs some two weeks after fertilization. Conception and fertilization, in other words, are no longer understood to be coterminous. Fertilization marks the beginning of the process of conception, a process that requires twelve to fourteen days to be complete. Only at the end of that period can we speak meaningfully of new "human life" and the existence of a unique "human soul."

An important pastoral concern has driven much of the research and resultant discussions that lie behind this position. It is one based on the purest of motives, that should not be confused with the various "agendas" referred to earlier. With the moral confusion caused by the proliferation of legal abortions in the United States and other developed countries, together with today's heightened sensitivity to the massive trauma caused by rape and incest, many theologians are frankly and openly looking for a means that would allow victims of sexual violence to end an unwanted pregnancy in a "licit" fashion, one that conforms to the Church's traditional moral teachings. If the distinction between the pre-embryo and the embryo is legitimate, then to terminate a pregnancy prior to implantation—that is, prior to completion of the process of conception with concomitant "ensoulment"—would not be considered "abortion" as that term is traditionally defined by various church bodies. In addition, to accept a medical and moral distinction between the pre-embryo and embryo would imply that the former represents potential rather than actual human life and is accordingly less qualified than the embryo to benefit from rights and protections extended by social convention to human individuals or "persons." One major consequence of accepting such a distinction is that it effectively eliminates moral objections to procedures such as *in vitro* fertilization (IVF) or embryo research and experimentation for therapeutic purposes.

While such pastoral and therapeutic concerns are laudable and well-meaning, they nevertheless presuppose a scientific view of embryonic development that is far from universally accepted by specialists in the field; and they rest upon a theological view of ensoulment, and consequent "personhood," that from an Orthodox perspective raises serious objections. Our aim in this chapter is to sketch out the argument put forth by three of the most prominent Roman Catholic ethicists who have addressed the subject, and to indicate why we believe their view should be modified on the basis of recent embryological research. We conclude with an evaluation of the theological implications of their position as read through the lens of Orthodox Christianity.

Shannon, Wolter and McCormick on the "Pre-Embryo" [3]

On the basis of recent findings in developmental embryology we can sketch out the following stages in the growth of the "pre-embryo."

Most cells in the human body are "somatic" cells, each of which contains in its nucleus forty-six chromosomes. The male sperm and female ova (oocytes or eggs), however, are germ cells or "gametes," each carrying twenty-three chromosomes.[4] The merging of these gametes into a single-cell zygote, containing a complement of forty-six chromosomes arranged in twenty-three pairs, occurs through the process of fertilization. Fertilization takes place at the far end of the fallopian tubes, near the ovaries. Sperm deposited in the female reproductive tract requires some seven hours to attain "capacitation," the ability of its enzymes to penetrate the outer wall of the ovum. An additional three hours is needed for sperm to make the arduous journey to the site where fertilization will occur. Of the millions of sperm deposited, normally a single sperm penetrates the tough, protective zona pellucida of the egg and makes its way through the cytoplasm to fuse with the haploid ("halved" or "single") nucleus. This produces what is known as "syngamy": a uniting of the two gametes to produce a genetically unique individual. The resultant diploid ("double") nucleus now contains a unique arrangement of genetic material (DNA)

3 Thomas A. Shannon and Allan B. Wolter, OFM, "Reflections on the Moral Status of the Pre-Embryo," *Theological Studies* 51/4 (Dec. 1990), 603-626, reprinted in T. A. Shannon, ed., *Bioethics* 4th ed. (Mahwah, NJ: Paulist, 1993), 36-60; and Richard A. McCormick, SJ, "Who or What is the Preembryo?," *Kennedy Institute of Ethics Journal* 1/1 (March 1991) 1-15 (who was apparently unaware of the Shannon-Wolter study). See as well Joseph Donceel, SJ, "Immediate Animation and Delayed Hominization," *Theological Studies* 31/1 (1970) 76-105, whose study initiated the present debate; and the responses by Germain Grisez, "When Do People Begin?," *Proceedings of the American Catholic Philosophical Association* 63 (1989), 27-47, revised in Stephen J. Heaney, ed., *Abortion: A New Generation of Catholic Responses,* The Pope John Center (1992), 3-27; and William E. May, "Zygotes, Embryos, and Persons: Part I," *Ethics and Medics* (Oct. 1991), 2-4, and "Part II," *Ethics and Medics* (Jan. 1992), 1-3.

4 Chromosomes comprise genetic material or genes: units of deoxyribonucleic acid (DNA) that determine hereditary characteristics—the physical composition, and to some degree the behavior, abilities and disabilities—of the human individual. Each chromosome, comprising about a meter of genetic material, contains 50,000 to 100,000 individual genes.

which determines the sex of the conceptus and provides conditions for "mitosis." This involves division or "cleavage" of the "blastomeres" or individual cells. The process begins with a two-cell, an a-chronic three-cell, then a four-cell stage, after which it progresses by multiples of two (8, 16, 32, etc.), until the embryo implants itself in the uterine membrane toward the end of the second week of pregnancy.

The time involved in this process is fairly well determined: approximately seven hours from intercourse to capacitation, another three for the sperm to reach the ovum, then twelve more for initial penetration. Fusion of the two cells (syngamy) takes another full day. The entire process leading to fertilization, therefore, requires from thirty-six to forty-eight hours to complete. By day four, the early embryo comprises some sixteen cells and is located near the mouth of the uterus.[5] The "blastocyst" stage is attained as the continually dividing cells form a sphere or disc, whose outer layer (the trophoblast) will give rise to the nutritive structures including the placenta, while the inner clump (the embryoblast) constitutes the embryo itself. At this time, the zona pellucida breaks down and the embryo "hatches," as it were, in order to attach itself to the wall of the uterus.

During this period of ten to twelve days, prior to implantation, there occurs the phenomenon known by the unfortunate term "wastage." It is estimated that from half to two-thirds of all fertilized ova are spontaneously aborted or rejected from the womb. They fail to implant and are "miscarried" (without the mother's awareness) for a variety of reasons, such as chemical imbalances in the reproductive system or defective genes carried by the embryo. When an embryo does implant itself successfully, it undergoes a restructuring known as "gastrulation" or "organogenesis," the rearrangement of cells into the embryonic ectoderm, endoderm and mesoderm. This is accompanied by definition of the primitive streak or primitive body axis, which leads to initial development of the embryonic nervous system. By the end of the eighth week the nervous system is fully integrated, and the growing child, now known as a *fetus*, is able to move and to experience pain.[6]

5 It is known at this stage as the "morula," from the Latin term for "mulberry," because of its shape: a mass of clustered cells that form the growing embryo.
6 See the *ACOG Committee Opinion* of the American College of Obstetricians and Gynecologists, No. 136 (April 1994): "Preembryo Research: History, Scientific Background, and Ethical Considerations."

Appealing to recent findings in the field of developmental embryology, Thomas Shannon and Allan Wolter argue with many others, both
embryologists and theologians, that a clear distinction must be made between the "pre-embryo" and the embryo proper.[7] The pre-embryo, they
maintain, is composed of a mass of essentially undifferentiated cells (blastomeres), each of which possesses "totipotency." Analogous to the hologram,
each individual blastomere is endowed with the same genetic information
that is possessed by the entity as a whole. This means that from the zygote
stage to formation of the primitive streak, each cell of the morula contains
within itself the capacity to develop into a full human individual. That capacity, however, is merely "potential," insofar as the conceptus must receive
additional genetic information from the mother after implantation, in order to attain "singularity" and develop into a true embryo. This is evi-
denced by the fact that the pre-embryo can "twin" or split into two
genetically identical entities (giving rise to identical twins); then, in rare
cases, the two can reunite to produce a single individual. This capacity for
twinning and recombining, they hold, persists until "gastrulation," also
called "restriction," when cell differentiation begins and totipotency is lost.
The zygote, in other words, cannot become a human embryo until it acquires supplemental genetic information provided not by the gametes but
by the maternal host.[8] Otherwise it can develop into a potentially cancerous
"hydatidiform mole," composed of placental tissue.[9]

7   Much of the current debate on this issue was initiated by Norman Ford, *When Did I Begin? Conception of the Human Individual in History, Philosophy and Science* (Cambridge University Press, 1988).
Ford argues for "delayed animation," claiming that the ontologically (and not merely genetically) distinct human individual comes into being only some two weeks after fertilization, with the appearance of the primitive streak. A highly perceptive analysis—and partial refutation—of many of Ford's
views is provided by Anthony Fisher, O.P., "Individuogenesis and a Recent Book by Fr. Norman
Ford," *Revista di Studi sulla Persona e La Famiglia: Anthropotes*, 2 (1991), 199-244. Roman Catholic
opinion is deeply divided over the issue of "individuation." For a review of recent literature on the
subject, see Lisa Sowle Cahill, "The Embryo and the Fetus: New Moral Contexts," *Theological Studies* 54/1 (March 1993), 124-142 (the author aligns herself with those who favor a theory of delayed
animation/hominization). Here we restrict our references to a very few representatives on each side of
the debate, whose work has prompted discussion particularly among Christian ethicists.
8   A clear and succinct statement of this position is provided by Carlos A. Bedate and Robert C.
Cefalo, "The Zygote: To Be Or Not Be A Person," *The Journal of Medicine and Philosophy* 14
(1989), 641-645. They conclude: "the formation of the embryo depends on a series of events
that will have to occur during the course of the ontogenesis, some of which are outside the control of the genetic program. The zygote does possess sufficient information to produce exclusively human tissue but not to become an individual human being" (644).
9   A hydatidiform mole is a tumor, formed in the uterus, that results from degeneration of the
fertilized ovum. It is often produced by "dispermy," fertilization of the ovum by two sperm,

Consequently, they maintain, it is incorrect to speak of the "embryo" as existing prior to implantation. During the first two-week period, while the process of conception is being completed, the conceptus should be referred to as a "pre-embryo," which does not yet contain the biological presuppositions of "ontological individuality" or, *a fortiori*, of "personhood." This indication, coupled with the phenomenon of "wastage," leads them to conclude that the pre-embryo cannot be said to possess an immaterial, rational "soul."[10] Accordingly, they defend a theory of "mediate" rather than "immediate animation,"[11] holding that "ensoulment" cannot occur prior to singularity and the profound rearrangement of cellular structure needed to produce the embryo. The pre-embryo, then, becomes by definition a candidate for morally licit abortion and scientific experimentation (although Shannon and Wolter do not explicitly state as much).

An equally careful and scientifically informed approach is taken by Richard McCormick in his article, "Who or What is the Preembryo?" He asserts that the term "preembryo" was adopted by the American Fertility Society and British Voluntary Licensing Authority "because the earliest stages of mammalian development primarily involve establishment of the nonembryonic trophoblast, rather than the formation of the embryo."[12] As we shall see below, this is a point that recent embryological research calls into question.

Fr. McCormick's article discusses various Roman Catholic statements which presuppose that the beginning of human individuality marks as well the beginning of human personhood. His purpose, like that of Shannon and Wolter, is to demonstrate that human individuality is not deter-

resulting in a karyotype or chromosomal count of 69 rather than the normal 46. Such an anomaly cannot be considered "human." (Even if one wishes to affirm that the human soul exists from fertilization, this does not mean that a hydatidiform mole is some grossly malformed human. While it is not the number of chromosomes that determines a human being, the *arrangement* of DNA in a hydatidiform mole from its beginning is such that it is "programmed" to be a mole and not a human individual.) Other lesser anomalies such as "trisomy 21" (an extra 21st chromosome) which produces Down's syndrome, do not at all diminish or otherwise affect the humanity of the individual.

10 Regarding "wastage," they state: "Such vast embryonic loss intuitively argues against the creation of a principle of immaterial individuality at conception" (619).

11 "Mediate animation" is also known as "delayed hominization." See Germain Grisez, "When Do People Begin?," and William E. May, "Zygotes, Embryos, and Persons—Part II" for critiques of the theory.

12 *Art. cit.*, p. 1.

mined by fertilization, but by the entire process that leads to singularity and formation of the primitive streak (after which, twinning is no longer possible). To do so, he makes a crucial distinction between "genetic individuality" and "developmental individuality." The former indeed exists from fertilization; but that is not to say that the conceptus has attained "personhood" or can be considered an "ensouled human person." For there must exist "a certain biological stability in the organism before personhood is possible. This stability is not present prior to the stage of primary embryonic organization," that is, prior to the appearance of the primitive streak.[13] Although he concludes that the pre-embryo should be treated as a person because it "in a sense is *personne en devenir*,"[14] he nevertheless retains the term "preembryo" because of its characteristic totipotency and capacity for twinning. The "preembryo," then, is not a "who," but a "what": one that is genetically unique and possesses "the potential to become adult."[15] But that potentiality can only be realized through acquisition of "developmental individuality," following the emergence of the primitive streak. The pre-embryo, he concludes, should be treated as a person, but only because it has "intrinsic potential" to become a person, and because the entire issue is surrounded with "many uncertainties," which he spells out.

Consequently, Fr. McCormick does not in principle rule out even non-therapeutic experimentation, because to his mind the pre-embryo cannot be considered to be in actuality an ensouled human person. Nevertheless, he would sanction pre-embryo research only when criteria for such research are established at the national level. Although he does not discuss the matter of pre-implantation abortions, the implication is that such would be morally permissible in cases where pregnancy results from sexual assault.[16]

13 *Ibid.*, p. 9.
14 *Ibid.*, p. 13.
15 *Ibid.*, p. 3.
16 Peter Steinfels, "Catholic Scholars, Citing New Data, Widen Debate on When Life Begins," *New York Times* (13 January, 1991), offers a perceptive summary of the McCormick and Shannon-Wolter articles that rightly questions the frequently proposed criterion of "brain birth." Some are arguing that a symmetry needs to be recognized between the onset of brain activity (brain birth) and its end (brain death). If brain death means the death of the person, they reason, then the birth or origin of the person should be determined by the beginning of brain function. As Fr. McCormick, echoed by Steinfels, notes, however, "Fetal brain activity

Jérôme Lejeune and the "Concentration Can."

How are we to assess these arguments for distinguishing between the pre-embryo and embryo, or between genetic and developmental individuality? The issue basically comes down to the accuracy of the scientific evidence supporting the "totipotency" of the blastomeres, together with the assertion by Fr. McCormick that "the earliest stages of mammalian development primarily involve establishment of the nonembryonic trophoblast, rather than the formation of the embryo." Although sound evidence has been advanced to affirm both points, other more recent studies support somewhat different conclusions.

Before noting these considerations, however, we need to stress the fact that the science of embryology is in a state of flux. In the United States and France in particular, debate is now focusing on such questions as the role of cytoplasm in conveying genetic information to the newly fertilized ovum, and on this and related questions there remain among specialists areas of significant disagreement. The evidence that is presently emerging tends nevertheless to support the theory that human life—individuated and, by implication, personal human existence—in fact begins not with implantation, but with the conclusion of fertilization and resultant syngamy, or at the latest with the two-cell stage of mitosis. To make this point, it would be useful to review a recent case that attracted widespread attention through the media, because it brought the arcane discipline of embryology into the sphere of civil law.

In April of 1989, the *New York Times* reported the pending divorce in Maryville, Tennessee, of Mary Sue Davis and Junior Lewis Davis. What made this particular action unique and an international *cause célèbre* is the fact that the Davises had resorted to *in vitro* fertilization, which produced a total of nine embryos. Two of these were transferred to Mrs. Davis' womb but failed to implant. The other seven were frozen for future use. With the pending divorce, Mrs. Davis sought custody in order either to receive the embryos herself or to donate them to a third party. Mr. Davis, on the other hand, argued that he should not be obliged to assume the responsibilities of

does not instigate a process of integrated organic development in the same way that adult loss of brain activity ends it." And no consensus has been reached concerning the point at which "brain birth" occurs.

parenthood subsequent to the divorce, and he therefore sought custody in order to liquidate the embryos as part of the couple's common property. Apart from the issue of cryogenic preservation and the likelihood that the embryos would perish in their "concentration can" because of delays in the legal system, the real moral issue came down to one basic question: were the embryos human infants with "rights" subject to legal protection, or were they simply joint property to be divided among the contending parties and disposed of accordingly? The matter was finally decided on appeal. Junior Davis was awarded custody, and presumably the embryos were destroyed.[17]

A principal witness for the defendant (the mother) was the eminent French geneticist, Dr. Jérôme Lejeune, who had gained world-wide recognition for his discovery of trisomy 21, the cause of Down's Syndrome. Lejeune's extended testimony is reproduced in his book, *The Concentration Can. When Does Human Life Begin?*[18] Although Lejeune (who is deceased) has been criticized for his "intégrist" views and ardent defense of conservative Roman Catholic teaching on abortion, his testimony is based on research, performed in England, France and the United States, that has been widely received within the scientific community. Very briefly, his argument is as follows.

In the late 1980s, research by the British geneticist Alec Jeffreys confirmed the genetic uniqueness of each fertilized human ovum; it established through scientific experimentation that the one-celled zygote is characterized by "genetic individuality." Further research by teams at Cambridge and Duke Universities has shown that a chemical process

17 Frozen embryos normally have a life expectancy of about two years, although newly developed techniques are expanding that time-frame considerably (cf. the recent outcry in England over the destruction of embryos preserved for five years). Before the legal proceedings, including appeals, were ended, the entire matter concerning the Davis embryos had become moot, since presumably they were no longer viable. With the recently developed technique by which unfertilized ova can be frozen for extended periods of time, it can only be hoped that cryopreservation of fertilized embryos will eventually become a thing of the past.

18 San Francisco: Ignatius Press, 1992; the French original was published in 1990, before final appeals in the case had been heard. The initial judgment, passed down by Judge Dale Young, found in favor of the defendant, affirming the humanity of the embryos from the time of fertilization. This is the judgment that was reversed on appeal. See R. Smothers, "Embryos in a Divorce Case: Joint Property or Offspring," *New York Times* (22 April, 1989); and (no byline) "Frozen Embryos' Fate Awaits L. I. Custody Battle," *New York Times* (25 June, 1994). The latter article deals with another woman who was seeking control of her frozen embryos in a divorce case.

known as "methylation" determines the information that will be conveyed by particular segments of DNA during fertilization. It was long thought that the chromosomes from the maternal gamete and the corresponding chromosomes from the male gamete, which merge to create the twenty-three chromosomal pairs of the diploid nucleus, were identical. The discovery of methylation showed that this is not true; rather, each male and each female chromosome provides the zygote with unique information. A methyl (CH_3) addition to the cytosine base of the DNA has the effect of "switching off" or suppressing certain gene activity so that with each successive division the cells become increasingly differentiated. In Lejeune's words, "the fertilized egg is the most specialized cell under the sun."[19] It contains *all* of the information necessary to produce a living human being. The "primary formula" for human life is derived from the unique alignment of chromosomal material in the nucleus of that original cell. As soon as fertilization is complete, that formula begins to direct cellular function.

This is true despite the fact that maternal RNA derived from the cytoplasm of the ovum governs development of the zygote until the two-cell stage of mitosis, when the embryonic genome is expressed or activated. This earliest developmental process occurs with syngamy. The genetically unique individual that results is constituted by the interaction of nucleus and cytoplasm, an interaction that continues even after the embryo's own genes are "switched on." Yet the "primary formula," which might be identified as the "soul," must be present from syngamy, to create the conditions for that interaction and to direct the zygote's growth.

Progressively, as the single-celled zygote undergoes mitosis, certain portions of its genetic information are "switched off" by methylation. Thereby differentiation can occur, allowing for development of the organism throughout the pre-implantation period.[20]

---

19 *The Concentration Can*, 44.
20 A leading figure in this research is M. Azim Surani of the Department of Molecular Embryology, Institute of Animal Physiology and Genetics Research, Cambridge, England. He and his research team have focused on methylation in mouse embryos. [See Surani et al., "Developmental consequences of imprinting of parental chromosomes by DNA methylation," *Phil. Trans. R. Soc. Lond.* (1990), 313-327; and "Genome Imprinting and Development in the Mouse," *Development 1990 Supplement* (1990), 89-98.] Their studies demonstrate that both a maternal and a paternal genome are necessary for the normal development of a mouse embryo, indicating that the genomes differ; and that initial genome imprinting occurs already in the germline, prior to fertilization.

If Lejeune is correct, cell differentiation is "written" or "programmed" into the conceptus from the very beginning of its existence. With the initial cleavage, genetic information is replicated, communicated from the first cell to the second. Lejeune posits a hypothetical three-cell stage of mitosis and argues that it is at this stage that *individuation* occurs. Such individuation (whether at the three or four-cell stage) is confirmed by the fact that beyond this point it is impossible to create a chimera (a being that results from the mixing of genetically dissimilar material, such as the sheep-goat anomaly known as a "geep"). As the cells undergo further division, other information is "switched off" and greater differentiation occurs. This means that cell differentiation begins not with implantation and "singularity" only at the end of the first two weeks of pregnancy. It begins rather with the single-celled zygote, when a unique "primal formula" describes and directs a continuing process that, under normal conditions, will result in the birth of a human baby. In Lejeune's view, then, it is simply erroneous to speak of the "pre-embryo" as an "undifferentiated mass of cells." Differentiation, which implies individual existence, occurs with completion of fertilization. Accordingly, fertilization and conception must be recognized as coterminous.

This implies as well that the very expression "pre-embryo" is misleading and should be abandoned. If fertilization and conception are coterminous, then the proposed distinction between "genetic" and "developmental individuality" is nonexistent. Fertilization normally marks the beginning of an unbroken, continuous process that involves progressive "individuation," through differentiation and specification, from the two- or three-cell stage of embryonic development. The beginning of human life, therefore, occurs not with "singularity" and formation of the primitive streak, however significant that stage might be in the growth of the embryo. Human life begins rather with *fertilization*, when the entire "code" or "program" inscribed in the zygote begins to direct cell-division and the exchange of genetic information.

Furthermore, the maternal (oocyte) cytoplasm contributes in a significant (but as yet poorly understood) way in that imprinting process. Coupled with the phenomenon of methylation, this evidence strongly supports the theory that cellular differentiation occurs in mouse embryos from the two-cell stage. Embryologists are not in agreement as to whether DNA methylation occurs in humans, although the consensus seems to hold that it does.

An Orthodox Assessment

The basic question raised by this entire debate concerns "individuation," the process by which developmental or ontological individuality—and therefore a distinct human individual and by implication a "person"—can be said to exist. At present, embryologists, and consequently ethicists, are of two minds on the issue. To some, totipotency and the apparent lack of differentiation among the blastomeres or early embryonic cells (together with the high percentage of naturally expelled fertilized ova) speak clearly for "delayed animation" and characterization of the pre-implantation conceptus as a "pre-embryo." To others, genetic individuality (that indisputably exists from syngamy), together with the developmental continuity manifest from fertilization through implantation and beyond, argue forcefully for "immediate animation." This means that from fertilization the embryo is a human individual, qualifiable as a "person" with rights to full protection under the law. [21]

The ethical issues raised by the debate are massive. If animation or individual identity occurs only with the appearance of the primitive streak at implantation, then one can reasonably argue for a gradation in levels of protection accorded the conceptus. Most who hold this view would agree that, as a potential human individual, the "pre-embryo" is to be accorded due respect and protection against indiscriminate manipulation. They would nevertheless accept embryo experimentation, to gain knowledge that could lead to improved techniques for such procedures as gene replacement, assisted reproduction through IVF, and contraception. They would likewise regard as morally acceptable the termination of pregnancies resulting from rape or incest, and might defend "elective" abortions as well.

If it is decisively proven, however, that cellular differentiation exists from fertilization, i.e., that animation or ensoulment occurs with syngamy, then to the minds of many ethicists the two-week "window" argued by Shannon, Wolter and others would be eliminated. "Totipotency" would be shown to be itself a chimera: a hybrid concept born of wishful thinking and defective science. *In vitro* fertilization and embryo experimentation of any

---

21 For an eloquent argument for the "personhood" of the embryo from its earliest formation, see Germain Grisez, "When Do People Begin?"; and his *Living a Christian Life* [Vol. 2 of *The Way of the Lord Jesus* (Quincy, IL: Franciscan Press, 1993)], 489-498.

kind would constitute manipulation that violates the individual's rights to protection. And irrespective of how the embryo was conceived, intentionally ending the pregnancy at any point would involve a morally illicit act of abortion because it destroys a developing human person.

Where does Orthodox Christianity stand on this issue? The Church's anthropology, grounded as it is in the double principle of the "sacredness and sanctity of life," calls for acknowledgment of human personhood from "the moment of conception." While modern embryology has demonstrated the ambiguity inherent in that phrase, the Orthodox rejection of abortion at any stage ("whether the fetus be formed or unformed," in the language of St. Basil) would align the Church's position squarely with the more conservative Roman Catholic view that defends immediate rather than delayed animation.

It would, however, take issue with the Catholic Church's doctrine of ensoulment, at least as it has been expressed in Aristotelian and Thomistic terms.[22] Language such as "ensoulment," "infusion of an immaterial rational soul," or simply "a principle of immaterial individuality or selfhood," sounds dualistic to Orthodox ears, a legacy of Origenism. From an Eastern patristic (and biblical) perspective, the soul or *nephesh* constitutes the very personhood of the individual (Gen 1:26-27; 2:7). Accordingly, one may properly affirm "I *am* a soul" rather than "I *have* a soul." The age-old debate over mediate (delayed) or immediate animation, therefore, appears to be grounded in a defective anthropology, one which views the material body as animated by a rational soul created separately from it and infused into it at fertilization, at implantation, or at some subsequent stage in its development.

Those who support a theory of delayed animation usually base their argument on two biological facts: monozygotic ("identical") twinning, and "wastage," the spontaneous expulsion of fertilized ova prior to implantation. Anthony Fisher has addressed both issues in his article "Individuogenesis" and provided arguments that are thoroughly compatible with an Orthodox point of view. While the problem of wastage can only be answered with reference to the problem of theodicy,[23] with respect to twinning we can add the following points.

22 In addition to N. Ford's study, see William E. May, "Zygotes, Embryos, and Persons—Part II"; A. Fisher, "Individuogenesis," 202f and 212-215; and Shannon and Wolter, "Reflections," 614-618.

23 As we pointed out in chapter one, Orthodox theology interprets passages such as Rom 5:12 to mean that what we inherit from Adam is not individual guilt, but *mortality*. It does not share

It is well established that the individual blastomeres possess a certain totipotency until gastrulation and attainment of singularity. One or more cells of the morula can be separated from the main mass and, because the separated cluster contains all the genetic information of the original zygote, it can develop into an "identical twin." Yet we must use the term "totipotency" or "totipotentiality" with caution. In fact, twins possessing similar genetic material are not at all "identical" in the strict sense of the word, as any parent of such twins well knows. While each develops from a common genome, they are—by virtue of methylation and the action of the oocyte cytoplasm (maternal RNA)—*genetically differentiated,* since (following Jeffreys and Surani) the blastomeres themselves are differentiated from the two-cell stage of mitosis, when genomic expression begins.

Pre-implantation cells, then, can twin; and in rare cases they can even recombine. The vexing question whether there is then "one soul or two," is not an issue if we regard each entity as "being" a soul rather than as "possessing" a soul; for by "soul" we mean the God-given power or *dynamis* (Lejeune's "primal formula") that actualizes individual, personal human existence. In cases of recombination, that personal identity is expressed no longer by two individual existences, but by one. "Identical twins," then, are not identical beings. Their identity is genetic, yet it is limited by methylation in such a way that each develops into a recognizably distinct and unique person.

The phenomenon of totipotency, limited as it is, thus presents no serious impediment to viewing the pre-implantation embryo as an individuated, personal human being. While formation of the primitive streak

the Western scholastic view that unbaptized infants (including fetuses) are eternally condemned [see, e.g., the quotation from Anselm of Canterbury, *De conceptu virginale et de originali peccato,* in Shannon and Wolter, "Reflections," 618, n. 59]. The premature death of embryos caused by "natural wastage" thus presents no more logical difficulty than the premature death of children caused by disease or accidents. If only the latter strikes us as inherently tragic, it is because of the loss of a personal relationship with the young child experienced by the parents and others who loved it. Obviously such a relationship does not exist between an embryo and the mother. Yet that fact does not deprive the embryo of "personhood," since (from an Orthodox viewpoint) that quality derives not from the infusion of a soul but from the relationship that God establishes with his (embryonic) creature. Personhood, then, depends neither on an "infused soul" nor on one's conscious relationship with others. It depends rather on the love of God that embraces the bearer of his divine image from conception, through death and beyond. This is why permanently comatose or PVS ("persistent vegetative state") patients are and remain *persons* in the fullest sense of the term: because they are perceived and affirmed as such by God himself.

means the end of totipotency and of the possibility for twinning, cellular differentiation begins not at this point but almost immediately after fertilization, at the two-cell stage of division.

Such early differentiation would seem to render moot Fr. McCormick's point that "the earliest stages of mammalian development primarily involve establishment of the nonembryonic trophoblast, rather than formation of the embryo."[24] The trophoblast at this stage is as much a vital element and condition in embryonic development as are "vital organs" that develop subsequently. This is true despite the fact that the placenta is discarded at birth. Milk teeth, hair, and in fact every somatic cell of every organ is discarded at some point in normal human development and replaced by others. It can not be argued, then, that organization and growth of the trophoblast in the pre-implantation stage precludes our considering the embryo to be an individual human life. For although the trophoblast may be the visible manifestation of that emerging life, the "program" or "primary formula" that will determine its further development into vital organs is already active, awaiting expression at the proper moment in the life-cycle.[25] Under normal circumstances, there is unbroken continuity in human development, from formation of the zygote, through implantation, to integration of the nervous system, and on to birth. At no point along that continuum *other than at its beginning* can it be said that "human life begins here and now."

This line of reasoning raises basic questions regarding the morality of procedures such as IVF and abortions, both therapeutic and elective. However desirable a two-week window of opportunity may be, whether to facilitate reproduction, to terminate tragic and unwanted pregnancies, or to allow for embryo experimentation, recent findings in embryology and genetics indicate that such a window in fact does not exist. If indeed cellular differentiation is present from the two-cell stage, then designation of the early embryonic life-form as a "pre-embryo" is at best misleading

24 "Who or What is the Preembryo?", 1.
25 Prof. Germain Grisez has noted in this regard: "The fact that the major developmental effort early on goes into trophoblast does not show at all that this development is not of the embryo. For the accessory materials that are discarded at birth are until then vital organs of the unborn individual, no less part of the person than your heart and lungs and kidneys and stomach are part of you. Naturally, development first produces the organs most essential at the early stages of life" [from personal correspondence, dated 7 September 1994].

and at worst deceptive. For such differentiation—strongly suggested by the phenomenon of methylation, by the impossibility of creating chimeras after the four-cell stage of division, and by the very nature of twinning properly understood (which significantly qualifies the usual notion of totipotency)—would verify the Church's traditional claim that human life begins with fertilization and resultant syngamy.

Yet even if embryologists should in the end demonstrate conclusively that such differentiation does *not* exist—that methylation does not apply to humans and that the "pre-embryo" is in fact simply a "mass of undifferentiated cells"—this would not alter the Orthodox conviction that human life begins with conception, meaning fertilization. This is due not to stubborn conservatism, but to the undeniable evidence that the human "soul," the divinely bestowed dynamic of animation, is present from the very beginning, when the pronuclei of sperm and oocyte fuse to form the zygote, thereby creating a new and unique human being. The life-principle or "primal formula" that produces a developmental continuum, leading normally to the birth of a human child, is manifestly present from that initial stage. No reasonable judgment regarding the morality of abortion, assisted reproduction or embryo experimentation can be made, therefore, without reference to that basic truth.

With this in mind, we want to turn now to the specific issues of abortion, medically assisted procreation and genetic engineering, to ask about the morality of these procedures in light of the conclusion reached above: that human life begins at fertilization and demands full respect and protection from that moment onward.

4

Affirming Life's Sacredness

Possibilities and Limits of Biomedical Technology

> "Thou didst form my inward parts,
> thou didst knit me together in my
> mother's womb."
>
> —Ps 139:13

> "The Lord remembered Hannah, and
> in due time she conceived and bore
> a son, and she called his name
> Samuel, for she said, 'I have asked
> him of the Lord'."
>
> —1 Sam 1:20

> "[I]f any one age really attains, by
> eugenics and scientific education, the
> power to make its descendants what
> it pleases, all men who live after it
> are patients of that power. They are
> weaker, not stronger..."
>
> —C. S. Lewis

As Orthodox Christianity faces the twenty-first century, one of its most difficult challenges will be to preserve and proclaim the central tenet of its anthropology: that God has created the human person in his own image. The freedom and responsibility conferred by that creative act imply that the *imago Dei* involves three basic conditions, usually referred to as "self-creation," "self-direction," and "self-realization." This means that within appropriate limits we are called by God to exercise dominion over our origin, our activity, and our ultimate end. Yet we do so as an act of "synergy" or cooperation with God that leaves the initiative, the authority, and even the effective working out of that dominion in the hands of the Holy Spirit. This is the paradox expressed by

145

the apostle Paul, when he condemns works-righteousness (Rom 3:20) yet summons us to "work out your own salvation with fear and trembling" (Phil 2:12). For as this latter passage continues, "God is at work in you, both to will and to work for his good pleasure."

Any evaluation of the dangers and possibilities inherent in modern biomedical technology must begin with this affirmation, which presupposes the transcendent origin and eternal destiny of the human person. Otherwise we reduce the person to a cipher, with neither purpose nor hope. Others have already carried out this reduction with the creation of "secular man" who believes nothing and ultimately cares for nothing. To Orthodox Christians today, perhaps more than ever, there falls the responsibility not only to *believe* that the person bears the divine image, but also to *bear witness* to that truth in a way that influences the attitudes and behavior of the societies in which we live. As it speaks especially of the principle of respect for human life, the voice of Orthodoxy needs to be heard in the halls of our legislatures as well as from the ambos of our churches.

In what follows, I would like to examine several related areas of concern that have become major issues within the past few years, largely due to rapid advances in biomedical technology. We will begin by looking at the ethical implications of both legalized abortion and medically assisted forms of human procreation. Then we shall consider several of the more important benefits and dangers of recent developments in the field of genetic engineering. My purpose is not to detail technological advances in these areas. It is to look rather at the way these advances present both a promise and a threat to Christian life and faith within today's world. The basic concern is to provide a theological evaluation of these issues, together with suggestions for a pastoral approach in dealing with them.

Abortion and the Sacredness of Prenatal Life

If we are to name the ills that afflict both technologically developed and more traditional societies today, we should no doubt begin with the problem of abortion. The *Roe v. Wade* and *Doe v. Bolton* decisions, handed down by the U.S. Supreme Court on January 22, 1973, legalized "abortion on demand" during the first trimester of pregnancy. Justice Harry Blackmun, author of the *Roe* decision, declared: "the word person as used in the 14th Amendment does not include the unborn."[1] In 1979, the now disbanded Ethics Advisory Board of the U.S. Department of Health, Education and Welfare acknowledged that the embryo is entitled to "profound respect." To their mind, however, that respect did not mean that the embryo could enjoy "the full legal and moral rights attributed to a person." This view was echoed five years later by the widely publicized report produced by Britain's Warnock Commission: the embryo possesses "special status," it affirmed, but not the status of a living child or adult.

Once this reductionist perspective on life in the womb was received by the general public, further legislation broadened the first-trimester limit to the point that no legal barriers exist for a woman in the United States to obtain an abortion for any reason at any stage of her pregnancy. The result is that in the name of "reproductive freedom" well over thirty million induced abortions have been performed in this country in the last twenty five years. More than 98% of those are elective, that is, performed for nonmedical reasons. According to recent reports, 43% of American women will have an abortion in their lifetime.[2]

With the development of the so-called "contraceptive pill," French researchers made 1987 the year of the do-it-yourself abortion. Although it is intended to be genuinely contraceptive, the French-manufactured RU-486 pill (named after Roussel-Uclaf, the laboratory where it was developed in the early 1980s) in fact acts as an abortifacient. By bringing on the menstrual period even after pregnancy, the pill allows women, as one news journal put it, "to abort in the privacy of their own bedroom."[3] As a consequence, abortion will soon be the modern world's preferred means of birth-control. If this state of affairs has provoked little outcry, even within the churches, it is because of a seismic shift in moral perspective that has occurred in the United States in the wake of *Roe v. Wade:* the conclusion that a woman's right to privacy takes precedence over a growing child's right to life.

1 Quoted in Wm. Brennan, *The Abortion Holocaust,* (Missouri: Landmark Press, 1985), 95. For an excellent evaluation of the early pieces of abortion legislation, see Richard McCormick's chapter "The Abortion Dossier," in *How Brave a New World* (Washington, DC: Georgetown University Press, 1981), 117-175.

2 This statistic opened the article, "Abortions in America," *U.S. News & World Report* (19 Jan., 1998, 20ff.) and was qualified as "astonishing." It continued: "It would mean that 25 years after Roe v. Wade, abortions are safe, legal, and not rare."

3 *Newsweek,* 29 Dec., 1986, 47. This explains why pro-life advocates often refer to the pill as a "chemical coat hanger."

The Orthodox stance on the issue of abortion has never been in doubt. From biblical times to the present, abortion has been regarded as the morally condemnable act of destroying an innocent human life. Euthanasia also involves killing an innocent person. There, however, the motive is to relieve suffering, and the act can be described euphemistically as "mercy killing." In the case of abortion, the killing is done in the sole interest of persons other than the victim. Therefore it is not, like euthanasia, a matter of simple homicide; it is murder. "Pro-choice" advocates decry use of the term "murder" to describe induced abortions, insisting that murder means the *illegal* taking of a human life; and since abortion is legal in this country, the expression is inappropriate. "Pro-life" advocates would respond that the Supreme Court decisions authorizing abortions are themselves inappropriate, since they 1) represent specious interpretation of the Constitution, and 2) result from usurpation by the judiciary of what is properly legislative authority.

The conviction that abortion is tantamount to murder (the willful taking of an innocent human life in the interests of someone other than the victim)[4] is solidly grounded in biblical revelation. The Psalms speak of life in the womb as created by God and personally known by God:

...Thou didst form my inward parts, thou didst knit me together in my mother's womb... Thou knowest me right well; my frame was not hidden from thee, when I was being made in secret, intricately wrought in the depths of the earth. Thy eyes beheld my unformed substance... (Ps 139:13-16)[5]

Isaiah and Jeremiah were called by God before their creation in the womb and destined by him to act as servants and prophets to both Jews and Gentiles.

The Lord called me from the womb, from the body of my mother he named my name... [He] formed me from the womb to be his servant, to bring Jacob back to him, and that Israel might be gathered to him... (Isa 49:1, 5)

"Before I formed you in the womb I knew you, and before you were born I consecrated you; I appointed you to be a prophet to the nations. (Jer 1:5)

---

4   However they may be judged on moral grounds, killing in war and capital punishment technically do not constitute murder because of a (presumed) lack of innocence on the part of the one killed, whether aggressor or criminal.

5   *The New Oxford Annotated Bible* (*RSV*) (New York/Oxford: 1973), 762. The note to these verses adds perceptively, "God formed him in the womb (poetically called *the depths of the earth*) and knew his character from his conception."

A similar theme appears in St. Paul's letter to the Galatians (1:15f): "when he who had set me apart before I was born, and had called me through his grace, was pleased to reveal his Son to me..." Both prophets and apostles are known by God in his infinite foreknowledge, then they are created and called for a specific function within the divine economy. As the psalmist indicates, however, God's creative works, together with the call he issues, pertain to every one of his human creatures. The implication of these passages is clearly that from conception onward, life in the womb represents individual human existence. Beyond that, they also imply that what we refer to as "fetal life" is recognized by God as fully "personal." Created by God through the agency of human persons (the parents), the new being is constituted by and reflects the divine image, which in itself bestows upon that being the moral and spiritual quality of "personhood."

As we indicated in the preceding chapter, the age-old debate over the time at which the fetus can be said to be human, and more specifically to be a personal being, is fundamentally misleading. It is based on the erroneous presupposition that the criteria for determining personhood are to be agreed upon by other people and then fulfilled by the fetus, whether those criteria include conception, implantation, quickening or birth. Returning to a theme stressed in chapter one, we have to affirm that from the perspective of Orthodox Christianity, *personhood is conferred by God* and not by physiological development, medical analysis or social convention. "Know that the Lord is God! It is he who made us, and not we ourselves..."[6]

Much has been made of the fact that the New Testament is silent on the issue of abortion. While it is possible that the condemnation of *pharmakeia* alludes to potions or drugs taken to induce abortions (Gal 5:20; cf. Rev 9:21, 18:23), the term more likely connotes sorcery or magic arts in general. Even the Old Testament, which in its Levitical legislation is far more concerned to govern specific behaviors, has little to say about abortion. One passage, in fact, seems to undermine the notion that fetal life is fully human and has value equal to that of a born child. The Israelite Book of the Covenant declares:

6   Ps 99[100]:3, LXX. Some Hebrew manuscripts read "and we are his." In either case, the psalmist's point is to declare the absolute Lordship of God over the whole of human life and activity.

When men strive together, and hurt a woman with child, so that there is a miscarriage, *and yet no harm follows*, the one who hurt her shall be fined... *If any harm follows*, then you shall give life for life, eye for eye, tooth for tooth... (Ex 21:22f)

Here the harm that follows seems to be suffered by the mother rather
than by the fetus, who may be presumed to be dead as a result of the miscarriage. An alternative interpretation holds that the first reference is to a
blow that provokes a premature birth with no further harm to the child,
while the second indicates that the child is seriously injured or has died,
and punishment is to be inflicted on the perpetrator(s) according to the
lex talionis or law of retribution. This alternative reading is nevertheless
forced. In either case the passage concerns the status of unborn life rather
than abortion per se.

The Septuagint rendering of this passage modifies the Hebrew text by
shifting the focus clearly to the fetus. Here a distinction, derived from
Greek philosophical tradition, is made between a child that is "formed"
(*exeikonismenon*) or "unformed" (*mê exeikonismenon*). If the child that
"comes out" as a result of a blow is unformed, the one who struck the
blow shall pay a fine determined by the woman's husband. If the child is
formed, however, the offender will suffer damages equivalent to those suffered by the child, including death. Provoking the fatal miscarriage of a
near-full-term fetus, in other words, merits the death penalty.

This passage, widely commented upon in ancient as well as modern
writings, deals only with miscarriage. Neither here nor elsewhere in Scripture do we find an explicit condemnation of abortion. (Although Josephus, in his apologetic work *Against Apion* [II.202], declares that Jewish
Law "forbids women either to abort or to eliminate the fetus," and he
equates such an act with infanticide, *teknoktonos*.) If Christian pro-life advocates can claim legitimately to base their stance on Scripture, it is rather
for its unequivocal affirmation of God's sovereignty over every aspect of
human existence, from conception to the grave, as well as for its witness
to the intimate communion God establishes with every human creature,
thereby conferring upon them the irreducible and inviolable quality of
personhood: "being-in-communion."

The patristic and liturgical traditions of the Church, on the other hand,
are outspoken and unambiguous in their opposition to induced abortion.
The *Didachê* or *Teaching of the Twelve Apostles* is a mid-second century writ-

ing with underlying tradition going back to the first century. It declares (2:2): "do not murder a child by destruction" (*ou phoneuseis teknon en phthora*), meaning by abortion; and it links the act with infanticide, adding: "do not kill a new-born infant" (*oude gennêthen apokteneis*). Modifying Jesus' commandment regarding the neighbor, the pseudepigraphical Epistle of Barnabas (early second century?) insists (19:5): "You shall love your neighbor more than your own soul." Then it adds the precise formula found in the *Didachê*, "do not murder a child by abortion" (*ou phoneuseis teknon en phthora*), suggesting that the phrase was a fixed element in early Christian catechesis. Similar prohibitions are found in the apologist Athanagoras (*Supplication for Christians,* ch. 35; ca. 177: women who induce abortions are called "murderers"), and in Tertullian (*On the Soul,* ch. 27; ca. 210: the substances of body and soul are formed at one and the same time, affirming "immediate animation"; similarly, Clement of Alexandria and Lactantius). Tertullian labels abortion "murder," irrespective of whether the fetus is "formed" or "unformed" (*Apology* 9).

In his attacks on what he considered to be the moral laxity of his contemporary, Bishop Callistus, St. Hippolytus of Rome in the early third century also condemned the use of "sterilizing drugs" and other means that would provoke a miscarriage. By allowing women of high estate to fornicate with slaves and others beneath them, forcing them to have recourse to abortion, Callistus, Hippolytus declares, "is introducing at one and the same time both adultery and murder!"[7] Others in the Latin West who wrote and preached on abortion include Saints Augustine, Ambrose and Jerome, each of whom condemned the willful destruction of prenatal life.

The fourth century Cappadocian bishop Basil the Great decrees that "She who purposely destroys the fetus shall suffer the punishment of murder." Like Tertullian, he adds—perhaps as a corrective to the Alexandrian Septuagint tradition, but in any case with a prophetic eye toward *Roe v. Wade*—"and we pay no attention to the distinction as to whether the fetus was formed or unformed" (Ep. 188, Canon 2). Basil's contemporary, St. John Chrysostom, considers abortion to be a worse crime than murder, and he lays equal blame for the act, as for the underlying sin of fornication, on

---

7 *Philosophoumena* 9.12.

the woman and the man. Inveighing especially against commerce with harlots "and the mother of it, drunkenness," he asks rhetorically:

Why sow where the ground makes it its care to destroy the fruit? where there are many efforts at abortion? where there is murder before the birth? for even the harlot you do not let continue a mere harlot but make her a murderess also. You see how drunkenness leads to whoredom, whoredom to adultery, adultery to murder; or rather to something even worse than murder. For I have no name to give it, since it does not eliminate the thing born, but prevents its being born... Why do you...arm for slaughter the woman who was given for childbearing?... [E]ven if the daring deed [of aborting her child] is hers, nevertheless the causing of it is yours![8]

The Church's canonical tradition is equally explicit in condemning abortion. The Spanish Council of Elvira, held in 305 or 306, excommunicates the woman who aborts her child, allowing her to receive the sacrament only on her death bed (canons 63, 68). Only slightly less severe was the penalty imposed by canon 21 of the Council of Ancyra, held in 314. The definitive formulation of canon law condemning abortion, however, was provided by the Council in Trullo ("Quinisext," 692), that based its decision on both Ancyra and Basil's canonical letters two and eight. Canon 91 in Trullo states, "Those who give drugs for procuring abortion, and those who receive poisons to kill the foetus, are subjected to the penalty of murder," meaning at least ten years of excommunication.[9] In the Church's canonical legislation, then, premeditated abortion is considered to be an act of murder that brings guilt upon both the woman who has the abortion and the person who provides the means whereby the act may be carried out. On the other hand, it does not develop the insight offered by some of the Church's early theologians, that the father shares equal responsibility with the mother for the death of their child.

It is in the liturgical tradition that we find the clearest evidence that the Church recognizes life in the womb to be both fully human and personal. The feasts of the Church include not only the birth of the Virgin Mary, John the Baptist and Jesus, but also their *conception* (December 9, September 23, and March 25, respectively). The Annunciation to the Holy Virgin, we should remember, is the liturgical celebration of our Lord's conception, just as the nuptial embrace of Joachim and Anna has

8 *Hom. 24 in Rom.*, in *NPNF* first series, vol. 11, 520 (translation slightly modified).
9 *NPNF* 14, 404.

been understood to represent the conception of Mary in iconographic form. Biblical grounding for these hymnic and iconic expressions appears above all in St. Luke's account of the meeting between Mary and her cousin Elizabeth. "When Elizabeth heard the greeting of Mary, the babe leaped in her womb." Filled with the Holy Spirit, Elizabeth blesses Mary and exclaims, "Behold, when the voice of your greeting came to my ears, the babe in my womb leaped for joy" (Lk 1:41-44). Taken together with the account of Jesus' virginal conception, this description of the Baptist's prenatal life leaves no doubt that the evangelist (and his underlying tradition) considered the unborn child to be fully human, conscious, and capable of experiencing human relationships and emotions.[10]

The matter, then, is clear: despite the conclusion of the U.S. Supreme Court that "a fetus, at least during the first two trimesters of pregnancy, is not an existing person within the meaning of the Constitution,"[11] Orthodox Christianity holds as fundamental the conviction that personal, human life begins, not at implantation or at quickening or at the moment of birth, but at *conception*, described in our preceding chapter as "syngamy," the creation of a genetically unique individual through the process of fertilization. For this reason, the Orthodox are morally obliged to accept a pro-life philosophy, one which is based on an authentic biblical anthropology rather than on social concerns or political correctness.

Orthodox Christians are not entirely in agreement, however, with the way that pro-life philosophy should be expressed or put into practice. In an article on "Abortion and Public Policy," Peter J. Pappas refers to polls in which Americans express the familiar theme, "I personally oppose abortion, but I feel the decision to abort must be made by every woman for herself"; or, "I personally feel abortion is wrong, but I think it should be legal." He adds, "While this position has never been supported by any official declaration of any Orthodox body in America, it is a position

10 For a further discussion of the biblical and patristic foundation of the Orthodox stance against abortion, see Frank Schaeffer's article, "The Church Against Abortion," in *The Christian Activist* vol. 3/2 (spring 1993); and ch. 18 of his book *Dancing Alone: The Quest for Orthodox Faith in the Age of False Religion* (Brookline, MA: Holy Cross Orthodox Press, 1994), 233-253. The former article includes information on various abortion techniques including "partial-birth abortion," which we discuss below.
11 Senate Judiciary Committee statement of 1982, quoted by A. Varga, *The Main Issues in Bioethics (Revised)* (New York: Paulist Press, 1984), 58.

which has been adopted by many of the faithful, clergy and laity alike."[12] True as this may be, many Orthodox, including several of our bishops, have taken a very active, public role in organizations such as "Orthodox Christians for Life," which, among other activities, coordinates Orthodox participation in the annual pro-life march in the nation's capitol. Many more of our faithful support their initiative wholeheartedly, even if they can not or prefer not to participate actively themselves. Others, however, have expressed concern that those who do become involved are allowing themselves to be co-opted by the national pro-life movement, with its perceived political and social agenda: an agenda which they believe to be incompatible with Orthodox life and faith.

If we are in basic agreement as to the status of the preborn child and to the immorality of elective abortions, we remain somewhat polarized with regard to the question: What sort of witness should the Church offer in the face of what has been appropriately termed the "abortion holocaust"? The answer to that question, it would seem, needs to be formulated in light of Jesus' chilling statement, "Whoever denies me before men, I also will deny before my Father who is in heaven" (Mt 10:33). Does this refer only to public, verbal confession of one's belief in Christ? Or should it be understood in terms of Jesus' teaching about the *neighbor*, whose very existence demands unqualified protection and love in Jesus' name (Mt 25:40; Mk 12:31; Lk 10:33-35)? And if the latter, is there a closer, more vulnerable "neighbor" than the unborn child? From this perspective, then, the only appropriate response to the abortion crisis is to oppose, peacefully but vigorously, the attitudes and laws that sanction it, and to do so by means of words and actions that reflect the Church's historical concern for prenatal life.

One element in the abortion debate that is making the issue so divisive is the way language is used to advance a particular agenda, either for or against elective abortions. If pro-life statements are crafted to arouse ire and indignation, "pro-choice" literature is replete with euphemisms. (An example of manipulation by language, of course, is this way of putting "pro-choice" in quotes: to stress the point that we are really talking about "pro-abortion.") This use or misuse of words is inevitable as long as we are

12 *SVTQ* 39/3 (1995), 233-255, at 234.

caught up in civil warfare over the issue of "rights." What is regrettable is the fact that all the sound and fury has tended to obscure a major issue that both sides need to address. Irrespective of the "rights" of either the fetus or the mother, what in fact is the *result* of an abortion on both mother and child? This leads to the issues of fetal pain and maternal depression.

The July 1996 issue of the popular journal appropriately named *Self* includes an article on "abortion options." After stressing that "abortion is one of the safest of surgeries," then detailing an awesome list of potential complications, it offers a table of various medical and surgical methods for terminating an unwanted pregnancy. The former include the RU-486 (mifepristone) pill, which causes an implanted embryo to be discarded along with the uterine lining; and the combination of methotrexate and misoprostol, which inhibits cell division and brings on contractions to expel the embryo.[13] Surgical options include "D&C": dilatation and curettage, used in early term abortions (the womb is emptied of its contents, including the child, by scraping or, alternatively, by vacuum aspiration); "D&E": dilatation and evacuation (the child is dismembered with forceps before being removed from the womb); and "D&X": dilatation and extraction, otherwise known as "partial-birth" abortion (described below). The article, by the way, does not include these descriptions. It does qualify D&X procedures by stating, "Performed only in extremely advanced pregnancies, usually over 24 weeks, when the woman's life is in danger or the fetus is severely damaged." As we shall see, this is another example of obfuscation through a blatant distortion of the facts: partial-birth abor-

13 Of particular interest is the article "Abortion Group to Advise Doctors on Drug Used to End Pregnancy," *New York Times* "National" (30 March, 1996). It describes the two-step protocol involving an initial injection of methotrexate (originally approved as an anti-cancer drug) "which interferes with cell division and kills the fetus." This is followed a week later by administration of the ulcer drug misoprostol, which produces uterine contractions and expulsion of the fetus. The article goes on to note that a recent survey indicated that a third of California gynecologists who currently do not perform abortions would do so using the drug combination. The protocol will be so simple, compared to later stage surgical procedures, that the number of early term (six- to eight-week) abortions is likely to increase dramatically. The report notes as well that some women who underwent clinical trials using the drug combination experienced cramping, nausea and diarrhea. Some were also troubled by the length of time it took for the fetus to be expelled, and by having to confront "the reality of what passes out of their body." Six months earlier, *Newsweek* published an article entitled "Blood and Tears," that illustrates the emotional damage done to women who have opted for a medical abortion using mifepristone (18 September, 1995, 66-68). Two women are reported to have expelled their fetal children at home, gazed at their "tiny fists," then flushed them down the toilet. The article goes on to state, "It is not clear how many women really want to see, or dispose of, their fetus."

tions, kept legal by President Clinton in 1996 and 1997 but still on the Congressional agenda in 1998, are not rare, nor are they limited to cases where the mother's life is at risk or the fetus is seriously deformed.

When the *Self* article speaks of pain, it addresses only the physical pain experienced by the mother during the procedure itself. It says nothing about the post-abortion syndrome, experienced by a large number of women (some research indicates up to 90% of those who have abortions), which can include depression, anxiety, acute feelings of guilt, loss of sexual functioning, compulsive eating and other compensatory disorders, suicidal ideation, and hospitalization for psychiatric care.[14] Nor does it speak about the effects of abortion on *men*, although recent studies have shown that fathers of aborted children often suffer serious and long-term depression as a result of what is basically the mother's choice. As one team of Roman Catholic therapists expressed it, "[As] for the man who stands up and opposes an abortion, under the law he has no legal recourse and cannot defend his child's right to life. His grief is punctuated with impotency and feelings of helplessness... Killing hurts the living too. It knows no gender bias."[15]

Most significantly, the *Self* article also fails to mention that the various surgical procedures "dismember"—the current euphemism for "tear apart"—the body of the unborn child. (In a classic example of "pro-choice" Newspeak, it states: "A cannula (tube) is inserted into uterus and attached to a vacuum, which suctions out contents of uterus." Those "contents," of course, include the mutilated remains of a growing human being.) Nor does it talk about the frequently used technique of salt poisoning, by which a needle containing a strong salt solution is inserted into the mother's abdomen so that the developing child inhales and swallows the salt. Within an hour or so the child is poisoned to death, and its body is burned and shriveled by the concentrated solution.[16]

14 See, for example, the brief report in the *ALA Journal*, Feb. 1997, 11 (with reference to the *Post-Abortion Review*, fall edition 1994); and especially David Reardon, *Aborted Women. Silent No More* (Chicago: Loyola University Press, 1987), ch. 4, "The Psychological Impact of Abortion."

15 V. M. Rue & C. Tellefsen, "The Effects of Abortion on Men," *Ethics & Medics. Catholic Tradition & Bioethics*, vol. 21/4 (April 1996), 3-4.

16 *U.S. News & World Report*, (19 January, 1998, 32) describes the widely used procedure of D&E as one "in which the fetus is cut into pieces with serrated forceps before being removed bit by bit from the uterus. 'If people object to D&X,' says the director of one clinic, 'what will they say when they get to this? D&E is the next battleground.'"

From what point in the gestation period does the child suffer from such procedures? Modern embryology has determined that the fetal nervous system is integrated and functioning by around the eighth week of pregnancy. Researchers, however, are divided on the question as to when the growing child actually begins to feel pain. The line of division tends to follow abortion philosophies: pro-abortionists usually claim that pain can only be felt once the cerebral cortex is fully developed, whereas anti-abortionists argue that such perception occurs much earlier in the pregnancy, perhaps from the eighth week onward. Although the "pain tracks" are only fully developed by around the twenty-sixth week, the consensus seems to hold that the cerebral cortex need not be fully developed for the fetus to experience pain.[17] If this is the case, it means that once the nervous system is functioning (from the eighth week), the child *in utero* feels the pain of having its body dismembered or poisoned. The same is a fortiori true in cases of D&X or "partial-birth" abortions. As the American public is by now well aware, this procedure—to distinguish it legally from infanticide—involves delivering most of the baby's body while leaving a portion of the head in the birth canal. Then the abortionist inserts scissors into the back of the skull to create an opening and suctions out the brain with a vacuum hose. This causes the skull to collapse and thereby facilitates extraction. In these usually late-term abortions, there is no doubt that the child experiences acute physical pain.

Aside from the fact that the "partial-birth" procedure is neither safe nor rare, it is *medically useless*. The group known as PHACT ("Physicians

---

17 Recent studies of pain responses in pre-term and full-term neonates have confirmed that development of the neural pathways occurs at a very early stage in the gestation period. Anatomical studies had already shown that nociceptive nerve endings in the skin of a fetus are "similar to those in adult skin," and neonates respond to noxious stimuli with a variety of complex reactions, including cardiovascular, respiratory, endocrine, metabolic, physiological, and behavioral modifications. In controlled studies, for example, stress levels and behavioral changes in infants given local anesthesia prior to circumcision were markedly less than in those infants who received no anesthesia, demonstrating that the body's response to pain is highly developed at birth. The fact that pain is experienced much earlier in the gestation period, however, is shown by the fact that neurons in the skin respond to touching, pinching and pricking very early in fetal life, although the degree to which the fetus can perceive pain prior to the end of the second trimester has not been determined. See Maria Fitzgerald and K. J. S. Anand, "Developmental Neuroanatomy and Neurophysiology of Pain," ch. 2 of *Pain in Infants, Children, and Adolescents* (N. L. Schechter, C.B. Berde, and M. Yaster, eds.; Baltimore & Philadelphia: Williams and Wilkins, 1993). I am indebted to E. M. Loutsch, M.D., of the Division of Child/Adolescent Psychology, New York Medical Center, Valhalla, NY, for providing me with this and related information.

Ad-Hoc Coalition for Truth," which includes more than 300 medical professionals) declared in the wake of the Clinton veto of the 1996 Congressional bill banning the procedure: "Partial-birth abortion is never medically necessary to protect the health of a woman or to protect her future fertility. In fact, the procedure can pose grave dangers to the woman."[18] As for the matters of frequency and safety, the "pro-choice" media themselves have reported that "thousands" of partial-birth abortions are performed each year, virtually all for convenience;[19] and even abortion activists admit that the procedure can lead to serious complications, including perforation of the uterus, hemorrhaging, peritonitis and sterility, not to mention the possibility of maternal death. Why then is it practiced? When asked the question, abortionists refer to various medical conditions of the fetus that purportedly make it necessary, such as hydrocephaly. Suctioning out the brain and allowing the skull to collapse allegedly allows for an easier birth. Why a live birth could not have been achieved by caesarean section is not discussed.[20]

In fact, *partial-birth abortion is nothing other than an expediency to avoid a charge of infanticide in the brutal killing of an unwanted child.* It is a barbarous procedure that should be banned as a matter of public policy, in part because of the severe pain it inflicts on the nearly full-term child, but basically because it kills a live infant. As Robert Bork pointed out in his aptly titled article, "Inconvenient Lives," the argument (advanced by the National Abortion and Reproductive Rights Action League and Planned Parenthood) that the child is killed by the general anesthesia given the mother is simply false. In any case, local anesthesia is most often used and provides little or no painkilling effect to the baby. Bork continues:

18 Quoted by Fr. Germain Kopaczynski, OFMConv, "Partial-Birth Abortion. What's at Stake in the President's Veto?", in *Ethics & Medics* 21/12 (1996), 2.
19 See, for example, the article in *Newsweek*, "A Bitter New Battle Over Partial-Birth Abortions," (17 March, 1997, 68).
20 Lies and intentional obfuscation on the part of pro-abortion activists have been well documented in recent press reports and other journalistic pieces. See, for example, the *Newsweek* article mentioned in the previous note, and the recent column by John Leo, "The First Crack in the Wall," *U.S. News & World Report* (10 March, 1997). They detail the admitted "untruths" uttered publicly in defense of the abortion cause by Ron Fitzsimmons, executive director of the National Coalition of Abortion Providers, misinformation that apparently influenced the Clinton veto of the proposed ban on partial-birth abortions. Leo quotes Dr. Martin Haskell, owner of two Ohio abortion clinics that specialize in the partial-birth procedure, as admitting that the fetus was "usually alive" when the stabbing and brain suction took place.

The vice president of the Society for Obstetric Anesthesia and Perinatology said the claim was "crazy," noting that "anesthesia does not kill an infant if you don't kill the mother." Two doctors who perform partial-birth abortions stated that the majority of fetuses aborted in this fashion are alive until the end of the procedure.[21]

Alive, that is, until a pair of scissors is thrust into the back of the baby's skull.

The Pulitzer Prize winning columnist Paul Greenberg, of the *Los Angeles Times* Syndicate, published a piece on 23 February, 1997, entitled "Partial-Birth Abortions Disguised by Partial Truth." After listing mind-numbing defenses put forth by defenders of the partial-birth procedure—including the argument that it serves the health interests of the *baby*—he concludes with a statement that needs to be heard above the clamor of the deceptive propaganda so loudly voiced today by pro-abortion activists:

> The essential purpose of a partial-birth abortion is no different from that of the vast majority of the million and more abortions performed in this country every year: *to kill the baby*. And not all the mindless, meaningless euphemisms being used to justify partial-birth abortions—Reproductive Choice!—can disguise that one stubborn fact.

In May of 1997 I taught an intensive course on bioethics at the St. Sergius Orthodox Theological Institute in Paris, France. Toward the end of the course I described briefly but as accurately as I could the procedure involved in partial-birth abortions. No one in the class had heard of it before. The two women present, both of whom were French, reacted with tears, while the male students, from a variety of ethnic and national backgrounds, stared in stunned disbelief. Later I went up to the women, who accosted me with a pair of angry questions: "How could anyone perform such a monstrous procedure?" "How could any mother resort to such an act, to kill her own child in such a barbaric way?" The only answer that came to mind, which I kept to myself, was a paraphrase of a widespread dictum from the 1960s: "Violent abortions are as American as apple pie."[22]

---

21 Published in *First Things* (Dec. 1966); reprinted in *The Christian Activist*, vol. 10 (winter/spring 1997).

22 Note the remarks made by Mary Ann Glendon, Learned Hand Professor of Law at Harvard University, before the Subcommittee on the Constitution of the Judiciary Committee of the U.S. House of Representatives, 22 April, 1996: "It is interesting to note that the question [of partial-birth abortion legislation] could not even come up in most other legal systems, for late abortions are forbidden or strictly regulated nearly everywhere... Typically, in the early weeks of pregnancy (ranging from ten in France to eighteen in Sweden), other countries do not criminalize abortion, but do require information, counseling, and material assistance in order

If there is ambivalence on the part of many Christians toward abortion, it is usually because of what are referred to as the "hard cases." These are instances where the circumstances of a particular case seem to call for Kierkegaard's "teleological suspension of the ethical," referred to in Orthodox terms as *oikonomia* or "economy." Certain situations, it is argued, not only justify abortion but make it ethically mandatory. The usual examples cited are 1) conditions such as ectopic pregnancy, eclampsia, or uterine cancer that directly threaten the life of the mother; 2) severe psychological stress experienced by the mother during the pregnancy that threatens her well-being; 3) pregnancy that results from rape or incest; and 4) a diagnosis, provided by amniocentesis or chorionic villus sampling (CVS),[23] that the child is genetically "defective" and will be born with serious physical or mental handicaps. In such cases, the reasoning goes, it is morally acceptable to terminate the pregnancy in the interests of a higher good. The moral injunction against killing the fetus (i.e., the ethical principle) is "suspended" in favor of the mother's ("teleological") right to life and personal well-being, which would otherwise be jeopardized if the abortion were not performed. Once again, the mother's legally sanctioned "right" to life, liberty and the pursuit of happiness takes precedence over the child's "right" to life at all.

Valerie Protopapas, a leading figure in the "Orthodox Christians for Life" movement, has written forcefully and eloquently against this appeal to "hard cases."[24] Her stance has been criticized as overly rigid, representing simply the opposite extreme to the pro-choice position: absolute protection of the woman's rights is replaced by absolute protection accorded to the fetus. Nevertheless, the conclusions she draws—which are well

to provide real alternatives to women facing what is often the worst crisis of their lives. After that initial period, most countries require strong justification for abortion and impose procedural safeguards to protect the woman and her unborn child." "'Medically Necessary' Killing," *The Human Life Review*, vol. 22/4 (1996), 56, 60.

23 Chorionic villus sampling or "chorion biopsy" can be performed during the eighth week of pregnancy, whereas amniocentesis is usually unreliable before the fifteenth week. Marc Lappé, "The New Technologies of Genetic Screening," *The Hastings Center Report* 14/5 (1984), 18-21, notes that there is an increased risk of spontaneous abortion with CVS. For articles detailing the procedure and its usefulness for detecting *in utero* a variety of chromosome abnormalities, see the journal *Prenatal Diagnosis*, published by the UCSD Medical Center, San Diego.

24 "Abortion, Oikonomia, and the 'Hard Cases'," *The Christian Activist*, vol. 5 (1995); see also her article "Common Pro-Abortion Clichés and the Pro-Life Response," reprinted in the Orthodox Church in America *Resource Handbook* (vol. 2/2, 1991) but originally circulated as a handout by "Orthodox Christians for Life" (available at P.O. Box 805, Melville, NY 11747; tel.: 516-271-4408).

worth studying in parish and other circles—are thoroughly consistent with the Orthodox view of the innate sacredness of human life.[25]

In discussing this issue, it is important to keep in mind the old law school maxim: "hard cases make bad law." This is as true in the area of ethics as it is in jurisprudence. Particularly in the abortion debate, pro-choice advocates have used the exceptional to establish the general: public policy that sanctions late-term abortions has been shaped in large measure by appeals made to the relatively few "hard cases" that seize the public imagination.

Reviewing such cases in light of the "best interests" of the woman's health, David Reardon draws the following conclusion: "these cases are the worst conditions under which to have an abortion... *The more difficult the circumstances prompting abortion, the more likely it is that the woman will suffer severe post-abortion sequelae.*"[26] That is, the likelihood that the mother will experience some degree of trauma increases significantly when an abortion is performed to terminate a pregnancy that threatens her life or mental stability, or to eliminate a genetically defective child.

We need to make an important distinction, however, among these various situations. The first instance, in which the woman's life is seriously endangered, represents a special case insofar as the woman has no real choice in the matter. (It should be noted as well that these cases, which are the only ones that can be considered truly "therapeutic," account statistically for fewer than one percent of the nearly 1.4 million abortions performed in the United States each year.) In cases of ectopic pregnancy, life-threatening eclampsia or uterine cancer, the only choice is to work to save the woman's life or else lose both her and the child she is carrying. Even in those exceptional cases where a late-term child might be saved if the woman's life is sacrificed, Orthodox tradition has held that priority should go to preserving the mother. This is not because her life has more intrinsic worth than that of her child, but because she has already established relationships and responsibilities with others who de-

---

25 Another useful resource for parish study groups is the "Orthodox Christian Study Guide on Abortion," prepared by Fr. Ed Pehanich, published in *Rachel's Children* ("Journal of Orthodox Christians for Life," edited by John and Valerie Protopapas, P.O. Box 805, Melville, NY 11747), vol. 10, no. 3 (1997).

26 Reardon, *Aborted Women.*, 163, emphasis his.

pend upon her. The same, of course, is not true with the unborn child.[27] The choice to preserve the woman's life is justified on grounds of the principle of "double effect." The direct intention is not to kill the child, nor even to terminate the pregnancy. It is to save the life of the mother. The fact that the therapeutic procedure ends the life of the growing child is a tragic and regrettable, albeit necessary and inevitable consequence.

As we point out in the appendix on "Orthodoxy and Abortion," however, a mother who willingly offers her own life in favor of the child growing within her exercises an authentic martyrdom out of love for another (cf. John 15:13). Nevertheless, that sacrifice can only be properly made by taking into consideration the needs and desires of other members of her family. Their dependence on her and the strength of their relationship with her is as great as that of her unborn child. In the great majority of cases, then, the tragic choice imposed upon her will lead her to preserve her own life rather than abandon those who relate to her in terms of emotion, memory, shared responsibility, and love.

With regard to the other three cases—rape, incest and genetic anomalies—the pregnant woman does have a choice. And except where mental instability caused by sexual violence tempts her to commit suicide, her life is not in jeopardy. Severe psychological stress accompanying a pregnancy can arise for various reasons: potential economic burden, the fear of "too many children," or pressure from the spouse. It can also be due to simple vanity: not wanting to bear the burden of a pregnancy because it might jeopardize the woman's career or mar her physical appearance. None of these reasons justifies taking the life of the child. Even there where the woman (often a teen-aged girl) is ostracized and rejected by her family, her psychological distress does not warrant destroying the life that is growing within her. In fact it has been amply demonstrated that aborting a child un-

---

27 Priority given to the life of the mother is something of a universal principle. Speaking to the issue from a Muslim perspective, Osman Bakar states: "As to why the saving of the mother's life is to be given priority over that of the child, a[n Islamic] jurist explains: 'For the mother is the origin of the fetus; moreover she is established in life with duties and responsibilities, and she is also a pillar of the family. It would not be possible to sacrifice her life for the life of a fetus which has not acquired a personality and which has no responsibilities or obligations to fulfill.'" "Islam and Bioethics," in *Orthodox Christians and Muslims* (Brookline, MA: Holy Cross Orthodox Press, 1986), 163. A number of Bakar's proposals reflect elements of Islamic teaching that are strikingly similar to Orthodox themes, especially those found in the writings of St. Maximus the Confessor.

der such conditions tends to increase rather than decrease the woman's urge to commit suicide.[28] Aborting the child tends to compound the guilt incurred by the pregnancy rather than alleviate it. And the bottom line remains the point that a moral solution to a regrettable situation (the unwanted pregnancy) cannot involve the taking of an innocent human life.

All of this, to be sure, is predicated on the conclusion we drew in the last chapter. The entity growing in the womb is not simply a bit of invasive tissue which the pregnant woman can dispose of as she sees fit. It is a living individual, a human being, a *person*—not merely "en devenir" or in the process of becoming such, but in its own right—because of its genetic uniqueness, but especially because, as Scripture makes abundantly clear, God considers it to be a unique personal being, a *child of God* and the object of God's infinite love.

Personhood, once again, is determined and bestowed by God alone. That personhood may be considered the "being in communion," with God and others, that is constituted by "the divine image" in which every human being is created. As such, it is characterized by a transcendent aspect that remains indelible, however much the person may succumb to the powers of sin and corruption. No human action or authority can deprive the child of that personal quality, however inconvenient that child may be to the mother or however "defective" he or she may be relative to social and medical standards of what is normal. As we shall note further on, the unborn child in this respect is like the patient who is irreversibly locked into a deep coma or persistent vegetative state. If Orthodox Christianity rejects the option of abortion (with the single exception noted above), it is for the same reason that it rejects euthanasia and the removal of vital organs from such persons: they remain in the fullest sense *persons* in the sight of God.[29]

---

28 See, for example, Reardon, *Aborted Women*, 167.
29 Writing about the reasons for Orthodox Christian opposition to abortion, Fr. John Garvey remarks: "Every life is valued by God. This includes the life of the unborn child, as well as the criminal, the enemy, the political oppressor, and the most annoying person we know. Although we fail in the task every day, we are called on, by our baptism into the death and resurrection of Christ, to reflect God's love for everyone who lives. Our model of love is not a sentimental pastel-colored greeting card, but Christ crucified. There are situations in which birth-giving is at least profoundly inconvenient, and others in which it may be absolutely terrifying. We should see something infinitely more terrifying, however, in a heart that is willing to kill life at its start, at its most vulnerable moment of being." "Orthodox Christians and Abortion," in the

What are the implications of this position for the twin issues of rape and incest? With regard to *rape*, we should recall in the first place that, mercifully, very few women who are subject to this vicious kind of violence become pregnant. Impediments to pregnancy may include the woman's infertility at the time of the attack (contraceptives, time of the menstrual cycle), lack of penetration, or sexual dysfunction on the part of the man. In any event, a woman who has been sexually attacked should immediately take precautions to avoid becoming pregnant. If she presents herself to a hospital emergency room within twenty-four hours of the attack, certain protocols (flushing the reproductive tract, hormonal treatment, etc.) can virtually guarantee that fertilization will not occur. It is true, however, that many of the most common post-rape protocols involve use of abortifacient drugs such as Ovral. Although touted as a contraceptive, Ovral's primary effect is to "render the endometrium hostile to a possible fertilized egg," that is, to provoke a miscarriage.[30] Therefore it is important that treatment be initiated at the earliest possible moment after the rape has occurred, to ensure, as far as possible, that an embryo is not formed.

The greatest obstacle to overcome in such cases is usually the shame or guilt experienced by the rape victim. After the incident she often feels dirty, exposed and vulnerable. The social stigma associated with rape is largely due to the unspoken feeling of many people that the woman is at least partly responsible: it is assumed—in total contradiction to the evidence—that she, consciously or unconsciously, provoked the attack. If the victim herself shared such feelings about rape before she was attacked, it will be especially difficult for her to take the steps necessary to obtain appropriate medical treatment.

This is a difficult and sensitive aspect of rape cases that needs to be given full consideration by those who attempt to help the victim, including family members and the clergy. It implies that rape is not a private matter, but rather involves the human community as a whole: family,

Orthodox Church in America's *Resource Handbook* (vol. 2/2, 1991). What distinguishes the Orthodox position from the prevailing attitude in contemporary society is precisely the conviction that "every life is valued by God," however inconvenient, intrusive, burdensome or worthless it may appear to human eyes.

30 See Fr. Steven P. Rohlfs article, "Pregnancy Prevention and Rape: Another View," *Ethics & Medics* 18/5 (May 1993), p. 1f.

church and the larger society. Accordingly, it is important that parents speak with their daughters at an early age, to explain various precautions to take to avoid such violence, and what to do in the event the violence occurs. More importantly, both families and the parish need to provide assurance that any woman who is so victimized will be materially, physically and emotionally supported and cared for in every way possible, to ensure her well-being and the well-being of the child she may be carrying.

The best way to help a woman through the trauma of rape, especially when it has resulted in pregnancy, is to surround her with unfailing love, understanding and concern. This includes accompanying her throughout the nine months and beyond, to provide appropriate care both for her and for her child. In cases where the woman feels she cannot keep the child, then that accompaniment will include supporting and aiding her through the birth as well as through the entire adoption process. [31] As for pastoral care, it will include frequent visitations, arranging for material and other means of support, and referrals to those who can provide professional services where they are needed, in the areas of social work, medical follow-up, and where appropriate, psychological counseling. But here especially, the pastor's primary responsibility will be to serve as a living witness to the Gospel of Love, and to work in every appropriate way toward creating conditions for her healing, within her family, among her friends, and within the fellowship of the Church.

A frequent form of sexual violence that receives little publicity is *marital rape.* Studies have shown that among sample groups more than ten percent of the married women surveyed had at one time or another, and on occasion repeatedly, been raped by their husbands. Most of them had been subjected to physical abuse as well. Until the late 1970s marital rape in the United States was not viewed as a crime. The courts simply accepted the husband's claim that he held "conjugal rights" over his wife. As one acquitted rapist put it: "You're my wife, you do what I

---

31 The Orthodox Church in America has established the Orthodox Christian Adoption Referral Service, presently under the direction of Mrs. Arlene Kallaur. Inquiries regarding any aspect of adoption may be addressed directly to her at the OCA Chancery (516-922-0550) or by e-mail (arlene@oca.org). The O.C.A.R.S. was created primarily to serve Orthodox women who have unwanted pregnancies. To date, only a very few women in these circumstances have availed themselves of it, and the organization has been primarily concerned to facilitate the adoption of children from Russia and other East European countries. The Lavra Mambre, an Orthodox monastery in Guatemala, is also offering children for adoption.

want."[32] Once abused women began to speak out publicly, political pressure from various quarters led most states to adopt statutes against marital rape. This kind of violence is especially difficult to detect, since it involves the most intimate aspect of a marriage relationship. But because sexual coercion is so frequent and potentially so devastating, it is important that the priest be attuned to cries of distress or cries for help, coming either from the husband or the wife. The sin of marital rape results from a pathology, but the violence it produces needs to be stopped before any real healing can occur. If the priest or other concerned person finds it impossible to deal adequately with the situation (very few of our clergy have been trained to handle domestic violence of any kind), they can always contact a rape victim hot line or other crisis intervention center in their neighborhood. Phone numbers can be found in the Yellow Pages.

Although some Orthodox Christians, including bishops, hold that "the Church should keep out of the bedroom," this attitude merely encourages violence and abuse where a sexual pathology exists. If a priest became aware of a situation of marital rape or some related form of sexual misconduct within a family setting, and then refused to intervene appropriately, he would betray his vocation as a pastor to Christ's flock—and open himself and the diocese to the very real possibility of a lawsuit.

The situation known as *date rape* represents a special case. If the woman has been drinking or engaging in sexual play, she bears at least some responsibility for creating the conditions that might lead to what she would consider unwanted intercourse. That, to be sure, in no way excuses the actions of the man who forces himself on her. It simply means that every woman needs to keep in mind the fact that certain conditions and actions will render her especially vulnerable to sexual pressure. The only dependable means to avoid the slippery slope that leads to unwanted sex is for both the man and the woman to accept the discipline of chastity. Date rape, of course, could be avoided altogether if the woman only dated men who shared her conviction that genital sexuality is not an option outside the context of marriage. On the other hand, the woman who has sex with one or more partners, yet decides with her present date that she does not want that degree of intimacy with him, is living in a state of

32 See the article "New Laws Recognizing Marital Rape as a Crime," The New York Times, 29 December, 1984.

moral ambiguity that can easily provoke abuse. It may sound crude to express it this way, but many men, married as well as single, are sexual predators. Their antennae are fine-tuned to pick up the message that the woman they are dating or are "in a relationship with" is sexually promiscuous. If she rebuffs their advances, their puzzlement and frustration can easily lead to pressure and even violence. In a word, virginity is its own best defense.

Closely associated with rape is the tragedy of *incest*. Statistically, the majority of pregnancies that occur as a result of intercourse between closely related persons are not technically cases of incest, since they result from a girl being impregnated by her step-father. In these cases there is no blood relationship, and the risk of genetic complications is no greater than with pregnancies within marriage. Nevertheless, the emotional impact is every bit as destructive as in instances of true incest. These latter cases (between father and daughter, for example, or brother and sister) can be devastating to the young victim. If all but a very few primitive societies have considered incest taboo, it is as much because of the damage it does to the child and to family relationships as because of the increased possibility of genetic defects. In any case, the guilt and shame that surround incest are at least as strong as in instances of rape.

Complicating the issue of pregnancy due to incest is the fact that incestuous relationships tend to go on for long periods of time before the young woman conceives. Once she finds herself pregnant, her reaction is often one of ambivalence toward the new life growing within her. A surprisingly large number of pregnant incest victims want to keep their babies, rather than abort them or put them up for adoption. The psychological reasons for rejecting the option of abortion are complex, usually having to do with her conscious or unconscious desire to stop the abuse. The perpetrator almost always imposes a strict rule of silence on their relationship ("Let's not say anything to Mommy," "This is something special that only you and I can share," "You breathe a word of this, and I'll kill you."). Although the media have made much of recent cases where teen-aged mothers have aborted babies which neither their families nor their friends knew they were carrying, an incest victim will often use the physical evidence of the pregnancy as a way of exposing the abuse she was afraid to talk about.

A major question remains to be addressed: Is it morally permissible to perform an abortion on a woman whose pregnancy results from incest? To reply in the negative seems unduly cruel and unjust. As in cases of rape, we want to ask: How can we expect a woman—especially an adolescent—to carry to term the product of sexual violence that will be a daily reminder of her victimization? This nevertheless raises a loaded question, one that obscures the real moral concern which is the existence of the new being—the new person—who is growing in the woman's womb. Once again, we can only reply that *no solution can be considered moral and acceptable if it destroys human life, whatever its stage of growth.* Yet this does not diminish the fact that a thirteen-year old girl who becomes pregnant by her father lives a tragedy that requires extraordinary strength and personal courage—not only on her part, but on the part of all those who feel themselves called to minister to her and to the child she has conceived.

There are two points that need to be made in this regard. First, it has been amply demonstrated that abortion is detrimental rather than helpful to the woman who is an incest victim. To quote Reardon's insightful observation, "just as with rape, there is no psychiatric evidence, nor even any theory which argues that abortion of an incestuous pregnancy is therapeutic for the victim—it is only more convenient for everyone else."[33]

The second and more important point concerns the lives involved. To abort the "evidence" of the incest would mean capitulating to the devastating "rule of silence" imposed by the perpetrator. The incestuous family requires healing. In order for that to occur, the act must be made known in appropriate circles: within the family, to the priest or pastor, to the family physician, and perhaps to a select number of close family friends who can aid in the healing process—and, if the perpetrator refuses to stop and to seek help, to the police or other civil authorities. The perpetrator must acknowledge that he is caught up in what is likely to be a severe form of sexual addiction, and agree to enter into regular therapy with an appropriately trained person, in order to be freed from this most destructive of passions. Then the same kind of intensive support and accompaniment as in cases of rape must be provided to the incest victim, to free her from the burden of shame and guilt, to enable her to carry the child to

---

33 Reardon, *Aborted Women*, 199.

term and to care for it appropriately (by keeping it or putting it up for adoption), and to surround her with tenderness, understanding and unqualified love. It is only in this way—and not by aborting her child—that real healing can occur.

Finally, there is the difficult matter of fetal life afflicted with serious *genetic defects*. Ordinarily such defects will provoke a spontaneous abortion—and women who carry mentally or physically handicapped children to term are often plagued by the question, "Why did my child slip through the net?" Sonograms, amniocentesis and CVS can reveal illnesses such as spina bifida, Down's Syndrome (Trisomy 21), cystic fibrosis, Tay Sachs disease, or the terrible and incurable Lesch-Nyhan syndrome, in which the victim suffers uncontrollable urges toward self-mutilation.[34] While it would be unconscionable to destroy by abortion or infanticide a Down's Syndrome child,[35] and while spina bifida can often be at least partially corrected by surgery so that those afflicted with it can lead fruitful and creative lives,[36] the decision to give birth to a child afflicted with a totally debilitating and painful disease (such as Lesch-Nyhan syndrome) is impossible to make without a crushing sense of moral ambivalence. Although the parents might be able to accept the stress and financial burden of intensive care provided for their child, what in fact serves the child's best interests? Is it preferable for the child to be born into the world, to suffer a very brief yet painful existence until death mercifully takes him after a few days or at most a few months, or to be spared that experience (during which he can have no sense of relationship,

34 *The Merck Manual* (15th ed.) (Rahway, NJ: Merck Sharp & Dohme Research Laboratories, 1987, 2143) characterizes the Lesch-Nyhan syndrome or "hereditary hyperuricemia" as follows: "Usually, affected males are severely mentally retarded, have marked hyperuricemia [high blood levels of uric acid], and exhibit a peculiar propensity to self-mutilation by chewing their lips and fingertips, which leads to tissue loss and scarring... Affected males can be detected prenatally, as with Hunter syndrome." The disease has no known cure, and because it severely reduces life-expectancy perinatologists routinely recommend that the afflicted fetus be aborted.

35 The syndicated columnist George Will, whose son has Down's Syndrome, has written eloquently on the subject. See, e.g., his 1980 article, "Trading Jimmy for a Corvette," (in *The Pursuit of Virtue and Other Tory Notions*, New York: Simon & Schuster, 1982, 113ff.), which sets the need for parents' "unconditional attachment" to their handicapped children against their "calculations of convenience."

36 See F. Dougherty, CP (ed.), *The Deprived, the Disabled and the Fullness of Life* (Wilmington, DE: Michael Glazier, Inc., 1985), which contains remarkable testimonies by handicapped persons, including those afflicted with spina bifida.

no real feeling of being loved, but only unrelieved pain) by being aborted? Is there a point at which the principle of the sanctity of life should yield to the compassionate concern to spare an infant the pain and futility associated with certain terminal diseases? That is, can an abortion ever *affirm* the sanctity of life position insofar as it provides a "compassionate" alternative to bringing into the world a child whose life will be painful, futile and short?

The same questions can be raised in the case of an *anencephalic* child, only here, presumably, the child is spared the anguish of intractable pain because major portions of the brain, including the "pain tracks," are not developed. Anencephaly is a condition caused by incomplete development of the neural tube. It is characterized by an absence of the cerebral hemispheres, together with insufficient development of the hypothalamus and other features of the upper brain. While the brain stem may be functioning—thus insuring heart beat, blood pressure, body temperature and related autonomic responses—the condition is inevitably fatal: infants are either stillborn or die within a few days of birth. The ethical issues surrounding anencephaly, like those raised by genetic defects generally, include the option to abort, postnatal care of the child, and tissue/organ donation.[37]

As with any genetically defective child, we can only affirm that in cases of anencephaly the condition itself does not reduce his or her humanity, or quality of personal being. Granted, there is no capacity for actualizing that quality by creating and sustaining human relationships. Nor is there

---

37 A great many medical professionals, including medical ethicists, would argue that anencephalic infants may be morally aborted because they lack the "necessary condition for human personhood." R. C. Cefalo states this position quite clearly: "With anencephaly a potential for cognitive function never exists. Therefore, it may be morally permissible to terminate the pregnancy if the fetus is afflicted with a condition that is incompatible with postnatal survival for more than a few weeks, and if it is characterized by the total or virtual absence of cognitive functions... Those who advise or chose [sic] to terminate pregnancy in which anencephaly has been clearly established cannot be said to be acting in a way that is morally wrong. Furthermore, the use of anencephalics after delivery, as a source of organs and tissues for transplantation is not a violation of personal dignity" ("Edges of Life: the Consequences of Prenatal Assessment, Diagnosis, and Treatment," in K.Wm. Wildes, S.J. et al. (eds.), *Birth, Suffering, and Death. Catholic Perspectives at the Edges of Life*, (Dordrecht/Boston/London: Kluwer Academic Publishers, 1992), 22, with ref. to Cefalo, R. C., and Engelhardt, H. T. Jr., "The Use of Fetal and Anencephalic Tissue for Transplantation," *The Journal of Medicine and Philosophy* 14 (1989), 25-29. Further relevant bibliography in H. T. Engelhardt, *The Foundations of Bioethics* (2nd. ed., NY: Oxford, 1996), 279, n. 24.

any possibility that the child—in this life—can enjoy any sense of communion with God. Yet that child, in some indefinable yet real sense, remains a "person" because it is created in the divine image and, however defectively, bears witness to that image by the sheer fact of its existence. We might ask if God can love a child who has no possibility of knowing or returning that love. The answer is offered by the loving gestures and words of virtually any mother who has just given birth to such a child and takes it in her arms. However deep her grief, this is still her child and the object of her maternal compassion. Can it be otherwise with God?

Accordingly, there can be no more question of organ donation with anencephalics than with any other person who is still alive. Although some transplant specialists will find this reasoning unconvincing, *the inherent sacredness of human life means that it is fundamentally immoral to remove vital organs from a living human being, including anencephalics.* For organs to be viable, of course, they need to be living rather than dead. Hence medical teams and potential donors (or their surrogates) are often under pressure to declare and accept that death has occurred, even when the patient is manifestly alive. This is particularly true with anencephalics because of the peculiar nature of the case and the presumption that they experience no pain. The only reason to reject such infants as live organ donors is a spiritual one. Yet the final answer to all of these ethical questions must be spiritual—that is, theological—rather than medical, social or economic. In the sight of God, the anencephalic child remains a person of infinite dignity and worth, and that child must not be reduced to a reservoir of spare parts.

This is not to say, of course, that measures should not be taken to limit the risks of bearing a child afflicted with anencephaly, spina bifida or some other genetic anomaly. In 1995, the Centers for Disease Control (CDC) began pressing for full implementation of the 1992 Public Health Service recommendation that all women who might become pregnant consume 0.4 milligrams of folic acid daily to reduce the risks of neural tube defects. Several months later the *Morbidity and Mortality Weekly Report*[38] included an article on folic acid that began: "Each year in the

---

38 Vol. 44/38 (29 September, 1995), 716ff. The *MMWR* is a weekly publication of the Massachusetts Medical Society "under the terms of a non-exclusive agreement with the Centers for Disease Control and Prevention."

United States approximately 2500 infants are born with spina bifida and anencephaly, and an estimated 1500 fetuses affected by these birth defects are aborted. Recent studies indicate that the B vitamin folic acid can reduce the risk for spina bifida and anencephaly by at least 50% when consumed daily before conception and during early pregnancy." Subsequent research has confirmed these findings. A massive education program is needed, in churches as well as in schools and the media, to convey the message to as many prospective mothers as possible.

In chapter 5 we discuss the matter of care for those who are in the final stage of life. For the present, we can simply affirm that anencephalic infants should be treated like any other terminally ill patient. Since the level of their sensory capacity cannot be precisely determined, they should be provided with warmth, comfort and other appropriate care, then be allowed peacefully to die.

Given the complexity of these issues, some would urge Orthodox couples to refuse any and all prenatal diagnostic tests, since they only lead to the temptation to abort the fetus if it is found to be genetically defective. Unfortunately, this is not an adequate solution. Hospitals will soon be making such tests on a routine basis, without parental authorization. Then again, as advances are made in the field of genetic therapy, no couple would want to risk ignorance when specific knowledge of a given disease, obtained through genetic screening, might lead to a cure. The problem is that diagnosis so often outpaces the development of an effective remedy. While such illnesses are detectable in the womb, genetic surgery and related therapies are still in their infancy. This inevitably raises for the mother or the couple the agonizing question whether or not to opt for abortion, especially when they are aware that many such illnesses would have been resolved by miscarriage. (We should recall that the rate of "wastage"—spontaneous abortions of embryos prior to implantation—may be as much as seventy percent.)

The real danger with genetic screening is once again the slippery slope. Many critics have referred to it as a "search and destroy mission," aimed at eliminating inconvenient and burdensome lives. The relentless quest for individual "happiness" and personal convenience endemic to American culture long ago pressured the noble art of medicine to devote much of its talent to cosmetic surgery and the dispensing of a drug-induced "peace of

mind." In such an environment, screening with the aim of aborting fetuses bearing serious genetic defects quickly degenerated into screening to
eliminate children with lesser defects, such as dwarfism or even the
"wrong" sex. Is there any reason to expect that more widespread use of
amniocentesis, CVS and similar tests—despite the very real dangers they
pose to the health of both mother and child—will be governed by moral
principles that will keep genetic screening from becoming the chief
weapon of the "new eugenics"? The key question that needs to be asked is
the one posed by George Will and others: *"Do we really want a world in
which there are no Down's Syndrome children?"* Or a world in which every
black man is seven feet tall and all white men *can* jump? Have we become
so blind—so hung up on physical accomplishment in a sports-saturated,
competitive culture—that we cannot see the beauty and personal value
that radiates from "handicapped" persons who have struggled courageously with their condition and, in moral if not physical terms, have
emerged victorious? Are we at the point where our only reaction to these
living icons is to abort them? Increasingly, distressingly, it seems so.

This atmosphere imposes a special burden on Orthodox clergy who
attempt to preach about the intrinsic sacredness of human life and the
dead-end solution to an unwanted pregnancy which is abortion. The experience of Orthodox pastors is that all too often our lay people make a
decision to abort *before* they consult with the priest, since they assume
that he will counsel against abortion on principle, regardless of the circumstances of their particular case. As our priests so often put it, "It's easier to obtain forgiveness than permission."

This said, however, it is important to stress the point that authentic
Christianity means personal freedom—freedom *in the Spirit*—that places the
responsibility for any decision to terminate a pregnancy primarily upon the
mother. As much as the child she carries, she is a person in her own right, and
must work out her salvation and bear her burdens before God in total dependence on his grace and forgiving mercy. This is why pastors, ethicists and
others in the Church can counsel but not command, urge but not impose.
Those of us who are males can hardly imagine the loneliness and anguish
many women go through who arrive at the tragic decision to abort. Each
one, after all, is a mother from her child's conception, not just from its birth.
As the title to Reardon's book implies, that death-dealing decision makes of

her an "aborted woman." Ending the life growing within her causes the death of a part of herself, and the resultant grief is deep and lasting.[39]

While we may inveigh with irony and even anger against the masses of "convenience" abortions that occur each year, the "hard cases" remain precisely that: hard, difficult, gut-wrenching and heart-breaking moments in a woman's life that she never wanted and never sought out, whatever the circumstances surrounding the pregnancy. Rather than glib criticism or outright condemnation, she needs—and deserves—our understanding, our love and our effective support.

A fine statement affirming that need appeared in the November 1990 *Greek Orthodox Observer*. In an article entitled "A Pastoral Approach to Abortion," Rev. Dr. Athanasios Demos offered some thoughts on pastoral care toward "aborted women" that bear repeating.

> In the cases where abortions have actually occurred, I have found that circumstances and situations: being unmarried, away from home and afraid to turn to anyone, being frightened with the idea of rejection by one's friends and family, being threatened or frightened by a spouse, or psychologically unable to cope with this new and added responsibility, plus a myriad of other reasons, contributed to the decision to abort the fetus.

> ... [The real] issue is to allow women to know that the Church is always there to help them in their time of need, to comfort them, guide them, and help them through any crisis. Our Church condemns the sin but not the sinner. Our Church is the Church par excellence of God's holy forgiveness...

> So why not focus on providing programs in our parishes to educate *everyone* about the sanctity of life...to provide the means by which a woman can come for help without fear of judgment or condemnation?

> We can find good homes for these yet unborn children. We can offer counseling and guidance, comfort and understanding, to those women who think in desperation that they can find only one way to turn.

> Incidentally...we cannot forget the responsibility of the man. He is just as responsible as the woman. His compassion and understanding are crucial in offering support to her in her hour of need.

> So let's not focus on the tragedy of what has happened, rather let us focus on how we can *prevent* abortions... Our focus should be on education and support which

39 For a moving account aimed at "understanding the needs of women in unplanned pregnancies," see Frederica Mathewes-Green, *Real Choices. Offering Practical, Life-Affirming Alternatives to Abortion*, (Sisters, OR: Multnomah Books, 1994).

hopefully will lead to prevention. And if an abortion does take place, then to focus on compassion and comfort which lead to forgiveness.[40]

In a culture as morally confused and hedonistic as ours, Orthodox Christians must continue to speak and act—peacefully but firmly—against the legalized destruction of unborn lives. To those who argue that "we cannot legislate morality," we need to point out that *every* law, to some degree or other, in effect legislates morality since it serves to shape human conduct. Our silence and inactivity will be taken as nothing other than tacit approval of immoral laws and practices that flaunt common decency and threaten social stability.[41]

On the other hand, our refusal to distinguish between the sin and the sinner violates a basic principle of Jesus' own teaching and behavior. It is important to recall that the woman caught in adultery (John 8) would have been stoned to death if Jesus had not intervened. But he not only preserved her from a death sentence mandated by the Mosaic Law (Lev 20:10; Dt 22:22). Speaking in the name of the God of Moses, he also assured her that he himself did not condemn her. Once she had heard that assurance, she was prepared to hear the command, "Go, and do not sin again." Judgment and condemnation can no more undo an abortion than they can an act of adultery. What is needed is healing, based on deep and lasting repentance. Genuine healing will occur, however, only where the person—in this case, the woman who has made the tragic and usually desperate decision to abort her child—is welcomed by the Church with forgiveness, love, respect, and unfailing pastoral concern.

Assisted Reproductive Technologies

There is no little irony in the fact that while millions of fetuses are aborted each year throughout the world, millions of dollars are being spent to de-

40 Quoted with the author's permission.
41 In his 18 January, 1998, communication on "Sanctity of Life Sunday," Metropolitan Theodosius, Primate of the Orthodox Church in America, underscored the point that the matter of abortion needs to be considered from a theological and spiritual—and not simply a moral or political—perspective: "Simply pointing out the deficiencies of present legislation regarding abortion or bemoaning the moral decay of our times is not enough. It is not sufficient simply to legislate morality. The Church must strive in 'truth and love' to appeal to the human conscience, the very core of human existence, which ultimately transcends all political and ideological platforms. We must seek not only to change human laws, but also to convert human hearts. Preaching the 'Good News' of the Gospel of Christ, we must strive to heal a divided community."

velop techniques for medically assisting the reproductive process. The new technologies raise in a most acute way the question of the limits that should be set to artificial involvement in the creation of human life.

As bearers of the divine image, men and women have received the command to "be fruitful and multiply" (Gen 1:28). According to Roman Catholic moral theology, based upon Natural Law theory, only "natural" means may be used to induce pregnancy or bring a conceived child to term. Accordingly, the "Instruction on Respect for Human Life in its Origin and on the Dignity of Procreation" (*Donum Vitae*)[42] unequivocally condemned such techniques as artificial insemination (AI), *in vitro* fertilization (IVF), and "surrogate mothering" (SM), more properly referred to as surrogate gestation. It held that any act of procreation through means other than those "natural" to the conjugal union is to be regarded as "illicit" and immoral.[43] The question that concerns us is whether Orthodoxy teaches a similar view. Do modern procreative technologies represent an unmitigated evil? Or may our faithful resort to them when conception does not occur through normal intercourse, as for example when the husband or wife is sterile?

As in the case of abortion, the question of assisted procreation must be resolved from a double perspective: the tradition of the Church, and the particular circumstances of the couple. Scripture and the preponderance of Orthodox tradition affirm that human sexuality is in essence good,[44] and that it is God's will that couples beget children. If the marriage ritual includes petitions for "a bed undefiled," it also asks that God will grant the couple "the enjoyment of the blessing of children." The same initial litany of the crowning ceremony, however, requests that God grant them "the fruit of the womb as may be expedient for them."

This qualification, "as may be expedient for them," is crucial to our evaluation of medically assisted means of procreation. For the inability of a couple to conceive in the usual manner may be understood in two ways. It may be seen as a divine indication that the bearing of children

---

42 English translation published by the Daughters of St. Paul, Boston, 1987.
43 Catholic moral theologians rightly speak of "procreation" rather than "reproduction." The latter suggests that the act of begetting children is purely biological, unrelated to God's work of creation.
44 See our discussion on this issue in chapter 2 above.

would not be "expedient" for them, meaning that they could then consider either adoption or a conjugal life without children. On the other hand, their inability to conceive might just as well be understood as a kind of illness: a weakness of the flesh that God-given advances in medical therapy can rectify. In the latter case, it would seem appropriate that the couple consider the possibility of certain means of assisted procreation. To do so as Orthodox Christians it is imperative that they consult beforehand with their spiritual director, in a serious and sincere effort to determine the will of God for their common life. Like Hanna, the mother of Samuel, they will ask their offspring "of the Lord," prepared to accept God's refusal as well as his gift of grace in the form of a child. For the spiritual director—priest or spiritually qualified layperson—to guide the couple effectively, however, he or she needs to be adequately informed, both as to the techniques available and to their potential physical and spiritual consequences for the life of the couple and the children they hope to raise.

In any case, there are definite limits which should be recognized and accepted by the couple as well as by the pastor, in order to observe the basic Christian principle of respect for human life. While the various methods of assisted procreation appear to be ethically neutral and therefore equally appropriate from a secular point of view, this is not and cannot be the view of the Church. An unbridgeable ethical gulf, for example, separates artificial insemination that uses the sperm of the husband (AIH or "homologous insemination") from that which uses sperm from a third-party donor (AID or "heterologous insemination").

Similarly, *in vitro* fertilization cannot be considered morally acceptable if it creates "extra embryos" that are destroyed, or used for medical experimentation or commercial exploitation. This is due to the fact, as we pointed out in chapter 3, that human life—with all the conditions for "personhood"—exists from conception. Because any embryo normally possess all the qualifications required for it to develop into an adult human being, there is no point after conception at which that embryo can be considered a subject for experimentation or other procedure that would not be appropriate (or legal) with a born child.

As for surrogate mothering, the fact that a third party is necessarily introduced into the procreative process makes it totally unacceptable from an Orthodox point of view. This is true whether the surrogate mother is impregnated with the husband's sperm, or whether she simply receives the zygote after its fertilization in a petri dish. In either case, the mordant expression "womb for rent" indicates to what degree even the secularized popular mind holds such a procedure to be ethically questionable.

The promise of procreative technologies lies in their capacity to provide offspring to couples who deeply desire to bear and nurture their "own" children. (Where adopted children are received and raised with loving concern and proper nurture, of course, they usually become the parents' "own" children, as fully as those who bear their parents' DNA. The bond between parent and child depends less on genetic make-up than on shared love, affection, play, and spiritual experience.) In her pastoral counseling, just as in her witness to contemporary society, the Orthodox Church must speak from a specific theological perspective that recognizes God to be the Creator and Lord of all life. The extent to which human cooperation or "synergy" is appropriate to achieve the *medically assisted* procreation of children must be determined on the basis of that perspective. Those who do acknowledge the sovereignty of God over the entire procreative process will hold certain basic convictions concerning cases of unintended pregnancy. While every act of sexual union need not have conception as its primary goal, nevertheless the couple is called to remain open at all times to the possibility that new life will be created; and when it is, they should welcome it with joy and thanksgiving. Once again, abortion used as a means of birth control is tantamount to murder and must be condemned as such. At the other extreme, the use of donor gametes or of surrogate wombs to provide offspring for otherwise childless couples must be condemned as a violation of the integrity of the marital union and the rights of the child to be born in and of its natural family.

Given these limitations, it *may* be appropriate for a couple to resort to certain procedures such as artificial insemination (AIH) and even *in vitro* fertilization (under conditions spelled out below), in order to conceive children of their own genetic heritage. The pastor first of all, though, will urge the couple to consider *adoption* as an alternative.[45] And any recourse

<hr>

45 Nearly 200,000 children are currently in foster care in the U.S., and most are candidates for adoption. Bureaucratic complications in America are such, however, that increasingly our citizens are adopting children from other countries. Against the popular stereotype, recent studies

to procedures such as IVF or AIH presupposes unconditional acceptance of the technique by both husband and wife. Above all, to determine whether such procedures are appropriate or not in any given situation requires a degree of spiritual discernment that comes only through patience and prayer.

Whatever the advantages and potential blessings of procreative technologies today, the dangers of abuse are perhaps even greater. It is no secret that human embryos are used every day in experiments to advance scientific knowledge or for strictly commercial purposes. In every case such experimentation means a violation of the rights and dignity of the conceptus and should be vigorously opposed by the voice of the Church. The principle of the separation of Church and State no longer holds when human life is at stake. While acts of violent protest such as the bombing of abortion clinics and the murder of abortionists can never be morally justified, in a democratic society we have both the possibility and the obligation to use all appropriate means to educate and persuade our own faithful, as well as our legislators and the public at large, to accept fundamental principles of human dignity, freedom, and personal welfare, even with regard to the unborn. Once again, the voice of the Church must be heard. But it can only be heard if Christian people speak with one mind and one heart, in consonance with their theology and their faith.

How, then, can we assess the various forms of medically assisted procreation that are available today? Any such assessment should be based on certain presuppositions that we have already discussed: the sacred character of human life from its inception at fertilization, together with the freedom and responsibility of persons (in this case, the parents) to make their own decisions before God. The following evaluations, therefore, should not be considered prescriptive. They represent my own impressions and opinions regarding issues about which Orthodox ecclesial authorities have not (yet) offered clear guidelines or made official statements. They are offered merely to help the reflection of couples who are struggling

have shown that children adopted by parents of another race tend to integrate well both into their adoptive family and into their own racial environment. From the pulpit and in the marketplace, Christian voices need to be raised against the unreasonable obstacles to adoption in this country, as against the lingering racism that either favors or discourages the adoption of children according to their racial or ethnic background.

with the often painful decision to resort to medically assisted procreative techniques in their desire to give birth to their own offspring.

AIH, also called "intrauterine insemination" (IUI), is a relatively simple and inexpensive procedure that consists in introducing the husband's sperm, via catheter, directly into the wife's uterus. It is particularly useful in cases where the husband is unable to ejaculate, or when the sperm count or motility is too low to enable its successful penetration into the uterine cavity and then into the fallopian tubes. The semen is usually procured by masturbation, which to some minds poses an ethical problem of the sort we discussed in chapter 2. Since the aim is to obtain semen only for purposes of procreation, however, there seems to be no serious objection on moral grounds (although this conclusion would not be shared by those who believe that masturbation is an evil in itself, always and invariably sinful). It is also possible to retrieve semen surgically from the epididymis, but this seems to be an unnecessarily complicated and risky procedure when it is not medically required.

It has been argued that AID (i.e., using the sperm of a donor) is morally acceptable in cases where the husband is unable to produce semen, or where there is a danger of male-transmitted hereditary disorders such as Tay-Sachs disease or Huntington's chorea. Our earlier discussion made clear the basic principle: *no third party in the procreative process*. In cases where the risk of hereditary disease is considerable, the couple would do well to avoid conception and consider adoption. Nor can instances of azoospermia (the incapacity of the male to produce spermatozoa) be considered justification for resorting to AID. Here again, despite the bureaucratic impediments and lack of genetic connection with the child, couples who desire children would fulfill both a parental and a stewardship role by electing to adopt.

Recently developed techniques for harvesting sperm from dying or deceased patients has given rise to the phenomenon of "post-mortem conception." After the husband's death, his wife is impregnated, via artificial insemination, with his previously frozen sperm. Apart from the fact that a child should be raised by two parents, a mother and a father, there is a further objection to this procedure that involves the very meaning of childbearing itself. Is it morally acceptable for a woman to conceive independently of a conjugal act of love? A "natural theology" approach to the question would certainly reply in the negative: the conjugal act, after all, must be performed by two persons who are alive. On the other hand, it could be argued that the couple's agreement to such a procedure in view of the husband's imminent death is ample evidence that the conception constitutes an "act of love." And it is understandable that a woman who has lost her husband would want him to "live on" in their offspring, even if it requires conceiving her child after the husband's death.

However that may be, I do not believe the procedure can be considered morally acceptable. To honor the "sacredness" of life requires that the *transmission* of life be accomplished by the "one flesh" relationship of two persons joined in a "monogamous, heterosexual, blessed conjugal union." That includes not only insemination (and therefore it does not exclude a priori the use of AIH). It involves both parents in the ongoing mutual love and support that will enable them to bear and raise their child as a couple. For that to occur, it is obvious that both must be living. In cases where a husband dies during his wife's pregnancy, the child, of course, should be brought to term and raised by the one parent. In this instance, unlike post-mortem conception, the pregnancy still results from a natural conjugal union between husband and wife.

A far more difficult procedure to evaluate is *in vitro* fertilization with embryo transfer (IVF-ET). The technique was originally developed to facilitate conception in women whose fallopian tubes are damaged or diseased. It has proved to be effective as well in cases of "unexplained infertility" in the wife and "male factor infertility." A typical IVF cycle includes hyperstimulation of the ovaries, oocyte ("egg" or ova) retrieval, semen collection, fertilization and embryo culture, and embryo transfer. The current average cost per cycle is between $6,000 and $10,000.

At the beginning of the cycle, the woman's ovaries are "hyperstimulated" by injections of gonadotropins over a period of about ten days. Rather than produce the usual single ovum during her monthly cycle, the woman will produce several. These ova can be retrieved by means of laparoscopy (requiring general anesthesia) or by the newer and more benign procedure of "transvaginal aspiration" guided by ultrasound. A sperm sample is provided, and the spermatozoa are separated from the seminal fluid, to be incubated and treated to improve chances for fertilization. Some 100,000 spermatozoa are combined with the ova in a glass dish and

182   THE SACRED GIFT OF LIFE

maintained at a temperature of 98.6º F (37º C). After 24 hours, where fertilization has occurred, the choice is usually made to select the most viable zygotes for ET and to freeze the rest. Those destined for implantation are held in culture for another 24 hours until they reach the four- to eight-cell stage of cleavage. Estrogen and progesterone are given to the woman in order to enhance possibilities for successful implantation. After 48 hours, the prepared embryos are transferred by means of a catheter inserted through the cervix and into the uterine cavity. Normally three embryos are transferred and one or two attach to the endometrium within a week after fertilization. A pregnancy test at the end of two weeks indicates whether or not the procedure has been successful. Success rates average around 18%. The extra embryos can be frozen for future use (cryopreservation) by being dehydrated and preserved in liquid nitrogen at -196º C.

Related procedures include the so-called GIFT (gamete intrafallopian transfer) and ZIFT (zygote intrafallopian transfer). The former is closer to AI, in that the gametes are retrieved and prepared as in IVF, but prior to fertilization they are transferred to the fallopian tubes where conception occurs *in vivo*. ZIFT, on the other hand, involves transfer of the zygote to a fallopian tube after at least 24 hours of culture *in vitro*. Its rate of success is superior to that of GIFT, particularly when the embryo has been cultured for 48 hours before transfer. Called TET (tubal embryo transfer), this last procedure is identical to IVF, except for the placement of the transferred embryo.

GIFT, it seems, presents no more objections from a moral point of view than traditional artificial insemination. As with AI (in which the spermatozoa are introduced directly into the uterine cavity), however, the procedure is morally acceptable only where the sperm is provided by the woman's husband.

A procedure developed in 1994 seemed to offer a solution to the problem of extra embryos. Called Intracytoplasmic Sperm Injection (ICSI), it involves injecting a single sperm—or fragment of the sperm, namely the head containing the nucleus—into an ovum by means of a microscopic pipette and hollow ICSI needle. The ovum is supported by the pipette, and the sperm or sperm head is injected by means of the needle through the egg membrane and into the cytoplasm surrounding the nucleus.[46]

46 Detailed photographs of the procedure, provided by the Advanced Fertility Center of Chicago, can be found on the Internet: www.advancedfertility.com/icsiimag.htm.

Developed to overcome problems of male infertility, ICSI also made it possible to achieve medically assisted fertilization without producing surplus zygotes that would have to be discarded, frozen, or otherwise disposed of.

Dangers with the procedure, however, are significant and need to be taken into account. The most serious has to do with selection of the particular sperm that will be used to fertilize the ovum. At the present time it is not possible to determine all possible chromosomal defects the given sperm might harbor. In normal intercourse, or even with AI, there is a "randomness"—or more accurately, a divine intentionality—that plays a crucial role in human conception. Even from a purely secular perspective it is recognized that only the strongest, most "fit" sperm can make the arduous journey to the locus of fertilization. ("Fitness" in this sense, however, refers only to sperm motility; it does not mean that the given sperm is free of genetic defects.) Of the millions contained in an ejaculate, only one sperm will normally arrive at its destination and penetrate the zona to begin the fertilization process. Orthodox Christians hold tenaciously to the notion that there is no such thing as "chance," that "all (unforeseen events) are sent by Thee," and that "Thy will governs all."[47] Sperm selection, then, is understood not as random, but as an example of divine-human synergy or cooperation. To put it in the simplest terms, selection of the gametes in any human conception can and should be made by God himself.

This view that God operates at the most personal and intimate level of human existence is fundamental to Orthodox theology. It implies that the entire process of human conception is a "mystery" of sacramental grace, in which divine intervention is the primary element. ICSI, on the other hand, with its selectivity according to strictly biological criteria, would seem to present a moral problem of major proportions, since it eliminates or at least interferes with the element of "divine mystery" in the selection of gametes. Scruples of this kind, of course, could lead to rejection of any form of assisted reproductive technology, as it could of genetic screening. With ICSI, however—from a religious or a secular point of view—the chief objection remains the inability to determine accurately whether or not the selected sperm contains serious genetic defects. With ordinary intercourse defective sperm do often fertilize an ovum, and produce either a miscarriage or

47 Morning prayer ascribed variously to St. Philaret of Moscow or to monks of the Optino Monastery.

a genetically "defective" child. But an Orthodox conscience or "mind" (*phronêma*) would attribute such an event to the divine economy rather than to chance, however we may explain the suffering involved. Genetic anomalies produced *in vivo*, therefore, bear a different moral weight than those produced by human ingenuity gone awry.

The few Orthodox statements that have appeared on the issue of "assisted reproductive technologies" (ART) tend to focus on the problem of extra embryos. If the problem can be eliminated by ICSI or by otherwise limiting the number of fertilizations, then what further objections remain to procedures such as IVF, GIFT and ZIFT?

The question can best be answered by reference to the slippery slope. The "father of the French IVF," Dr. Jacques Testart, warned back in 1986 of the dangers in opening the Pandora's Box of assisted procreation.[48] Among the bizarre scenarios he envisioned (some of which have been realized in the intervening years) are: 1) fertilization of a woman's ovum by the *ovum* of another woman, as in the case of two lesbians who wish to have their own children without male intervention; a process possible by the fusion *in vitro* of the two female gametes (achieved already in 1977 using the ova of mice); 2) female "self-procreation," in which a woman's ovum would be fertilized by a donor's sperm that would activate mitosis and be immediately removed ("gynogenesis" would occur as the first division of the egg is chemically inhibited, allowing the nucleus to attain the diploid state of forty six chromosomes); and 3) cloning, already widely practiced in agriculture and animal husbandry (we discuss its implications for human reproduction in the next section).

To these, we need to add practices such as the one euphemistically labeled "fetal reduction." Because of the cost and the difficulty of the procedure, several ova at a time are retrieved in an IVF cycle, and several embryos are fertilized and then transferred to the prospective mother's uterus. If more than one or two embryos implant, producing a multiple pregnancy, one or more of them may be intentionally killed by an injection of lethal drugs. The aim is to give the remaining children a greater chance of survival throughout the gestation period. (In April, 1988, the

---

48 *L'Oeuf Transparent* (Paris: Flammarion, 1986), esp. pp. 135-144, "Les perversions de la FIVÈTE."

New England Journal of Medicine warned that selective reduction could provoke the spontaneous miscarriage of *all* fetuses.) Since the "reduction" often occurs well into the fetal stage of growth, it is not merely a "therapeutic abortion." It comes perilously close to infanticide.

With the increasingly common practice of freezing extra embryos, there will certainly be repeated instances of the kind widely publicized in 1983. An American couple, Mario and Elsa Rios, traveled to Melbourne, Australia, where several of Elsa's ova were fertilized by AID, that is, by donor sperm. Three "pre-embryos" were selected, one for transfer to her uterus and the other two for cryopreservation in case the first did not implant. After ten days the transferred embryo was spontaneously aborted. In the Spring of 1983, before an attempt was made to transfer the remaining two embryos, the couple was killed in a plane crash in South America. The question at issue was what to do with the frozen embryos, particularly since the family was very wealthy, and it raised the issue of inheritance. In the meantime, there have occurred similar cases that pose the same kind of dilemma. The families involved, as well as ethicists and the medical teams, have had to agonize over the decision to destroy the embryos (or allow them to deteriorate and die), or to bring them to term using a surrogate mother. Much of the agony involved in the decision is due to the fear that subsequent legal action could lead to the judgment that refusal to bring the children to term, in order for them to profit from their inheritance, constitutes a violation of their rights.

Then there are the errors that occur with IVF. In December, 1993, twin boys were born to a blond, blue-eyed Dutch couple. One of the twins was white and the other black. The clinic involved (the University Hospital of Utrecht) claimed that there had been accidental insemination with the sperm of another man, a native of Aruba, in addition to the fertilization achieved using the husband's sperm. Clinic administrators suggested that a technician had used a contaminated pipette to introduce the sperm into the petri dish. Since pipettes are normally used only once, then discarded, critics contended that the hospital was engaged in willful experimentation.[49]

Perhaps more disturbing are intentional manipulations via IVF that also raise serious moral objections. A case in point is Arceli Keh, a 63 year old

49 *New York Times* "International," 28 June, 1995.

woman who, in November 1997, gave post-menopausal birth to a child. Another concerns the girl named Jaycee, the "child" of John and Luanne Buzzanca, who was conceived using the sperm and ovum of anonymous donors and brought to term by Pamela Snell, a surrogate mother. The question is, Whose child is she? In 1997 a California judge declared that Jaycee "in the eyes of the law...effectively had no parents." John had filed for divorce a month before her birth and denied responsibility for her upbringing; and Luanne had no more legal standing than did the surrogate. The child's only genetic connection was with two anonymous gamete donors.[50]

The situation in some ways is becoming ludicrous as technology moves us toward the scenario described in the old country song, "I'm my own Grandpa!" Over a decade ago a South African woman served as a surrogate mother for her daughter, who had been born without a uterus. The daughter's ovum was fertilized with her husband's sperm, then transferred to the womb of the future grandmother. Although the daughter and her husband were listed as the parents on the infant's birth certificate, and the older woman merely provided her womb, the latter is the child's "gestational mother" as well as her grandmother. The first American woman to serve as surrogate mother (SM) for her daughter was 42-year old Arlette Schweitzer. On October 12, 1991, she gave birth by C-section to her own grandchildren, a boy and a girl.[51]

By providing this surrogate service, these women undertook what in some sense is a very gracious act of charity (especially since no money was involved, contrary to usual SM arrangements). But what does one tell the children born under these circumstances? Personal identity is largely established in the framework of family relationships. Will these children eventually experience an "identity crisis" because of a lack of clear lineage or clear relationship with one or another family member? A child may not (yet) be able to become its own grandparent, but what is the impact on one whose close relative is both its mother and its grandmother? How is it to be explained to the child, and how can the child reasonably explain it to teachers and other children, without becoming the butt of withering jokes? (Perhaps an even greater danger is that the other kids will regard it

---

50 *Newsweek*, 2 February, 1998, 68f.
51 *New York Times* (13 October, 1991).

as "cool," thereby further lowering their threshold of tolerance to medical wizardry that is inherently unethical.) However a family may decide to resolve the matter, those who have resorted to surrogate mothering in any form report that they are torn between secrecy and disclosure. What indeed is best for the child? Clearly, it is to avoid the situation altogether.

Extra embryos, unwitting selection of defective genes, surrogate mothering, anomalous ("unisex") forms of procreation, manipulation of embryos for purposes of cloning or other experimentation, conceiving children for their "spare parts" (like the girl conceived to provide bone marrow for her sister, in 1991), sex-selection and other eugenic practices: all of these militate against the manipulation of human gametes outside the womb, and consequently against procedures such as *in vitro* fertilization.

Yet it must be said as well that there are a great many couples today who are joyfully and gratefully parenting IVF offspring. And there is no question that significant and highly beneficial advances have been made toward healing genetic anomalies, thanks to scientific research using human germ cells. How do we reconcile such procedures and protocols with the instinctive Orthodox reluctance to create life *extra utero* and to use human gametes for purposes of research? Dr. Leon Sheean, of the Case Western University School of Medicine, recently addressed both of these issues in e-mail correspondence. A specialist in IVF technologies and an active Orthodox Christian, Dr. Sheean made two points in particular that deserve serious consideration. First of all, he would allow for research and experimentation "on degenerating cells [human gametes] which are not capable of normal development...since this is akin to the evaluation of pathological tissue." This seems fully reasonable, given that the research is potentially of such value to the overall issue of human health, and that the cells are not capable of fulfilling their normal function: that is, they have lost their capacity to produce a viable embryo.

Second, he addresses the problem of extra embryos. In younger women, where there is a greater likelihood of retrieving several ova and the choice is made to fertilize more than will subsequently be transferred, a decision has to be made concerning the surplus embryos. While cryopreservation and future transfer to the genetic mother seem to pose few risks, and represent the least offensive way to resolve the matter, there will nonetheless be cases where the mother will not want her extra embryos.

In such cases, Dr. Sheean suggests, those embryos could perfectly well be donated to an infertile couple. Although this would violate the principle that no third party should intervene in the procreative process, it could also be considered as *adoption* of the embryo by the gestational mother. Considered in this light, the embryo has the same moral standing as an adopted child, with the added advantage that the gestational mother and her spouse experience pregnancy and the child's birth. While the Orthodox "mind" would certainly prefer that no spare embryos be created in the first place, in order to enable couples to resort to IVF and yet assure that no embryos be destroyed or subjected to unethical procedures, donation of the extra embryos might well be ethically justifiable: that is, in conformity with God's will.

Perhaps what we need to conclude is this: There where assisted reproductive technologies can be helpful to an otherwise infertile couple, it is reasonable and appropriate to explore their potential. Certainly it is to be regretted that so many viable embryos have been destroyed in developing IVF and related procedures. But now that the technology is available, and possibilities exist for preventing or adopting "extra embryos," perhaps it is not unreasonable (or sinful) for a couple to avail themselves of it, so long as certain caveats are respected and appropriate criteria are applied to determine which procedures might be morally acceptable.

Once again, there seems to be no inherent objection to AIH, given the ease and safety with which it can be achieved. As for IVF, together with ZIFT, the couple needs to have assurance that extra embryos will not be created (or will be limited to those that might be donated for "adoption"), and that a small enough number of fertilized eggs will be transferred to avoid the necessity for "fetal reduction" if they all implant. The parents must also be willing and able to bear the *consequences of defects or anomalies* caused by the procedure that will impact on their life and the life of their child.[52] Finally, the parents, together with the Church community, should welcome the child thus conceived with the same degree of intimacy and love as if it had been conceived "naturally." Before they decide

---

52 This is not an insignificant consideration. Data from Australia, France and elsewhere suggest that the various reproductive technologies are two to three times more likely to produce disease and physical abnormalities in the children conceived by these methods. See the article by Cynthia B. Cohen, "'Give Me Children or I Shall Die!' New Reproductive Technologies and Harm to Children," *Hastings Center Report* 26/2 (March-April, 1996) 19-27.

to resort to ART, however, it is imperative that the parents, together with friends and spiritual advisors, devote themselves to deep and focused prayer, in order to discern what is actually God's will *for them* in the miraculous and mysterious procreation of human life.

A further word at this point needs to be said about the all too common phenomenon of *miscarriage*. Traditional Orthodox prayers for a woman who has suffered a spontaneous abortion imply that she is in some way responsible for the accident and that it involves her sinful participation: "Have mercy on thy handmaiden *N.* for the voluntary or involuntary sin she has committed that has caused the death and the miscarriage of the child she had conceived; forgive her every sin, both voluntary and involuntary... In the abundance of thy compassion, speed the healing of her weakened body...; for we were conceived in sin and iniquity, and each of us is impure in thy presence, O Lord..." (then the petition is repeated which requests that she be forgiven the voluntary or involuntary sin that caused the death and miscarriage of her conceived child). Because of this repeated emphasis on the sinfulness of the mother, groups of Orthodox Christians, including bishops, are presently working toward a partial rewriting of the traditional prayers. Their aim is to preserve the acknowledged link between human fallenness and physical illness, while avoiding the implication that the mother herself is morally responsible for the death and "abortion" of her child.

Today we are aware that virtually every fertile mother experiences multitudes of "mini-miscarriages" of which she is completely unaware. (Recall that 50-70% of all fertilized ova are spontaneously evacuated before implantation). In addition, it is now well known that the causes of miscarriage are highly complex and are usually due to chemical imbalances, anatomical abnormalities or genetic defects over which the mother has absolutely no control. Except in the rarest of cases, it is totally inappropriate to impute to her sinful motivations or actions. It has been demonstrated, for example, that a woman's mental condition, whatever her level of stress or regret over the pregnancy, is incapable of provoking a miscarriage. Those miscarriages that are certifiably sinful are usually the result of botched abortions, although they can also arise from alcoholism and other forms of substance abuse.

A woman who has suffered a spontaneous abortion is often burdened by an overwhelming sense of grief. Her pain needs to be acknowledged, accepted and palliated through words and gestures of understanding, sympathy and love, offered by her family and the parish community. Especially in those cases where the mother has seen or even held her dead baby, it is appropriate for the parents to *name* the child and to request that the priest celebrate a modified service for the departed (*Panykhida*). (In this regard, it would be of immense pastoral benefit for our bishops and liturgical commissions to produce a special service for miscarried infants.) Thereby the parents, with the entire Church, can affirm that human life begins with conception, that this deceased fetus is a "child" in the fullest sense, and that their gestures on its behalf serve to introduce the deceased child into eternal life in the communion of saints.

Genetic Engineering and Procreation: The Manipulation of Human Life

While abortion and assisted means of procreation may not directly affect those who oppose them, the same cannot be said of genetic engineering (GE). The manipulation of genetic material, whether of plants and animals or of human beings, has biological and social consequences that affect virtually everyone. If we oppose abortion because it violates the rights and destroys the life of an innocent person, then the dangers inherent in certain forms of GE—especially in the newly developed cloning techniques—make the guarantee of control even more necessary, since misguided genetic manipulation, whether willful or accidental, can have disastrous consequences for entire populations.

Before we turn to specifics, it would be useful to define a few key terms. "Eugenics" generally designates that science which aims at improving the human gene pool—and thus human nature itself—by improving both environmental factors and the overall human condition.[53] "Genetic therapy" involves both the screening of prospective parents to determine whether their children risk inheriting genetic disorders, and prenatal or postnatal intervention to correct such disorders. Its aims are *therapeutic* and not eugenic or "innovational." It seeks to cure a defect rather than to enhance characteristics deemed desirable. "Genetic engineering," properly so-called,

53 See Häring, *Ethics of Manipulation: Issues in Medicine, Behavior Control and Genetics* (New York: Seabury, 1975), esp. p. 173.

involves manipulation of genetic material (deoxyribonucleic acid or DNA) in the gametes or embryo for either therapeutic or eugenic purposes. Gene therapy, then, is a branch of genetic engineering.[54]

The human organism is composed of two kinds of cells: "germ" or reproductive cells (gametes), and "somatic" or non-reproductive cells. The nucleus of each normal somatic cell contains 46 chromosomes (23 pairs). Germ cells possess 23 chromosomes, so that the union of sperm and ovum produces a combination of 46 chromosomes that is unique except in the case of identical twins. Each chromosome comprises some 100,000 genes: segments of DNA that determine the genetic code of inherited characteristics. Genetic engineering is made possible by the fact that, rather like a hologram, every nucleus of a somatic cell contains the genetic code of the entire organism. Through "recombinant DNA" technology (rDNA), it is possible to alter the genetic make-up of an organism by introducing foreign genes into it, either directly through a process called "transformation" or by viral transmission known as "transduction." The technology referred to popularly as "gene-splicing," while thus far limited to bacteria and some plants, opens the way for genetic manipulation of any form of life, including human.[55]

By means of a "gene-sequencing" machine developed at Caltech (announced in June, 1986), scientists were able to begin the mapping of the genetic composition of the entire human organism. As the "human genome initiative" moves ahead, we know ever more precisely which genes perform which functions and where they are located on the strands of DNA. Coupling this with knowledge of the mechanism that "turns genes on and off," it is already possible to perform highly selective modifications of genetic material, both somatic and germ line. This in turn *provides scientists with the power to manipulate human life at its most basic biological level.*[56]

54 According to the *Journal of the American Medical Association* vol. 220 (1972), 1356, GE can be "considered as covering anything having to do with manipulation of the gametes or the foetus, for whatever purpose, from conception by other than sexual union, or the treatment of disease *in utero*, to the ultimate manufacture of a human being to exact specifications." (Quoted in Häring, *op. cit.,* 174). This definition, which includes under GE assisted forms of procreation including AI and IVF, is too broad. The expression "genetic engineering" should be restricted to actual manipulation of genetic material for purposes of eliminating defective genes or inserting others to enhance desired traits.

55 For over a decade scientists, using techniques of gene-splicing, have been able to create such novelties as tobacco plants that glow in the dark—by introducing into them genetic material from fireflies! (*Time* Magazine, May 4, 1987, 110).

56 For a sound introduction to and evaluation of the human genome project by an Orthodox specialist in the field, see the article by Gayle E. Woloschak, "Bioethical Issues Raised By the

While genetic modification of somatic cells affects only the immediate individual, any modification of the germ line cells is inherited by succeeding generations. The spiritual and physical consequences of such manipulation are mind-boggling, and they explain why activists such as Jeremy Rifkin condemn all forms of GE as inherently unethical because they are inherently uncontrollable. By transforming the genetic composition of a living organism, including a human being, we may be transforming its very nature.[57]

Nevertheless, there can be no question that GE in the area of agriculture and livestock production, as well as in the field of medicine, has already led to a welcome revolution of extraordinary proportions. To date, scientists have been able to develop plants that resist herbicides, and they are improving techniques to enable plants to produce their own insecticides, nitrogen fertilizer and frost inhibitors. Manufactured enzymes that break down and consume industrial waste were patented over a decade ago. Today, "bioremediation," using microbes such as bacteria and fungi to dispose of toxic chemicals—organic compounds such as pesticides, but also PCBs, oil and various carcinogens—is a big "eco-business," here and throughout the world. By genetically increasing photosynthesis, scientists

Human Genome Initiative," *Synergia* 10/2 (April 1996), 1ff (publication of the Orthodox Christian Association of Medicine, Psychology and Religion [OCAMPR], P.O. Box 958, Cambridge, MA 12238). The human genome comprises some 50,000-100,000 genes with an estimated 3 billion base pairs. The mapping of genes (determining where they lie along segments of DNA known as chromosomes) has proceeded apace and is nearly complete. The much more difficult process of sequencing the genome has only recently begun, and to date only about 3% has been completed. For an alternative strategy that is attempting to speed up the process, see John Travis, "Another Human Genome Project. A Private Company's Plan Shocks the Genetics Community," *Science News* 153 (23 May, 1998), 334-335.

57 The Nobel Prize winner Hermann J. Muller argued in the 1950s and 60s that GE can produce superior human beings, suggesting that attitudes of love and altruism can be genetically programmed into an individual. See his well-known article "Better Genes for Tomorrow," in *The Population Crisis and the Use of World Resources* (The Hague: Dr. W. Junk, Pub., 1964), 315. The fallacy in this argument, as in similar arguments by ethicists such as Joseph ("If it can be done, do it") Fletcher, is that they fail to recognize the reality of human sin, the element of the tragic inherent in human nature. In an article published in 1967, the eminent Catholic theologian Karl Rahner declared: "Genetic manipulation is the embodiment of the fear of oneself, the fear of accepting one's self and the unknown quantity it is," because it is *predetermined*. "Accepting this necessarily alien determination of one's own being *is* and *remains*, therefore, a fundamental task of man in his free moral existence." *Theological Investigations*, vol. 9 (NY: Crossroad, 1981), 244ff; reprinted in Lammers & Verhey (eds.), *On Moral Medicine* (Grand Rapids, MI: Eerdmans, 1987), 384. Much modern discussion of the ethics of GE moves between these poles of a utopian naïveté and a God-centered realism regarding the significance of GE in the fulfillment of human potential.

hope for a new "green revolution" that will meet the needs of a rapidly growing world population, particularly in the developing countries.

But this projected agricultural boon is seen by many as a bane. Citizens' groups have blocked experiments in California and elsewhere that would have released new strains of bacteria into the atmosphere. Where such experiments have taken place, no serious adverse effects were immediately detected. Nevertheless, reports have appeared over the years, in the *New York Times, Newsweek* and elsewhere, warning that scientists have often ignored rules governing the release of genetically altered bacteria and viruses. Some critics have argued that we are preparing an eco-disaster greater than the one brought on by introduction into this country of the gypsy moth. Others warn that through GE there will be a narrowing of genetic diversity by the production of uniform crop species, with a consequent weakening of their resistance to insects and changes in weather conditions. Still others express concern about the unpredictable and irreversible consequences of genetically engineered crops crossing with other varieties, to create "super weeds" and related hybrids that jeopardize ecological stability.[58] With ecological disasters increasing across the globe (the 1998 fires in Southeast Asia and Florida, for example, together with the rapidly diminishing ozone layer), prophets of doom are finally being given what is certainly a well-deserved hearing.

Similar progress, but with different dangers, is being made in the field of livestock production. Genetic engineering can improve an animal's weight, size, strength, quality of meat, etc. Cloning techniques—long successful with frogs, mice, and, reportedly, a pony—took a major leap (in which direction?) with the conception and birth of Dolly, the ewe supposedly cloned from an adult somatic cell. The Scottish scientists who produced Dolly have admitted that she may in fact have been cloned in the old-fashioned way, using an embryonic cell. The experiment was reproduced, nevertheless, with

58 This point, together with an articulate assessment of the overall situation, was recently made by Dr. Elizabeth Theokritoff, in personal correspondence dated 11 May, 1998. Her objections to genetic manipulation of plants, as of animals, are essentially theological: "Except where genetic engineering actually increases suffering among creatures—e.g., the mouse especially designed to be susceptible to tumours—it is very difficult to cite clear ethical principles which are being violated. I would suggest, however, that the very language often applied to genetic engineering—that of 'creating'—and the view of this 'creation' as a product which can be patented, suggest an alarming degree of human *hubris*. It seems we are coming dangerously close to a parody of God's creative acts, 'creating' living things according to our own image and solely for our purposes."

the subsequent cloning of mice from adult somatic cells, and the technique seems applicable to other species. However that may be, human genetic material is being introduced into various animals to produce medications and other products, and cloning will make those products available on a global scale.

The danger inherent in this kind of manipulation is twofold: violation of the dignity and integrity of created life-forms; and interference in the micro-evolutionary process of natural selection which, as with plants, can narrow the gene pool with unforeseeable consequences. The introduction of human growth hormones into pigs, for example, has produced a leaner variety—but one afflicted with strabismus and arthritis. And while mythological creatures such as fauns, mermaids, centaurs and other chimeras remain on the GE drawing-board, experimentation is going on in several countries to combine human genetic material with that of bovines, primates and other life-forms, as well as to successfully clone a human being. But at what ecological price? At what cost to our basic humanity?

In considering the potential bio-possibilities and bio-hazards connected with human genetic engineering, we should distinguish between therapeutic and eugenic or innovational techniques. In the former category, GE can manufacture human insulin, growth and other hormones, vaccines, and interferon (a protein that defends against virus infection). Gene therapy seeks to detect and to correct genetic defects *in utero*, at the earliest embryonic stage, before damage can be inflicted upon the brain and nervous system. Cures are emerging, or at least envisioned, for inherited illnesses such as hemophilia, muscular dystrophy, sickle-cell anemia, cystic fibrosis, and other debilitating or fatal diseases whose genetic markers have now been discovered. Already in 1987 the *New York Times* announced that scientists had transplanted foreign genes into the bacteria that make up the tuberculosis vaccine, opening the way for a "multi-disease vaccine" that can be used in the treatment of such diseases as leprosy and malaria. And the progress continues.

Even depression and schizophrenia, now widely recognized as illnesses of biochemical origin, seem susceptible to treatment by genetic therapy: by increasing the neurotransmitter norepinephrine, for example, or the Beta-endorphin enzyme that acts as a natural analgesic.[59] Research is advancing

59 The hugely popular SSRIs ("selective serotonin re-uptake inhibitors") such as Prozac appear to work

toward alleviating or eliminating degenerative diseases such as Parkinson's and Alzheimer's, together with various cancers. Advances in the treatment of immunological disorders such as ADA (adenosine deaminase deficiency) suggest that the ultimate victory of GE might be the cure of AIDS.

The line between therapeutic and eugenic techniques is difficult to draw. While theoretically it is possible for GE to replace *homo sapiens* with a superior *homo novus*, such "enhancement technology," is far in the future, for economic if for no other reasons: the costs of research and application of technology to modify height, hair or eye color, or even intelligence, would seem to far outweigh any conceivable benefits. Nevertheless, the potential for "improving" on God's blueprint for human life is such that serious ethical questions must be addressed here and now, by the Churches as well as by public and private regulatory bodies.

Among the most pressing ethical issues raised by GE are the following:

— The allocation of scarce and expensive resources. How do we determine who benefits from the new technology, and who *profits* from it? Karl Rahner and others have warned that GE could fall under the "heartless rules" of the marketplace.[60] The "managed health care" system of America's burgeoning HMOs has amply demonstrated the injustices that arise from allowing private enterprise and human greed to govern medical treatment. Will life and death ultimately depend on one's ability to pay?

— Closely related is the whole issue of control. Who will set standards and limits on experimentation, and using what criteria? The U.S. Patent and Trademark Office announced in May of 1987 that it "considers non-naturally occurring nonhuman multicellular living organisms, including animals, to be patentable subject matter."[61] A license to manufacture and patent life has been delivered into the hands of corporate America. If past experience is any indicator, "control" of the new technologies will be largely determined by the profit motive.[62]

---

by stabilizing serotonin and other neurotransmitters in the brain. While they are not the direct result of GE, under controlled conditions they can complement certain forms of genetic therapy.

60 See Häring, *op. cit.*, 187.

61 *Time Magazine*, 4 May, 1987, 110.

62 On various religious objections to gene patenting and a discussion of the present debate, see the dossier by Mark J. Hanson, "Religious Voices in Biotechnology: the Case of Gene Patenting," *Hastings Center Report* (Nov.-Dec. 1997), 1-21.

— As techniques of genetic screening have grown more sophisticated, it has become possible to detect a wide range of genetic disorders that may or may not be curable within a foreseeable future. Screening, in fact, may become legally mandatory. This raises a number of intriguing and perplexing questions: (1) Should *any* form of genetic screening be made obligatory, since in cases where genetic surgery or other therapy cannot correct the anomaly *in utero*, the mother may be urged or legally compelled to abort? (2) Should prospective spouses be required to submit to screening and refused a marriage license if genetic defects indicate that their offspring would likely weaken the human gene-pool? (3) Should mandatory sterilization be imposed in cases where the parents carry defective genes? (Since everyone has an average of six defective genes to begin with, it would be necessary, of course, to prioritize defects according to their potential danger.) (4) The Western world presently finds itself in a dangerous slide towards broad acceptance of active euthanasia, both voluntary and involuntary (a subject we discuss in the next chapter). As a result, the issue of *infanticide* is being aired publicly in a way unthinkable a generation ago. One of the most difficult questions in this regard concerns so-called "defective neonates" or genetically impaired newborn infants whose medical prognosis is hopeless. Should consideration ever be given in such cases to some form of active euthanasia, to spare the infant from unrelieved pain for the brief duration of its life, and to spare the parents from prolonged anguish and crushing financial liability? These are difficult questions, and to many minds their implications are repugnant. They need to be faced openly, however, by the Orthodox as well as by other Christians, in order for the voice of the Church to be heard in a world that all too often chooses knowledge over wisdom and expediency over compassion.

— Finally, there is the issue of responsibility. Who will assume responsibility for ecological disasters, epidemics, and generally the future products of GE that have a deleterious effect upon individuals or society? We certainly can't count on the insurance companies. With legalized abortion, insurers are increasingly reluctant to pay for the care of a child whose genetic defect could have been detected *in utero* and who might subsequently have been aborted. Similarly, diagnostic tests revealing genetic defects in workers could cause cancellation of their insurance policies and even loss of their jobs. Once again, when diagnosis outpaces the possibility for cure, justice is often the victim.

The possibility of accidental contaminations and epidemics, together with the threat of unacceptable manipulation of human and other life-forms, underscore the need for the Churches, through their theologians and medical professionals, to insist that the *federal* government regulate experimentation in the area of genetic engineering. Such regulation is needed not only to guarantee public safety, but to preserve the very integrity of God's creation.[63] And of course the regulatory agencies must be granted the necessary authority to set guidelines and to fix enforceable penalties, since asking the bio-tech industry or even the scientific community to establish its own ethical code and enforce it effectively, would be merely inviting a conflict of interests.[64]

Given the present possibilities of the various "technologies of manipulation," it would seem appropriate to suggest that the following limits be placed on genetic experimentation.

— First, with a growing number of research scientists and medical professionals today, we as Orthodox Christians ought to call for a moratorium on all experimentation with human germ line cells (as the Orthodox Church has done regarding human cloning, in a statement published in the Spring of 1998). The only exception to this should be in those cases where the cells have begun to degenerate and are incapable of normal development. The quest for therapeutic measures to correct genetic defects in somatic cells is laudable and should be pursued. There where the dignity and integrity of the human or animal subject are fully respected, such a quest should be encouraged and, where appropriate, subsidized by public funding. Germ line experimentation, however, runs a morally unacceptable risk of transmitting to future generations irreversible consequences of unintended but nonetheless disastrous mistakes.

— Similarly, a clear and unambiguous stand should be taken against any form of human experimentation that would violate the freedom, dig-

---

63 This theme, co-opted by default by the World Council of Churches, is one that needs to be addressed by every ecclesial body. Groundwork for an Orthodox approach to ecology and the integrity of creation has been admirably laid by Metropolitan John Zizioulas, in a series of articles that have appeared in *Sourozh*, the journal of the Moscow Patriarchate published in England, and in other Orthodox journals.

64 Häring, *Ethics of Manipulation*, 187, observes: "...as long as society legalizes, without any therapeutic indication, the killing of healthy foetuses, there is little hope that scientists will respect the human life of the 'mishaps' of their own engineering."

nity or integrity of the person. Such procedures include commercial use of embryos, the mixing of human and non-human genetic material (except *perhaps* in those cases where significant medical benefits can accrue through techniques that are strictly therapeutic), as well as all forms of human cloning. (The ultimate consequences of human cloning, by the way, are perhaps not as horrendous as they at first seemed. As we pointed out in chapter 3, natural twinning of the embryo at the pre-implantation stage is a form of cloning. Artificially produced clones are basically artificially produced identical twins. Since a given individual is much more than the product of his or her genetic heritage, and since cell differentiation begins with the earliest stages of cleavage, even "identical" twins are not truly identical; each constitutes a unique individual, and in humans, a unique person. This fact, however, should never be taken to imply that the cloning of human beings represents a moral good. Under any circumstances, because it places determination of human life as well as human qualities and characteristics—i.e., the human *soul*—in the hands of men rather than of God, it remains an unqualified moral evil.)

— Finally, we should urge a reversal of the decision to grant patents on newly developed animal life-forms. Genetic engineering of bacterial and plant life can produce results that morally justify wide-ranging experimentation and commercial exploitation, provided adequate safeguards remain in place. The custom-designing of animal life-forms, however, will inevitably lead to what Rifkin has termed "the ultimate form of technological reductionism."[65] From insider trading, to megamergers with massive layoffs, to health care and insurance companies that honor above all the bottom line, the marketplace creates its own set of values that have little to do with the Christian Gospel. It is up to the Churches, then, to speak out clearly and firmly against decisions, in both private and public sectors, that would open the door to wanton exploitation of God's creation.

A Pastoral Assessment

The new procreative and other biomedical technologies affect every stage of human life, from conception to death. At each stage, as we have seen,

---

65 Jeremy Rifkin, *New York Times* (27 April, 1987). See the ensuing debate on this issue in the *New York Times* Science section, 9 June, 1987.

they raise two closely related questions. How do we determine which scientific achievements are potentially good? And how do we determine their good or morally appropriate use in any given case? The respirator, for example, is undeniably good. Its use on a terminal cancer patient, however, might not be.

This leads us back to our original concern: to stipulate criteria that will help us with a theological evaluation and pastoral approach regarding these issues as they affect the lives of each of us.

Such criteria would begin with recognition and joyful acceptance of the absolute sovereignty of God as Creator, Redeemer, and Judge over all life and all human endeavors. They would include a vision of the human person as bearer of the divine image, called to manifest and to grow continually in the divine likeness. This implies growth in authentic "personhood" that transcends fallen human nature and reflects the self-giving love that unites Father, Son and Spirit in a personal communion of divine life. In addition, we must perceive virtually every experience, including personal suffering, as an occasion for drawing closer to God and to the ultimate meaning of human existence. Not all suffering is "redemptive," particularly as it involves protracted and totally absorbing physical or mental agony. Nevertheless, many apparent tragedies can be transformed into channels of grace. Thus, for example, a couple that anguishes over their inability to bear children could answer their own longing and meet an important need by accepting to adopt. Similarly, there where a Down's syndrome or other genetically "defective" child is accepted and loved, the impairment often proves to be a blessing for the entire family.

Finally, we should remember the importance of our own participation in creating the world and our own lives, from moment to moment. The realizing of eschatology is not only God's concern. It involves us as well. It engages us in an ongoing effort to prepare ourselves and the world as a whole for the Parousia: God's future, when the work of creation and redemption will be complete. Christian ethics is eschatological and teleological as well as deontological. It judges and counsels in terms of ultimate ends as well as of present obligations. Thus it concerns not only our responsibility *before* God, but also our cooperation *with* him, with the intent to transfigure the creation according to his will and purpose.

An Orthodox theological perspective leads to specific conclusions concerning the *pastoral approach* we need to take regarding the issues of medically assisted procreation and genetic engineering.

Traditional Roman Catholic thought over the past two or three decades has consistently condemned what it calls "non-natural" means of procreation. In Rahner's terms, such means put procreation outside the realm of "man's sphere of intimacy...the proper context for sexual union."[66] This fails to appreciate the fact that love is not only expressed in the intimacy of sexual intercourse. The "sphere of intimacy" in fact includes the whole gestation period—indeed, the entire marriage—no less than the specific act of sexual union that leads to conception.

Assisted means of procreation, then, within the limits prescribed above, would seem to be consistent with Orthodox moral theory. These would include artificial insemination using the husband's sperm, and *in vitro* fertilization where all embryos are transferred to the mother's womb and there is no resorting to "fetal reduction." On the other hand, AID and "surrogate mothering" are *not* ethically acceptable because they introduce a third party into the procreative process and are vulnerable to commercial exploitation (sperm banks that sell the semen of Nobel Prize winners, women renting their wombs, etc.).

As for genetic engineering, we can accept and counsel in favor of both prenatal and post natal therapeutic measures that aim at preventing or correcting illness and deformity. Today such counsel remains largely hypothetical (except for genetic screening, which now leads many pregnant women to abort genetically impaired or otherwise undesirable children). Corrective surgery, nevertheless, is already being performed *in utero* as well as on defective newborn infants. In the not too distant future, it should be possible to eliminate deleterious genes at the embryonic stage (via IVF) or even to correct potential genetic anomalies in the gametes prior to fertilization. The research needed to perfect these therapeutic techniques can be supported by the Church, but only where research is limited to degenerating germ cells that are incapable of normal development, and excludes all experimentation on viable human embryos.

Eugenic or enhancement procedures, on the other hand, whether to improve certain traits or to create a superior or inferior "race," should be vehemently opposed as a fundamental violation of divine sovereignty and the rights of mankind as a whole. Concern has been expressed especially

---

66 *Art. cit.* (in *On Moral Medicine*), 385.

about the possibility of enhancing certain characteristics by GE that would produce a "super-race," a fulfillment of the Nazi dream. In fact, the greatest danger today seems to be the relentless attempt to produce a *sub-species* of humanoid that would function as a slave-class. On Thursday, May 14, 1987, Uli Schmetzer of the *Chicago Tribune* announced that Italian biogenetic scientists had successfully bred an anthropoid with a chimpanzee mother and a human father. Although the experiment was interrupted at the embryo stage because of "ethical problems," there seems little doubt that patent offices will soon be obliged to pronounce on the patentability of "ape men." The matter is so ludicrous it seems amusing. But in fact, it portends the ultimate in human manipulation, and its consequences are at least as far-reaching and potentially disastrous as with the development of nuclear weapons.

Whenever it is a question of human manipulation, regardless of the ends, it is important to keep in mind one thing. In Jesus Christ we love and are loved, not for what we can accomplish, but simply for who we are.[67] Love is called for as an unconditional gift, apart from any consideration of potentials or defects proper to the loved one. And we should recall as well that Christ came for the physically handicapped and the deformed, as well as for those who are spiritually ill (cf. Mk 3:1-6; Lk 14:12-14).

Today, as fully as in Byzantine times, the Church must act as the *conscience* of society, through evangelization and moral persuasion. It must accept this role with regard to abortion, procreation and genetic engineering, as well as to economic and social justice, national defense, ecology, and the like. As stewards of God's creation, we are called to use all appropriate means—i.e., non-violent means consistent with the Gospel—to transform both the attitudes and the priorities of a pluralistic society (and today *all* societies are pluralistic), in order to serve God faithfully within and for his world.

---

67 See Leon R. Kass, "The New Biology: What Price Relieving Man's Estate?", in Thomas A. Shannon (ed.), *Bioethics* (Revised), (NY: Paulist Press, 1981), 379-402. Kass states: "The family is rapidly becoming the only institution in an increasingly impersonal world where each person is loved not for what he does or makes, but simply because he is" (p. 394). This statement, originally published in 1971, sounds naïve today, with the deterioration of the family in American society. The Church is perhaps the last "institution" to which it truly applies. Charles Curran, "Moral Theology and Genetics," in *On Moral Medicine*, 381, states: "The Christian view of man does not see his value primarily in terms of what he does or can do for himself or others, but in terms of what God has first done for him."

With its scriptural and patristic moral perspective, Orthodoxy has a unique witness to offer in this necessarily ecumenical endeavor. For too long we have avoided making that witness by pretending to give priority to "spirituality" or by condemning such involvement as "activism." The Church, however, is called to speak: to proclaim the will and the purpose of God as he seeks to lead the creation into his Kingdom. The question is, do we have the courage and the conviction to make that voice heard?

5

"A Blessed Pascha":
Approaching the End of Life

*"Thou art the Resurrection, the Life
and the repose of Thy servants, O
Christ, our God..."*

—Orthodox Burial Service

*"Release Thy servant, [O Lord], from
this unbearable suffering and this
continuing bitter illness, and grant
him/her rest."*

—Prayer for the terminally ill

*"In the womb, the fetus practices
many of the acts it will need to
perform once it is born, such as
kicking and swallowing. Similarly,
in the world, a person practices the
acts he or she will need to perform
after death, especially knowing and
loving, the two values emphasized by
all the saints, mystics, wise men, and
resuscitated patients."*

—Peter Kreeft

Our purpose in this chapter is to address the issue of appropriate care for those who are facing imminent death. This includes both terminally ill adult patients and handicapped newborn infants, so-called "defective neonates." To determine what kinds and levels of care are morally appropriate in such cases, we need to look first of all at the Orthodox Christian approach to sickness and death, and to the relation between "sanctity/sacredness of life" and "quality of life" approaches that influence end-of-life judgments. This will lead to a consideration of the meaning and importance of physical and mental suffering in human experience, particularly as it concerns the terminally ill. Finally, we will take up the question of protocols or guidelines in the treatment or non-treatment of the dying patient, together with the ethical significance of "active" and "passive" forms of euthanasia.

The Hippocratic Oath declares, "I will use treatment to help the sick according to my ability and judgment, but never with a view to injury and wrong-doing." Out of this vow have grown the dual principles of (1) *beneficence*: the commitment to further the vital interests of the patient, and (2) *nonmaleficence*: the commitment to avoid harm to the patient through either intentional action or neglect.[1] These two principles, together with the Oath itself and the sixth commandment of the Hebrew Decalogue, provide a philosophical safeguard against active euthanasia or "mercy killing," even in cases where the patient is in a persistent vegetative state or is enduring intractable pain. They reflect the view, normative for the Judeo-Christian tradition, that the principle of the sanctity or sacredness of life takes precedence over concern for the quality of life.

Until very recently, this normative religious perspective seemed straightforward and unquestionable. If God is the author of life, he is equally Lord over death and the dying process. With the development of life-support technology (dialysis, chemotherapy, respirators, etc., including the possibility of transplanting vital organs such as the liver and the heart), however, new moral issues arise that in an earlier age were either undreamed of or seemed settled once and for all.

It is now possible to maintain biological existence artificially for prolonged periods of time, even when there is no hope for a cure. This fact obliges us to reopen the question between the "sanctity" or "sacredness" of life and the "quality" of life. And it raises as well ancillary issues such as the allocation of limited resources and the potential financial burden upon the patient and his or her family. As a result, three lines of ethical reasoning have emerged. The first, mentioned earlier, is "vitalism," which holds that biological life should be sustained at all costs and by any means available. While this sounds like a noble defense of the "sanctity of life" principle, it is in fact a form of biological idolatry, which places the abstract

1   See Robert Weir, *Selective Nontreatment of Handicapped Newborns* (New York: Oxford University Press, 1984), 199.

value of sustained physical existence ahead of the personal needs and ultimate destiny of the patient.

The second line of reflection, supporting various forms of "euthanasia," argues that terminally ill patients should be allowed to choose the time and the way by which they will die. It thus promotes what it terms "death with dignity." As recent ethical debate has shown, however, the slogan "death with dignity" can be used to justify a multitude of attitudes and practices that have little regard for the patient's ultimate physical or spiritual welfare.[2] And insofar as it encourages any form of active euthanasia, it unwittingly fosters the ultimate "death with *indignity*" by promoting homicide or suicide.

The third view is much more in keeping with a Christian perspective. It maintains that at some point in the dying process, nontreatment (the withholding or withdrawing of life-support systems) may be morally appropriate, thereby allowing the patient to die a "natural" death.

Yet even this last line of reasoning raises a host of vexing questions. Does the choice of what is termed "selective nontreatment," popularly referred to as "pulling the plug," merely "allow nature to take its course"? Or does it amount to an illicit form of euthanasia? In other words, is selective nontreatment—usually labeled "passive euthanasia"—*ever* morally justified, given the fact that its purpose is to hasten the patient's death, even from natural causes? And what of the differences between various forms of nontreatment: is a moral distinction to be made, for example, between turning off a ventilator and withdrawing a feeding tube? Finally, can the "benign neglect" of nontreatment be ethically condoned as truly "passive"? Or does nontreatment, by virtue of its intentionality, always amount to *active* intervention, a form of euthanasia that qualifies as homicide if not murder?

Questions of this kind usually arise in regard to patients who are in the late stages of potentially fatal diseases such as cancer. They apply equally, however, to those newborn infants who, because of genetic anomalies, severe fetal alcohol/drug syndrome, birth trauma, or some other reason are classified as terminally ill "defective neonates." In all such terminal cases, the basic question to be resolved is this: *what are the limits to which medi-*

---

2   See the articles by P. Ramsey, R. S. Morison, and L. R. Kass in *On Moral Medicine. Theological Perspectives in Medical Ethics,* ed. Lammers & Verhey (Grand Rapids: Eerdmans, 1987), 185-211.

cal technology should be employed to sustain biological existence? In looking for an answer, we may begin by noting specific cases that have recently focused national attention on the problem of euthanasia.

On 23 October, 1991, Michigan pathologist Dr. Jack Kevorkian made national headlines by providing the means by which two women ended their lives. Previously he had engaged in "physician-assisted suicide" (PAS) in the case of Alzheimer's patient Janet Adkins. These persons were chronically ill but would not have been diagnosed as "terminal," that is, according to the generally accepted definition of the expression, as having less than six months to live. Their deaths represented clear-cut examples of suicide, with the aim of ending what they considered to be the unbearable burden of their illness. In the meantime, while the nation hesitates to engage in a serious debate over the issue, allowing the courts to deal with it on a state-by-state basis, Kevorkian has "assisted" another fifty or so persons to put themselves to death.

In an effort to sanction yet provide legal controls over medical intervention in such activity, right-to-die groups presented "Initiative 119" to the voters of Washington State on 5 November, 1991. Although the Initiative was narrowly defeated, its proponents and like-minded groups have continued relentlessly to press for its most important and ominous provision: the legalization of physician-assisted suicide.

The Initiative contained three basic provisions. First, with reference to Washington's "Natural Death Act" that allows for Living Wills, it would have expanded the list of life-support technologies that a patient may refuse, to include feeding and hydration tubes. Second, it would have permitted the signer of a Living Will to stipulate that no life-support should be used if the person enters into a clinically diagnosable persistent vegetative state (PVS). These two modifications had been previously endorsed by the Washington State Medical Association. Opposed by the Association, and by many other religious and medical bodies, was the third provision. This would have allowed physician-assisted suicide by terminally ill patients on the basis of their written request, together with certification by at least two medical doctors that the patient had less than six months to live.[3]

---

3   The official summary of the Initiative ran as follows: "This initiative expands the right of adult persons with terminal conditions to have their wishes, expressed in a written directive, regarding life respected. It amends current law to: Expand the definition of terminal condition to include

Euthanasia or right-to-die proponents continued to press their case over the next three years. In November of 1994, Oregon voters, by the narrow margin of 51%-49%, made their state the first and only jurisdiction in the world to legalize physician-assisted suicide.[4] Now that Measure 16 is no longer tied up in the courts, terminally ill adult residents of the state are able legally to request a physician's prescription for drugs with which they can, through self-medication, end their own life. Provisions of the Measure require a 15-day waiting period, one written and two oral requests by the patient, and the opinion of a second physician to determine whether the patient is suffering from mental illness or depression. There is no legal obligation for the patient to notify next of kin.

Coming in the wake of the Washington Initiative and a similar proposal narrowly rejected by California voters, Oregon's Measure 16 represents a monumental victory for proponents of the right-to-die movement. As the first of what will undoubtedly be many such victories, it raises a multitude of complex ethical questions concerning medical care at the end of life. Those we want to consider here include the relation between a "sanctity/sacredness of life" and a "quality of life" ethic, together with appropriate treatment of the terminally ill, including those in an irreversible coma or PVS.

The "Sacredness of Life" and "Quality of Life" Debate

Two cases first reported in February 1994, attest to a significant shift in attitudes toward terminal life-support in the United States. In a Sarasota, Florida, case the court ordered a hospital to maintain life-support for a thirteen-year-old, brain-dead girl. While the medical staff sought legal permission to have her removed from what they regarded as futile treatment, the mother insisted that the hospital do everything to "keep her

irreversible coma and persistent vegetative state or condition which will result in death within six months; Specify which life-sustaining procedures may be withdrawn; Permit adult persons with terminal conditions to request and receive aid-in-dying from their physicians, facilitating death." Quoted in A.R. Jonsen, "What is at Stake?" *Commonweal* [Supplement on Euthanasia: Washington State Initiative 119], 9 August, 1991, 3.

4   Although in the Netherlands "aid-in-dying" has long been openly practiced by physicians, and has become the focus of an intense debate over the merits of physician-assisted suicide, the practice remains illegal. When doctors follow certain accepted guidelines, however, they are virtually exempt from prosecution.

daughter alive." One medical ethicist familiar with the case stated: "The hospital has an obligation to take her off the ventilator. Now they are treating a corpse."[5]

A second case involved a decision by the U.S. Court of Appeals of Virginia ordering a hospital to continue treatment of "Baby K," a female child born in a semi-anencephalic condition. Although the infant was totally and permanently devoid of sensory perception and relational capacity because most of her brain was missing, the mother insisted on continued life-support.[6]

In each of these cases, the medical team held that life-support should be ended because they deemed the treatment to be futile. In earlier years, hospitals tended rather to insist that apparently futile treatment be continued even against the wishes of family, of health-care proxies or, in certain cases, of the patient herself, as in the celebrated case of Elizabeth Bouvia.[7] To some extent this reluctance was motivated by the fear of litigation if the medical team did not do "everything possible" to sustain even minimal biological existence. Increasingly, however, the courts are accepting judgments of health-care specialists which call for the cessation of treatment based on the patient's "quality of life." To some, this is long overdue acceptance of an element essential to making any medical judgment. To others, it represents the fast track down the slippery slope. To Christian bioethicists, it poses in an acute way the question of how quality of life (QL) considerations can be reasonably and faithfully integrated into a more fundamental sacredness of life (SL) philosophy.[8]

Christian ethicists, including those who insist on the fundamental sanctity or sacredness of human life, find themselves obliged by virtue of modern biomedical technology to make moral judgments that take into consideration the "quality" of the life in question. What remains unclear,

5 *New York Times*, 12 February, 1994.
6 L. Greenhouse, "Court Order to Treat Baby with Partial Brain Prompts Debate on Costs and Ethics," *New York Times* (20 February, 1994), A 20.
7 G. Pence, *Classic Cases in Medical Ethics* (New York: McGraw-Hill, 1990), 29-44.
8 The latter pole is usually referred to as the "sanctity of life." Use of the expression "sacredness" throughout this chapter is based on our discussion in the Introduction. There we distinguished between the inherent "sacredness" of human life (a function of human nature, a given in human existence) and its "sanctity" (a hypostatic or personal function, attained through ascetic discipline and acquisition of Christian virtues).

however, is how various traditions use the expressions "sacredness" or "sanctity," and "quality." This lack of clarity has led to fruitless debates between (1) apparent "vitalists," who hold that the mere fact of biological existence is a good in itself [9] and should therefore be preserved at all cost, whatever the condition of the patient; and (2) apparent "relativists," who argue that life has neither meaning nor worth if it lacks certain capacities or attributes necessary for maintaining self-consciousness and the ability to relate to others.

The sacredness of life position, usually but not necessarily identified with a particular religious tradition, is generally based on the following pair of convictions. First, human life by its very nature is "sacred," that is, it is intrinsically good and always deserves respect and protection. Its worth is not contingent on any particular condition or attribute which might characterize it. Second, all human lives are of equal value, at whatever stage of their development from conception to death. This implies that all human lives have the same "right" to life. [10]

Debate concerning the "sacredness of life" (SL) and "quality of life" (QL) approaches has been hampered by a tendency on the part of some proponents of a SL ethic to criticize the QL position as inherently and inevitably in conflict with SL principles. Leonard Weber, for example, first notes that the SL approach defends the two propositions just mentioned concerning the sacredness and the equality of human lives. Then he adds, "The quality of life ethic finds neither of these two propositions acceptable." [11] To the contrary, however, a great many representatives of the QL ethic would accept these propositions, provided they are not absolutized into a vitalist position. As Weber points out, QL considerations include the "value" of the life in

---

9 In Roman Catholic parlance, physical life so viewed is a *bonum honestum*, as contrasted with a bonum utile, a useful but not ultimately valuable property or condition.

10 On this entire issue, see the collection of articles in James J. Wolter and Thomas A. Shannon, *Quality of Life. The New Medical Dilemma* (New York: Paulist, 1990). Presuppositions behind the SL and QL ethic are discussed particularly by Edward W. Keyserlingk, "The Quality of Life and Death," 35-53; and Leonard J. Weber, "Who Shall Live?," 111-118. For specific critiques and applications of SL and QL principles, see also John R. Connery, "Quality of Life," 54-60; Warren T. Reich, "Quality of Life and Defective Newborn Children: An Ethical Analysis," 161-175; and Richard C. Sparks, "Protected Quality of the Patient's Life—A Critique," 176-187. A useful assessment of QL issues and public policy (the 1989 Oregon Basic Health Services Act) is provided by David C. Hadorn, "The Oregon Priority-Setting Exercise: Quality of Life and Public Policy," *Hastings Center Report* 20 (May/June 1991), 11-16.

11 "Who Shall Live?," 111.

question, both to the patient and to others. The term "quality," however, has been defined in ways both broad and narrow, and no consensus has been reached as to the selection and application of QL criteria in specific cases. To some, the QL approach implies the following: 1) the value of human lives is unequal and depends on individual conditions or capacities; 2) human life is to be understood as a possession rather than as a gift, therefore it is governed by the principle of autonomy rather than that of stewardship; and 3) the ultimate "meaning" of human life resides in the self rather than in God or some other transcendent principle. Understood in these terms, a QL ethic would tend to offer unqualified support to abortion on demand, to physician-assisted suicide, and in fact to any procedure that serves one's personal comfort, gratification or sense of purpose.

Where a QL perspective holds that human lives are of unequal worth because of certain conditions or the lack of certain values and capacities (as in cases of mental retardation or ill health), then it is indeed incompatible with the sacredness of life position. As James Wolter has pointed out, however, "quality" must not be "defined by reference to an attribute or property of physical life." For this reason he prefers to speak rather of "the quality of the relationship which exists between the medical condition of the patient, on the one hand, and the patient's ability to pursue life's goals and purposes (purposefulness) understood as the values that transcend physical life, on the other."[12]

The quality of life position founders whenever it focuses on the quality of an attribute or condition, rather than on the quality of a *relationship*. That relationship, as Wolter rightly insists, can only be between the actual condition of the patient and his or her capacity for pursuing life's transcendent goals. A similar point is made by John Paris: "What within the Christian tradition is the significance of life? It is that life is destined for God. Its ultimate goal is the restoration of the kingdom. Thus, it is eternal life and not life itself which is the ultimate."[13]

Human life in its aspect of biological existence cannot be considered an absolute good that must be preserved *for its own sake*. Its ultimate value

12 "The Meaning and Validity of Quality of Life Judgments in Contemporary Roman Catholic Medical Ethics," in Wolter and Shannon, *Quality of Life*, 80-82.
13 John J. Paris, S.J., "Terminating Treatment for Newborns: A Theological Perspective," in Wolter and Shannon, *Quality of Life*, 151-160.

and meaning lie outside itself, beyond the limits of earthly existence. This is the truth that any genuinely Christian "quality of life" stance is based upon. It avoids the bio-idolatry of both vitalism and relativism, while recognizing that the true sanctity of human life resides *in the person* rather than in the sheer fact of physical existence. From this perspective, then, there is no conflict between sacredness of life and quality of life approaches. The two are necessarily complementary, since the former points to the ultimate source and meaning of human existence, while the latter, properly understood, charts the pathway that leads from earthly life to life in the Kingdom of God.

Ethicists of all moral and religious traditions recognize that medical decisions today inevitably involve quality of life considerations. Very few would be inclined toward "heroics" simply to maintain minimal physiological functioning in a clearly hopeless case—as with anencephaly or higher-brain (cerebral or hemispheric) death—simply because the technology exists to do so. That such a case is indeed hopeless, however, is a quality of life judgment: it weighs the relationship between the patient's condition and the treatment options, and concludes that attempts to sustain biological existence would be unnecessarily burdensome or simply futile. Judgments made in light of "futility" or the "burden-benefit calculus" are necessarily based on evaluations of the "quality" of the patient's life. Such quality, however, must always be determined in light of the patient's own personal interests and well-being, and not on grounds of the burden imposed on other parties, the family, for example, or on the medical-care system with its economic considerations and limited resources.

Debate over "sacredness" or "sanctity" versus "quality" has usually turned on questions of patient *autonomy* and *beneficence*, i.e., the "rights" of individuals to exercise control in their treatment, and the "duty" on the part of care givers to avoid harm (as expressed in the "nonmaleficence" clause of the Hippocratic Oath),[14] while offering the patient appropriate treatment and/or care.[15] Orthodox Christianity, on the other hand, begins with the af-

14 On the issues of autonomy, nonmaleficence and beneficence, see Tom L. Beauchamp and James F. Childress, *Principles of Biomedical Ethics,* 4th ed. (New York: Oxford University Press, 1994), 120-325.
15 Some would distinguish between "treatment" and "care" by maintaining that the former may be discontinued under appropriate circumstances but that care must never be denied. A critique of the resource paper, "Nutrition and Hydration: Moral and Pastoral Reflections," published by the

firmation that human persons are created in the image of God (Gen 1:26-27) and are called to exercise obedient and loving dominion or "stewardship" over the created order. "What are human beings that you are mindful of them, mortals that you care for them? Yet you have made them a little lower than God, and crowned them with glory and honor. You have given them dominion over the works of your hands..." [Ps 8:4-5, NRSV]

Human life by its very nature is sacred insofar as it bears and manifests the image and purpose of its Creator. As we stressed earlier, it is precisely that image and purpose that determine our "personhood." Yet we must also affirm that this essential, personal quality is in some measure independent of the capacity to convey the love of God in a direct and active way. Even an embryo or a patient in deep coma retains the quality of personhood. This is not because of any capacity for interpersonal relationships or self-consciousness; in these cases such a capacity manifestly does not exist. Rather, it is because the individual bears the image of God from conception to death and into eternal life. As we shall see, however, this does not mean that in terminal cases life-sustaining treatment may never be withheld or withdrawn, or that the relationship between burdens and benefits cannot be taken into account in the making of health-care decisions. Considerations of "sacredness" and "quality" remain intertwined.

From a Christian perspective, then, the question of the "quality" of a human life can only be approached theologically. Rather than see a SL ethic as opposed to a QL ethic and therefore irreconcilable with it, we need to ground quality of life considerations in the more basic perspective of *the sacredness of the human person.* This requires that we address the question of suffering in human experience and its relation to the primal Christian vocation of stewardship.

Committee for Prolife Activities of the National Conference of Catholic Bishops on 2 April 1992, points out, however, that these are relative concepts: one person's treatment option is another person's ethically mandatory expression of "care." Consequently, the true measure for moral decision making is not "treatment vs. care" but the relationship between benefits and burdens, and the significance of that relationship for the patient. See *Issues. A Critical Examination of Contemporary Ethical Issues in Health Care,* vol. 7, no. 3 (May/June, 1992), 8.

Illness and the Mystery of Suffering

A familiar caricature of the quality of life ethic depicts it as focusing nearly exclusively on the pain and suffering experienced by a terminally ill patient. If the level of distress rises to the point that it interferes significantly with personal relationships or demands an exorbitant expenditure of energy just to cope, then, it is argued, appropriate measures may be taken to relieve that suffering, including heavy sedation or, in "hopeless" cases, active euthanasia. Viewed in this light, suffering is perceived as an enemy to be defeated or avoided by any means possible.

On the other hand, where quality of life considerations focus on the *relationship itself* between the patient's medical condition and his or her ability to pursue ultimate goals (rather than simply on the value or quality of relationships with others), then suffering assumes a very different aspect. If it is experienced within the limits of human tolerance, suffering can be decidedly *beneficial*, both for its direct effect on the patient and for its ability to foster communion with God and others.

Orthodox theologians approach the problem of suffering from a perspective rather different from that of St. Augustine or the Western scholastics. Eastern Church tradition views pain and suffering as evil consequences of the Fall, unintended by God but allowed as a kind of spiritual pedagogy. Generally speaking, suffering is not considered to be punishment for sin inflicted by a God of wrath, nor is it explained simply as a function of theodicy. Nor does Orthodox tradition understand suffering to be a condition or essential prerequisite, a necessary "price to pay," for our redemption and salvation. To recall the apostle Paul's assertion to the Corinthians, "You have been bought with a price!" That is, our redemption from the slavery of sin and death is accomplished entirely by Christ's own suffering and death. As the Suffering Servant foreshadowed in Isaiah 53, Christ bore his passion for us, on our behalf. Although we can share in his sufferings through acts of "martyrdom" or witness, such "works" are never understood to be the *condition* for our liberation from the consequences of sin and death.

And yet Orthodoxy also knows that human suffering can unquestionably possess what is called *redemptive value*. How, then, are we to explain the apparent contradiction which holds God to be the unique

Author of human life and redemption, yet views our active participation in the redemptive process to be indispensable? This leads us once again to the question of "synergy" and our response to God's work on our behalf. Perhaps we can best indicate the role of synergy as it involves suffering, particularly at the end stage of life, in the following way.

Created in the "image" of God, human persons are called to grow toward the divine "likeness," to assume the very qualities or virtues of divine life itself. This process of growth toward *theosis* or deification is nevertheless the result of God's own initiative, the free gift of his unbounded love. The sanctifying, deifying grace that effects the transfiguration of human existence consists of divine *energeia*, "energies" or attributes of God, infused into the personal life of the believer through the action of the Holy Spirit.

Divine initiative, however, must be complemented by human initiative.[16] *Theosis*, accordingly, is the result of the human will working with the divine will in the process of synergy, or cooperation between God and his human creatures. Its purpose is to lead the human person back to the primal state of perfection mythically depicted in the creation story of Genesis 2-3. This "primal state" is prelapsarian, untainted by sin and consequent death.

This implies that death is an anomaly within the created order. It is an unwilled and unintended intrusion into earthly affairs that must be overcome if human life is to attain its true potential and its true goal. While the death of the physical organism may be considered either a blessing to bring an end to man's alienation from God, or as a natural and necessary part of the life cycle,[17] it remains from the point of view of Orthodox theology and experience a spiritual enemy that is as much a *cause* of human sin as it is a consequence of it.[18] Insofar as the dread of death provokes rebellion, aggression and alienation from God and other persons, it leads to a multitude of sinful behaviors, all of which are "attempts to fill voids" of

16 See our discussion of Orthodox anthropology in chapter 1.
17 See the article by Leon Kass, "Averting One's Eyes, or Facing the Music?—On Dignity and Death," in *On Moral Medicine*, pp. 200-211, esp. 206 on "Death as Natural."
18 In addition to our discussion in chapter 1 above, see the articles by D. Weaver, published in *SVTQ* vols. 27/3 (1983) and 29/2-3 (1985) under the title "The Exegesis of Romans 5:12 Among the Greek Fathers and Its Implications for the Doctrine of Original Sin: the Fifth to the Twelfth Centuries"; and John Meyendorff, *Byzantine Theology* (New York: Fordham University Press, 1974), 143-146.

meaninglessness and threatened annihilation. The dread of death, in other words, is a primary motivator of our behavior. Consequently, death itself can hardly be considered as morally neutral.

God has chosen us not for death, but for life, whose *telos* or ultimate goal is eternal communion with the Persons of the Holy Trinity. From a Christian perspective, this means that *our true death and rebirth occur at our baptism*: the moment we are plunged into the regenerating "waters of the Jordan" and, in the name of the Holy Trinity, are raised up and united to the communion of saints, both living and dead, who constitute the Body of the glorified Lord. Therefore it might be argued that because of the Cross of Christ, physical death no longer threatens us. It has lost its sting. The "last enemy" has been transformed into a welcome passage, a glorious Pascha, leading to everlasting life and joy.

As true as this may be, however, the "last enemy" continues to hold sway over us in the form of the *dying process*. Anticipation of prolonged and meaningless suffering, far more than the event of death itself, is the chief cause of anxiety and despair for the terminally ill.

This perspective on death and the dying process has profoundly shaped the Orthodox understanding of suffering, as it has the question of care for those who are facing imminent death. It provides the insight that enables us to perceive and accept suffering, both mental and physical, as truly "redemptive."

The spiritual exploits of the desert fathers and other Christian ascetics testify eloquently to the reality of "redemptive suffering." Certain forms of physical and mental suffering, distinct from but often associated with pain, can further spiritual growth in numerous ways. In the first place, they make undeniable the reality of our own sin, frailty and susceptibility to temptation. Unlike Job, our patience is limited, and suffering presents us with the constant temptation to "curse God and die." Yet insofar as we can accept and embrace our inability to save ourselves, or even to endure certain intensities of pain and emotional distress, we can, like Job, obey the God-given impulse to throw ourselves on the divine mercy as our only source of hope and strength. Then again, by forcing us to choose constantly between God and despair, suffering can attain the quality of an ascetic discipline, overcoming the destructive passions of both flesh and spirit.

These aspects are common to all forms of suffering, whatever our life circumstances may be. In the case of persons who are afflicted with disease, and especially the terminally ill, mental and physical suffering (again, as distinct from but closely related to the matter of pain) can be experienced as "redemptive," as actually promoting spiritual growth, in the following specific ways.

1. Suffering can make us aware of our total dependence on the inexhaustible love and mercy of God. Like no other experience known to us, it focuses our attention on our weakness and vulnerability, and on God as the unique source of mercy, grace and ultimate healing.

2. As a corollary, suffering can bring a heightened self-consciousness and, with it, an awareness of our personal limitations. More than perhaps any other experience, pain and suffering signal the fact that we are *not in control.* This is a profoundly humbling experience, one that can lead either to despair or to previously unknown heights of faith and hope.

3. Suffering can also have the effect of purging and purifying the passions, that is, the desires and deceptions that corrupt our relationship with God, with others, and with ourselves. At the same time, it draws our attention to the present moment, forces us to reorder our priorities, and invites us to seek above all "the one thing needful" (Luke 10:42).

4. Suffering also brings awareness of our mortality. In Christian monastic tradition, the monk rises to pray with the admonition, "Remember death!" There is nothing morbid about the memory of death. Rather, it is a joyful expression of hope, based on the conviction that by his death, Christ has once and for all destroyed the power of death.

5. Suffering can also foster ecclesial communal ties with others on whom we depend. In return, their own spiritual growth can be enhanced by the experience of sharing another's pain through their prayer and gestures of care.

6. Finally, suffering offers the possibility to share in the life and saving mission of the crucified and risen Lord. For the dying patient, this means to take up one's cross and to follow Christ to his own passion and death. To endure one's suffering for the sake of Christ, in the certainty that one will rise with him into the fullness of life, is also to offer to others the most eloquent and effective witness or *martyria* possible.

It is this last aspect that prompts some theologians to affirm that the suffering which accompanies the dying process should be experienced to the fullest extent that one can tolerate. This is extreme. It runs the risk of absolutizing suffering by seeking it for its own sake. There is no point to suffering—it possesses no redemptive value whatsoever—as a phenomenon unto itself. *Only when pain and anguish are surrendered into the loving and merciful hands of God can they have ultimate meaning and value.* Otherwise they all too easily lead either to despair or to a perverse form of pride, a kind of spiritual masochism or auto-idolatry. We need to keep in mind the *vicarious* nature of Christ's suffering. He voluntarily offered his life *for us*, on our behalf, to accomplish what we could not do for ourselves. This said, however, it remains true that where physical pain and mental anguish are borne with courage and the desire to assimilate them to the Lord's passion, they are unquestionably vested with "redemptive value."

Not all suffering, however, is redemptive. Beyond a certain point, severe physical pain or protracted mental anguish can break down the will and thwart the best intentions of the heart. Many have experienced it as simply "dehumanizing," depriving them of hope and leaving them focused on nothing but their own misery. Such suffering can be produced by factors exterior to us and beyond our control: torture, excessive physical pain due to an illness, or mental anguish brought on by external threats. Newborn infants afflicted with genetic disorders such as myelomeningocele or Lesch-Nyhan syndrome (hyperuricemia, which causes uncontrollable urges toward self-mutilation), adults suffering from amyotrophic lateral sclerosis (ALS: "Lou Gehrig's Disease") or pancreatic cancer, and third-degree burn victims of any age, can be so consumed with physical distress and excruciating pain that life itself becomes a permanent, unrelieved burden. In such cases, the ability of the patient to pursue life goals or to perceive transcendent meaning often vanishes.

Researchers have become particularly aware in recent years that other forms of suffering can be equally degrading and apparently devoid of redemptive quality. Our individual susceptibility to mental anguish is as important a factor as our threshold of pain in determining how we will react to various intensities of suffering. Not everyone is a St. Ignatius, prepared psychologically and spiritually to brave a martyr's death in the arena. Pain thresholds are relative, but both genetic and environmental factors seem to play a role in their development. Victims of child abuse,

for example, or persons who have experienced severe loss or abandonment, can be so deeply wounded that the very fear of increased suffering—perceived as further punishment—can provoke uncontrollable
dread and hopelessness. Then there are the elderly infirm who suffer both
from their physical ailment and from the loss of a beloved spouse. Their
grief is deep and at times unbearable. Too often they feel abandoned not
only by the deceased, but by family, friends, and the parish community.
For Sartre, hell may have been "other people." For the aged who are desperately sick and desperately lonely, hell is their own pain and their own
solitude. With no realistic hope that their physical condition will improve, they tend to spiral downward into depression and finally despair.
Once their condition becomes serious enough, they often see "physician-
assisted suicide" as their only ray of hope, their only way out.

The most serious and dangerous temptation of those faced with mental or physical suffering is that they perceive their affliction to be absurd
and devoid of ultimate meaning. To the Eastern Church Fathers, however, convinced as they were that God is at the origin of all human life and
experience, suffering is perceived as a function of God's plan of salvation.
To their mind, suffering always has *redemptive potential.* Yet to affirm this,
we need to be clear that God does not inflict suffering as vengeful retribution or vindictive punishment for our sin. Although he uses pain and mis-
fortune as part of a "divine pedagogy," we cannot simply assume that God
"wills" tragedy in human experience. In the ninth chapter of St. John's
Gospel, Jesus affirms unequivocally that suffering and guilt are by no
means necessarily connected. God *allows* tragedy, yes. But that does not
mean that one suffers in direct proportion to one's sinfulness. In the
morning prayer of the Optino Fathers referred to earlier, we beseech God
to "teach me to treat all that comes to me throughout the day...with firm
conviction that thy will governs all... In unforeseen events, let me not forget that all are sent by thee." Yet it is unthinkable that the God of mercy
and compassion should will—in the sense of want or desire—torture, ter-
rorist bombings, or the tragedy of death itself. If we affirm that "nothing
occurs apart from the will of God," then we must likewise insist upon a
fundamental distinction between what God *wills* and what he desires, in-
tends or permits; that is, between his "accepting will" and his "intentional
will." God does not desire that his creatures, however rebellious they may

be, should be victims of dehumanizing suffering. Yet in the unfathomable mystery of the divine economy, he may indeed "will" such experiences.[19]

It is this awareness that leads the Church Fathers to seek an explanation of the origin of evil and suffering in man's rebellion against the divine will, in his relentless quest for self-destructive "pleasure" rather than for authentic joy.[20] St. Maximus the Confessor, for example, attributes suffering to the Fall and declares that its purpose is to cleanse the soul from "the filth of sensual pleasure" and to "detach it from material things." This, he adds, "is why God in his justice allows the devil to afflict men with torments."[21] As the prologue to the Book of Job indicates, even if God wills that affliction come upon men, the actual agent by which that affliction occurs is not God himself, but Satan, the Adversary and Tempter.

The consensus among the Fathers, then, is that suffering originates with the divine will and that it has, potentially, the capacity to purify human persons from sinful passions and restore them to communion with God. The fifth century ascetic Mark the Hermit expresses this truth in the following concise way: "The mercy of God is hidden in sufferings not of our choice; and if we accept such sufferings patiently, they bring us to repentance and deliver us from everlasting punishment."[22] "Let all involuntary suffering teach you to remember God," he adds, "and you will not lack occasion for repentance."[23]

---

19 Palladius' early fifth century *Lausiac History* expresses this distinction in the following way: "Two causes are responsible for every event: either the will of God, or His permission. Everything that takes place in conformity with virtue occurs by the will of God, whereas everything that produces damage and danger as a result of unhappy circumstances or weakness, occurs by God's permission" (47.5).

20 Hilary of Poitiers († 367) makes a basic distinction between suffering and pain, the former being a function of human nature, the latter a secondary—we might say, "accidental"—aspect of human experience. Therefore he can hold that Christ in his incarnate body "felt the force of suffering, but without its pain." "He had a body to suffer," Hilary continues, "but he did not have a nature [weak as ours from sin] which could feel pain." (*de Trinitate X.23; NPNF* vol. 9, 187f.). Hilary has often been accused of holding a docetist or monophysite Christology. His purpose, however, is to affirm that physical pain—as distinguished from suffering—is a consequence of sin, therefore of fallen human nature. The implication is that Christ perfected that nature by uniting it to his "unique" (i.e., divine) nature. Thus he could truly *suffer*, and thereby accomplish our redemption, but without feeling *pain*. Similar reflection led to the belief, expressed in aspects of the Church's liturgical tradition, that the *Theotokos* or Mother of God experienced no pain when she gave birth to her Son.

21 St. Maximus the Confessor, *Philokalia* vol. 2, 178, no. 64.

22 *Philokalia* vol. 1, 136, no. 139.

23 *Philokalia* vol. 1, 114, no. 57. Compare 1 Pet 4:1, "whoever has suffered in the flesh has ceased from sin..."

Christian stewardship obliges us to accept personal suffering and to seek spiritual healing through it. Even though our "outer nature" may be "wasting away," as the suffering apostle knew, "our inner nature is being renewed every day" (2 Cor 4:16). Within the limits of tolerance, certain levels of pain and hardship can serve as spiritual blessings which promote inner peace and strength, the strength that emerges in the midst of our weakness (2 Cor 12:9-10). As St. Paul further declares, "It has been granted to you that for the sake of Christ you should not only believe in him but also suffer for his sake" (Phil 1:29). Here the apostle is referring specifically to persecution. Nevertheless, as in the following well-known passage from his letter to the Romans, his aim is to stress to his readers the redemptive, sanctifying value of suffering courageously endured.

> We rejoice in our sufferings, knowing that suffering produces endurance, and endurance produces character, and character produces hope, and hope does not disappoint us, because God's love has been poured into our hearts through the Holy Spirit which has been given to us. (Rom 5:3-5)

It is precisely that quality and abundance of divine love that enable the sufferer, according to Christ's own admonition, to "endure to the end" (Mt 10:22; Mk 13:13).

Over thirty years ago an American monk, who himself has known considerable physical suffering, translated a small book by Archimandrite Seraphim Papakostas, entitled *For the Hours of Pain*. It contains a lesson that bears repeating:

> If Christ had to march to glory, through sufferings, is it strange that we his followers must do the same? If the absolutely sinless and holy One, upon whom affliction and pain had no claim, passed through every measure of affliction and pain for our sake, is it strange that all those who are being sanctified through Him need to be cleansed and purified in the crucible?

> Learn this, then, dear Christian. If man had not sinned, if we weren't sinners, we would certainly march to divine glory without afflictions and sufferings. Now, however, there is no other way to this glory, but through suffering and pain. The leader of our salvation Himself, marched on that road.[24]

When tragedy strikes, bringing in its wake inconsolable pain and distress, our most natural response is to question God's purpose and the depths of our own faith. The age-old question, "why do bad things hap-

---

24 Athens: Zoe Brotherhood, 1967, 43.

pen to good people?," seems unanswerable. Theologians respond by speaking of "theodicy." The suffering layman, on the other hand, wants to know how to reconcile his belief in the omnipotence of God with the biblical claim that "God is love." If God is all-powerful, and if he is indeed a loving God, how can he permit *me* to know such affliction? And particularly if the intensity of my suffering is such that I can no longer pray, because my mind and body are totally focused on what I experience as unbearable. If I can direct my thoughts toward God at all, it seems, it is only with frustration, anger and rebellion.

Whatever the immediate cause and nature of our suffering, we need to bear in mind two things. On the one hand, suffering is always communal, that is, *ecclesial.* It involves the whole Body of Christ, since we are "members of one another" (Rom 12:5). This means that the redemptive value inherent in our suffering can also contribute to the salvation of other persons in addition to ourselves. Just as our sinfulness leaves its mark on the entire Body, our suffering—insofar as it is accepted in faith and offered to God in love—can transform others within that Body. How this occurs is a mystery that no one in this life will ever fathom. *That* it occurs, however, is a matter of ecclesial experience. Even there where suffering seems to be meaningless and unbearable, the very act of surrendering it to God, in faith and in love, enables the one who suffers to participate directly and intimately in Christ's own crucifixion. The angels at the Tomb identified the risen Lord as "the Crucified One" (*ho estaurômenos,* Mk 16:6; Mt 28:5); and the French Catholic philosopher Pascal echoed this message when he declared, "Christ is in agony until the end of the world." The Risen Lord remains forever the Crucified One. Those who are united to him, then, are united as well to his once-for-all crucifixion, whose meaning and power endure throughout the ages. Although Christ's passion and death have fully accomplished the world's redemption, our personal affliction—offered as a sacrifice of praise and thanksgiving for the gift of life he has bestowed upon us—can become the means by which we are united with him and with all those who courageously and faithfully bear their own affliction. Suffering, therefore, can become an effective means for creating a deep and intimate communion with Christ and with the afflicted members of his Body.

Yet a second point needs to be made as well. Our suffering not only enables us to participate in the passion and crucifixion of Christ. It also provides a primary means for Christ to participate in the reality of our own "sickness unto death." Despite what may appear to be an element of the absurd—an utter lack of meaning and purpose—in our affliction, the biblical and patristic witness is unequivocal: *God accompanies us in our suffering.* He is not only aware of it; he shares it to the full, he drinks its bitter cup to the dregs. Thereby he transforms our meaningless anguish into a truly redemptive experience.

This is true, even where the person is incapable of sensing that redemptive quality because of the intensity of mental or physical pain, or because they have entered into a coma or persistent vegetative state. In this case, it is the responsibility and the privilege of the Church—the family and parish community—to "assume" the person, through their prayer and love. Thereby they do what the person cannot do for him or herself, namely offer their suffering and their very life to the grace and mercy of God. This is the gesture that most faithfully responds to the petition of our litanies: "Let us commend ourselves *and each other,* and all our life to Christ our God."

In cases where the afflicted person is incapable of experiencing his or her own suffering as redemptive, there nevertheless remains what can be termed "vicarious redemptive suffering," accomplished through the presence and sanctifying power of the Crucified One, as well as through the presence, intercession and love of others who share the afflicted person's burden. This complementarity, this synergy of love and mercy between Christ and other persons, can thereby transform human suffering from a cruel mockery of our frailty and a judgment on our sinfulness, into a vehicle for our sanctification and a promise of eternal blessedness to come. He who endures to the end—by bearing his own affliction with courage and hope, or by allowing others to bear it for him in prayer and love—that person "shall be saved" (Mk 13:13).

When viewed in this perspective, in the radiant light of Christ's own sacrificial passion and death, it is clear that virtually *all* suffering is potentially redemptive. The corporate prayer and solidarity of members of Christ's Body can make of even the most "meaningless" tragedy a witness to the Cross and to the truth that Life has triumphed over death.

Euthanasia and the Care of the Terminally Ill

What do reflections of this kind imply with regard to life-support for the terminally ill? Can "quality of life" considerations ever justify "active euthanasia," whether in the form of direct medical intervention or of physician-assisted suicide?

The Meaning of "a Good Death."
The Park Ridge Center publication, *Choosing Death*, includes several statements by Orthodox ethicists on the matter of active euthanasia, the intentional medical termination of a human life.[25] They reflect a consensus that has emerged in recent years and can be summarized as follows. 1) Human life, created by God and bearing the divine image, is sacred by its very nature and must always be respected and protected as such. 2) The principle of stewardship demands that the moment of death, like that of conception, remain in the hands of God; he alone is sovereign over life, death and the dying process. There is "a time to live and a time to die," and that time must remain God's determination. 3) Every effort must be made to restore the patient to an optimal state of health; the patient's life, however, retains its irreducible value and worth, even when full health cannot be restored. 4) In cases of terminal illness (where the dying process is irreversible and death is imminent), it is nevertheless permissible to withhold or withdraw life-support that represents nothing more than a burden to the patient. Particularly in cases of brain-death, it is immoral—and not merely "useless"—to maintain the patient on life-support systems.[26] 5) On the other hand, there can be no justification for

25 Ron Hamel, ed., *Choosing Death. Active Euthanasia, Religion and the Public Debate* (Philadelphia: Trinity Press, 1991), 90-95. Without careful reading the passage could give the impression that "Eastern," "Greek" and "Russian" views represent distinct denominations. Orthodox Christians of any ethnic origin, however, speak out of a common tradition that is informed by common liturgical celebration, creedal confessions and sacramental experience.
26 In the words of Fr. Stanley Harakas, who is widely recognized as the "dean" of Orthodox ethicists in the United States today: "when over-arching evidence supports a prognosis that the patient is terminally ill, the practitioner, the individual patient, the family and all others associated with the situation are not morally obligated, and ought not to feel obligated, to expend energy, time and resources in a misdirected effort to fend off death." (*Choosing Death*, 92). Note that "resources" is included in this burden-benefit assessment. See further his statement in *Living the Faith. The Praxis of Eastern Orthodox Ethics* (Minneapolis: Light & Life Publishing, 1992), 129: "The medical use of drugs, surgical operations, and even artificial organs are legitimately used when there is a reasonable expectation that they will aid the return in due time to normal or close to normal functioning of the whole organic system. Their use is therapeutic. However,

the active taking of (innocent) human life, even in cases of terminal illness accompanied by severe suffering.[27] Active euthanasia, including physician-assisted suicide, is therefore forbidden by an Orthodox ethic, whether or not the patient expresses the desire to die, that is, whether or not there is informed consent.[28]

The rationale behind these conclusions is essentially theological. Fr. Stanley Harakas declares, "The only 'good death' for the Orthodox Christian is the peaceful acceptance of the end of his or her earthly life with faith and trust in God and the promise of the Resurrection."[29] A litany from Orthodox liturgical services includes a petition that asks for "a Christian ending to our life, painless, blameless and peaceful." And the prayers offered for one who is dying request "the peaceful separation of soul and body." A "good death," then, is one that preserves a maximum of consciousness with a minimum of suffering, together with the peaceful surrender of one's life into the merciful hands of God.

Traditional Orthodox piety expresses the desire to be spared from "a sudden death." To most Americans today, such a request is incomprehensible: "Let it be swift, clean, and if possible, in my sleep..." A genuinely Christian attitude, on the other hand, recognizes the need to prepare for death: to allow time for the dying patient to seek reconciliation and fellowship with family members and friends, time to seek reconciliation with God through confession, and time for a final communion in the life-giving Body and Blood of Christ. This need to prepare for the end of earthly existence is what explains the frequency of prayers in the Ortho-

there is an ethical limit to their use. The discrete organs may be artificially aided to function when the total organic system has ceased functioning. If, especially, there is no evidence of brain activity in conjunction with the systemic breakdown, we can safely say that the patient is no longer alive in any religiously significant way. Only certain organs are functioning. In this case the use of artificial means to keep organs functioning is wrong." This crucial distinction between the death of the *whole* organism and death of the organism *as a whole* offers a key to the difficult issue, which we discuss further on, of patients in deep coma or PVS.

27   The qualification "innocent" is needed here, since Orthodox Christians are divided over questions of capital punishment and participation in warfare.

28   From this perspective, it is appalling to most of us that the debate has so swiftly shifted from the morality of PAS in cases of repeated demand on the part of the patient, to the question of the "morality" of terminating the lives of those who do not or can not express such consent. See, for example, Gerrit van der Wal, "Unrequested Termination of Life: Is it Permissible?", *Bioethics*, vol. 7, no. 4 (1993), 330-339. The author answers his title question with a qualified "yes."

29   S. Harakas, *Contemporary Moral Issues Facing the Orthodox Christian* (Minneapolis: Light & Life Publishing, 1982), 176. Quoted as well in *Choosing Death*, 94.

dox tradition that implore God, "Lord, spare me from an unexpected death!" To "die well," then, requires *time* as much as it requires inner peace, appropriate care, and love.

What does this imply with respect to particular case situations and the establishment of protocols to provide appropriate medical care at the end of life?

Both Roman Catholic and Orthodox ethicists today generally accept as morally "licit" a decision to remove life-support systems in terminal cases, when such removal clearly represents the desire of the patient and continued usage would serve no demonstrable good (an evaluation made on the basis of "futility" and the "burden-benefit" ratio).[30] This leaves us, however, with a problem of definition: what determines a "terminal illness," and does suspending life-support constitute "euthanasia?"

A "terminally ill" patient is usually defined as one having a prognosis of less than six months to live. This is so broad that it would seem more appropriate to define the "terminally ill" patient as one who, according to professional medical opinion, is engaged in irreversible biological processes that will lead to imminent death.

Catholic and Orthodox ethicists are also in basic agreement that removing life-support under these conditions does not constitute "euthanasia" as that term is used today. The expression "euthanasia" originally meant simply "a good death." In recent years, however, it has become so closely identified with the eugenics movement on the one hand, and with the Kevorkian syndrome on the other, that it would perhaps be best to discard it altogether. With recent technological developments and our inability to draw a clear distinction between active therapeutic intervention into the dying process and merely "allowing nature to take its course" while providing pain management and other palliative care, it would be better to forego as well the terms "active" and "passive" euthanasia. Where "euthanasia" signifies "to put an end to a patient's life by a specific act," then neither Orthodox nor Roman Catholic traditions can sanction such an act.

---

30 On this issue see the essays by R. McCormick, "To Save or Let Die: The Dilemma of Modern Medicine," and, (with R. Veatch), "The Preservation of Life and Self-determination," in *How Brave a New World? Dilemmas in Bioethics* (Washington, DC: Georgetown University Press, 1981) 339-351 and 381-389; S. Harakas, *Contemporary Moral Issues* (Minneapolis: Light & Life Publishing, 1982) 170-173; and J. Breck, "Selective Non-treatment of the Terminally Ill," in *St. Vladimir's Theological Quarterly*, 33/3 (1989), 261-272.

Nearly twenty years ago Catholic ethicists published a document on "euthanasia" which held that the term is ambiguous, misleading, and should be avoided in reference to certain actions and decisions concerning end-of-life care. Although the Orthodox have not made a formal pronouncement about the term itself, the Roman Catholic position on the matter is thoroughly compatible with an Orthodox understanding of so-called "mercy killing." The word "euthanasia," they argue, should be used

1) neither to designate the actions involved in *terminal care* which aim at making the last phase of an illness less unbearable (dehydration, nursing care, massage, palliative medication, keeping the dying person company...);

2) nor to designate the decision to stop certain medical therapies which no longer seem to be required by the condition of the patient. (Traditional language would have expressed this as "the decision to give up extraordinary measures.") It is thus not a matter of deciding to let the patient die but, rather, of using technical resources proportionately following a reasonable course suggested by prudence and good judgment;

3) nor to designate an action taken to relieve the suffering of the patient at the risk of perhaps shortening his life. This sort of action is part of a doctor's calling: his vocation is not only that of curing diseases or prolonging life but—much more generally—also that of taking care of a sick person and relieving his suffering."[31]

An important element in the "right to die" debate has recently surfaced in the medical literature, while being curiously neglected by the popular media. It concerns the recent Supreme Court ruling that rejects physician-assisted suicide (*Washington v. Glucksberg*, 117 S. Ct. 2258 [1997]). Writing in *The New England Journal of Medicine*,[32] Yale Law School professor Robert A. Burt points out that the Court's decision to uphold New York and Washington statutes prohibiting assisted suicide "effectively required all states to ensure that their laws do not obstruct the provision of adequate palliative care, especially for the alleviation of pain and other physical symptoms of people facing death...By authoritatively pronouncing that terminal sedation intended for symptomatic relief is not assisted suicide, the Court has licensed an aggressive practice of palliative care."[33]

31 Statement, published by the Vatican Press in 1981, entitled "Question of Ethics Regarding the Fatally Ill and the Dying," in *Medical Ethics: Sources of Catholic Teachings*, 116.
32 Vol. 337, no.17, 23 October, 1997, 1234-1236.
33 *Ibid.*, 1234.

The Supreme Court, in other words, has upheld "a Constitutional right to palliative care," while rejecting the active intervention of assisted suicide.[34] This is a significant development, in that it removes one of the major barriers to effective pain management, namely the attending physician's fear of a law suit if he or she resorts to opioids that might shorten the life span of a terminally ill patient.[35] Palliative care in clearly terminal cases where metastasized cancer or other conditions cause intolerable and refractory pain and suffering may include even "terminal sedation," where respect is paid to the principle of double effect. This, once again, is not "euthanasia." It is a morally appropriate—indeed, imperative—treatment offered in those cases where the only alternative is to allow the patient to die in protracted anguish and misery.

Thus neither palliative care, nor withholding or withdrawing life-support in "futile" cases, nor administering adequate pain medication, even when it might slightly shorten the patient's life (as with morphine and other opiates), constitutes "euthanasia." Here once again the principle of "double effect" comes into play. The intention is not to kill the patient or to limit his or her life span. It is to provide the patient with comfort and other appropriate care, so that the dying process will lead, as much as possible, to "a painless, blameless and peaceful" end.

If the terminally ill patient has declared, either through a Living Will or via a health-care proxy, that he or she wants no "extraordinary" means used *which would merely prolong the dying process*, then we are morally obliged to respect that request. The same is true of a "DNR" ("Do Not Resuscitate") order recorded on a patient's chart. The *principle of patient autonomy* requires such respect from the care providers, the family, and any others who may be concerned, including the law courts. Otherwise we lapse into a form of "paternalism," which presupposes that the medical team or some other party is more capable than the patient of making health-care decisions and of determining what is in the patient's best interest.

34 Burt cites Justice Sandra Day O'Connor's concurring opinion that adds: "I agree that the State's interests in protecting those who are not truly competent or facing imminent death, or those whose decisions to hasten death would not truly be voluntary, are sufficiently weighty to justify a prohibition against physician-assisted suicide," *ibid.*, 1235.
35 Burt adds, "Armed with their patients' constitutional right to adequate palliative care, physicians could protect themselves in judicial forums against state regulatory boards ignorant or dismissive of the evidence that high-dosage prescriptions of opioids for treating pain and other distressing symptoms are safe, effective, and appropriate," *ibid.*, 1236.

The traditional notion of "paternalism" tended to stress patients' perceived *needs* rather than their *rights*. It was assumed that the medical team was in a better position than the patient to assess those needs and consequently to determine the most appropriate treatment. With the development of life-support technology, and the conflicting values of a pluralistic society, ethicists have proposed a "weak" or limited paternalism that respects the need for *informed consent* on the part of the patient, together with *patient autonomy*, while recognizing that in certain instances intervention might be needed to prevent the patient from self-harm (e.g., from committing suicide). Respect for personal freedom or autonomy needs to be balanced by concern for the patient's roles and responsibilities within social, family and church communities. This concern justifies some limited forms of paternalism. Such paternalism, however, should be persuasive rather than coercive.

A "good death," then, requires both physical care and spiritual nurture. It can be achieved on the one hand by guaranteeing to the patient both informed consent and autonomy, the freedom to make his or her own choices regarding end-of-life treatment, and on the other hand by providing loving *accompaniment* of the dying person through the presence of family and friends. Ultimately, it requires that the community of the Church exercise its priestly function by *offering* the dying person to God in prayer, through gestures of love, compassion and intercession on his or her behalf.

Pain Management.
Proper treatment of the terminally ill demands not only that they be able to give their informed consent and that their autonomy be respected. It also requires that they be given *adequate pain medication*. Techniques for pain management are so sophisticated today that few patients need to suffer unbearable pain and distress. When they do, it is usually because they are being given inadequate medical care. Yet a great deal remains to be done toward the research and development, as well as the appropriate administration, of pain-killing drugs. This is a crucial issue that has been largely neglected, even in medical schools.[36] One of the great dangers

---

36 Note the remarks of Gregg A. Kasting, "The Nonnecessity of Euthanasia," in *Biomedical Ethics Reviews* 1993 (Totowa, NJ: Humana Press, 1994), 24-45: "The argument that assisted death is unnecessary cannot be made on the claim that pain in terminal illness is amenable in full or in part to presently available analgesics and anesthetic techniques...[T]he empirical

with passage of legislation such as Oregon's Measure 16 is that it will relieve medical researchers of what today is perhaps their primary obligation: to develop a wide variety of pain management techniques that are effective, inexpensive, and readily available.

Although in Canada and Western Europe morphine and other drugs can be given freely to alleviate chronic or acute pain, the same is far from universally true in the United States. Advances in pain management have been hampered in this country by laws that prohibit certain drugs from being used medicinally at all. The most obvious of these is heroin. Because of the widespread, devastating use of street drugs, we are reluctant to consider measures that have become routine in other countries: use of the heroin- or morphine-based "Brompton's cocktail," used so effectively in the St. Christopher hospices in England, for example, and other less potent drugs such as marijuana. (Developed for terminal illness therapy, the Brompton's cocktail is an alcohol solution with morphine or heroin, plus codeine and an optional tranquilizer. Its value lies in the fact that tolerance to it does not develop. In addition, it has been observed that patients who self-medicate with the cocktail require lower dosages than other patients, apparently because they are "in control": as their level of anxiety decreases, so does their level of perceived physical pain.)

It is entirely unreasonable to argue, as many people do, that drugs which are adequate for pain management may not be used in terminal cases because they are addictive. This is especially true if by "terminal" we mean patients already engaged in the dying process. In cases of increasingly debilitating terminal disease—for example, throat tumors, bone and colon cancer, advanced multiple sclerosis, AIDS—compassion and elementary respect for the dying person require that any and all available measures be used to relieve the pain that can lead to hopelessness and despair. We need to remember that the dread of death is in many cases dread of the dying process and its attendant physical suffering. Adequate pain management, therefore, should be given the highest priority, to relieve the

claim that all terminal pain is relievable is not supported by the medical literature" (41). In the same volume, David C. Thomasma, "The Ethics of Physician-Assisted Suicide," 93-133, addresses the responsibility of medical specialists to intensify their efforts to provide adequate care to the terminally ill: to prescribe more adequate pain control, but also "to be more engaged with the dying patient as a person," through the development of hospices and medical school programs that offer specific training in care for the dying.

patient's anxiety and guarantee that his final days and hours be spent in a state of tranquil alertness, with a minimum of physical distress.[37]

PVS, Deep Coma and "Brain Death."

To this point we have presumed that the dying patients are conscious, that they experience no more than a tolerable level of pain and distress, and that appropriate caregivers, including family and clergy, are present to minister to their needs. But what of those who are not conscious, who have slipped into a deep and, according to the best diagnosis, irreversible coma, or who exist in a persistent vegetative state?[38]

"Deep coma" is a state of profound unconsciousness characterized by complete unresponsiveness to external stimuli. In severe and prolonged cases, avoidance reflexes tend to disappear altogether. It is caused by an interruption—provoked by accident, illness or ingested poisons—in the interaction between the cognitive functions of the cerebral hemispheres and the arousal mechanisms of the reticular formation, a system of nerve cells and fibers, located primarily in the midbrain and upper brain stem.[39] The condition is usually irreversible, as in the celebrated cases of Karen Ann Quinlan and Elaine Esposito. Quinlan was a permanently comatose patient who died in June, 1985, more than nine years after she was taken off a respirator.[40] Esposito, who was comatose for more than thirty-seven years after receiving general anesthesia, died without ever regaining consciousness. The major ethical question raised by these two cases is the same. Did modern medical technology such as artificial feeding and hydration actually keep these women "alive"? Or did it merely prolong the process, begun with their respective accidents, that would inevitably lead to their death. Did life-

---

37 This line of reasoning holds as well with regard to the medical use of marijuana. Insofar as various illnesses, and particularly the nausea associated with chemotherapy, can be relieved by its use, it seems only reasonable to make it legally available under doctor's prescription. Certainly, tight controls have to be maintained, and strict penalties have to be applied if a physician orders the substance without sufficient medical justification. On the other hand, it is unconscionable that many ordinary American citizens have to take to the streets in quest of a drug dealer who can provide them with the only medication that offers them effective relief.

38 For a description of PVS, see "Deciding to Forego Life-Sustaining Treatment: A Report on the Ethical, Medical, and Legal Issues in Treatment Decisions," President's Commission Report (Washington, DC: US Government Printing Office, 1983).

39 For a discussion of coma and related conditions, see *The Merck Manual of Diagnosis and Therapy*, 15th ed. (Rahway, NJ: Merck Sharp & Dohme Research Laboratories, 1987), 1331ff.

40 See in this regard William J. Curran, "Defining Appropriate Medical Care: Providing Nutrients and Hydration for the Dying," in Th. Shannon, ed. *Bioethics*, 3rd ed. (New York: Paulist Press, 1987), 209-214.

support, in other words, actually maintain *life?* Or did it simply prolong the dying process? And if the latter, what does that imply about the moral obligation to provide nutrition and hydration to patients in deep coma?

Unlike patients in deep coma, the eyes of PVS patients are often open, and they seem to experience relatively normal sleep-wake cycles. Occasionally they emit sounds that others mistakenly take to be attempts to speak. The vegetative state is induced by damage to the cerebral hemispheres that deprives the person of any sense of self-awareness. Autonomic and motor reflexes, however, remain intact. The condition is often reversible, but once it has persisted for several months, complete recovery seems impossible. In early 1995 the media reported that Japanese researchers had succeeded in reviving a number of PVS patients by stimulating the midbrain. It is still too early to know whether this or similar techniques will offer a medical solution to the problem.

These issues of deep coma and PVS raise the question of just how we determine "death." Are patients in these conditions alive or dead? And what constitutes appropriate treatment in each case? The matter is complicated by the fact that medical texts often refer to PVS as "cerebral death."[41] This kind of language clearly stacks the deck against the interests of the patient, insofar as the conditions may be reversible. The question remains, however, whether irreversibly comatose or PVS patients should be regarded as "dead," and thus considered suitable candidates for the harvesting of vital organs. In any case, unless and until their actual death can be medically confirmed, it is imperative that they be considered and treated as living persons, however we may judge their "quality of life." What in fact is the quality of life of a comatose patient? Can the words of the maiden in the Song of Solomon possibly apply here: "I slept, but my heart was awake" (Song of Sol. 5:2)? Perhaps the abyss of unconsciousness is like the abyss of Sheol in the vision of the Psalmist: "If I ascend to heaven, Thou art there; if I make my bed in Sheol, Thou art there!" (Ps 138/139:8).

From a Christian perspective the most basic requirement for "personhood" is the unity of body and soul. However we may define "soul," it is clearly related to brain function (although it is certainly not limited to that). That is, once "brain death" occurs, the organism is dead. The ques-

41 *The Merck Manual*, 1335.

tion remains, though, as to how we define "brain death." To some, it means death of the *whole brain*: the brain stem, the limbic system and the cerebral cortex. The brain stem regulates such functions as breathing and heart rate,[42] while the limbic system (including the hypothalamus and pituitary gland) regulates eating, sleeping, balance and, in general, bodily homeostasis. The limbic system is also involved in various emotional responses such as the sex drive, the "fight-flight" mechanism, and overall self-protection. None of these functions, however, establishes distinctively *human*, or a fortiori *personal*, existence. The gift of human life depends rather on the cerebrum (left and right hemispheres) and its covering of nerve cells known as the cortex. The cortex enables us to make decisions, organize our lives, remember experiences, communicate with others, and perform various creative activities (art, music). It is here as well that our capacity for reflective activities resides: the ability to philosophize, to speculate, to wonder and to pray.

In cases where accident or disease have irreversibly destroyed higher brain or neocortical activity, we must conclude that the person in question is no longer alive. Bodily functions governed by the brain stem and limbic system do not constitute personal human existence: these are merely support systems for what makes us truly human, truly personal beings. Even if midbrain and brain stem functions (blood pressure and temperature, respiration) can be maintained by artificial means, the organism *as a whole* is no longer "alive" in any meaningful sense. In such cases, we can say that the biological mechanism is being sustained by technology that in effect replaces the human soul or life-force. If it can be determined, therefore, that *the death of the brain as a whole* has occurred, that the cortex does not and cannot function, then it is only reasonable to declare the patient dead.

It is this very determination, however, that has proven so difficult and has led many physicians and ethicists to insist that the patient be pronounced dead only in cases were there is *death of the whole brain*, meaning the brain stem as well as the cerebrum.[43] In this regard, however, we need

---

42 It appears that the cerebellum of the brain stem records some memories from learned responses. Most memories, however, are stored in the limbic system. The breakdown of this latter may be responsible for symptoms related to Alzheimer's Disease.

43 For a sound defense of this view from a nonreligious perspective, see David Lamb, *Death, Brain Death and Ethics* (New York: State University Press, 1985).

to hear the opinion of a leading Orthodox ethicist, H. Tristram Engelhardt. Concerning the criteria for death he states, "A human body that can only function biologically, without an inward mental life, does not sustain a moral agent...The death of a person marks the passing of an entity that can make promises and fashion strong moral claims. To underscore this point with regard to definitions of death: a body with whole-brain death, or with death of the whole brain except for the brain stem, does not support a mental life, much less the life of a person."[44] Personhood, in other words, requires the capacity for higher brain function. When that capacity is irretrievably lost, the "person" or "soul" is no longer present, and there is no longer *human* life in any meaningful sense. Attempts to sustain biological functioning in such cases are not simply futile. They are immoral. "The time to die" has come and gone, the soul has departed the body, and further "life-sustaining" treatment merely delays the "release" and "rest" requested by our prayers for the terminally ill.

Where does this leave us with regard to patients in deep coma or PVS? The literature on the subject is sharply divided. A growing consensus holds that food and water may be morally withheld or withdrawn from such persons precisely because they are only marginally "personal." This kind of approach, however, comes dangerously close to the misdirected "quality of life" thinking that evaluates the person's capacities and conditions, rather than the relationship between the effectiveness of treatment and the possibility for pursuing life goals.

A basic imperative, therefore, emerges from this debate: *every appropriate diagnostic procedure and treatment protocol should be used to bring about recovery.* From a Christian perspective, grounded in the principles of stewardship and the sacredness of life, this can be stated as the moral requirement to "choose life" (cf. Dt 30:19). In cases of PVS or deep coma, there must be a presumption of life and a bias towards life, as there must be in all cases where the patient is not demonstrably brain-dead. If it can be determined, however, that such a patient is indeed brain-dead—that cerebral and cortical functioning have been irretrievably lost—then it is medically accurate and morally appropriate to declare that the person has died. In

---

44 For an important discussion of this entire issue, see Engelhardt's *The Foundations of Bioethics* (2nd ed., New York: Oxford University Press, 1996), 239-287, on "The Endings and Beginnings of Persons: Death, Abortion and Infanticide." (Quotation, 242f).

cases of higher brain death, once again—even when lower brain function can be artificially maintained—either the soul has already departed from the body, or life-support measures are hindering it in its struggle to do so. In either case, it is morally imperative that we "let the person go."

Insofar as such a determination cannot be made with certainty in cases of PVS and deep coma, it would be morally wrong to remove the patient from life-support systems. Only when efforts to promote recovery have persistently failed, and there is clear evidence that neocortical function has been permanently lost, can withdrawal of food and hydration be considered morally acceptable.

This conclusion is based in part on consideration of the futility of treatment. But it finds its ultimate justification in the sacredness of life principle itself. If the United States is plummeting down the slippery slope today, it is largely because we have so dramatically and tragically distorted the meaning of death. From a Christian perspective, however, death has "lost its sting." By his own death, Christ has destroyed the power of death, transforming it into "Pascha," a passover or passage from life in the flesh to eternal life in the loving presence of God the Father.

> Death is swallowed up in victory. O death, where is thy victory? O death, where is thy sting? The sting of death is sin, and the power of sin is the law. But thanks be to God, who gives us the victory through our Lord Jesus Christ! (1 Cor. 15:54-57) [45]

Nutrition and Hydration for the Terminally Ill.
Another major question, raised in a particularly sharp way by Washington's Initiative 119 and Oregon's Measure 16, concerns a form of terminal life-support that has long been considered "ordinary" rather than "extraordinary." This is the matter of providing terminally ill patients with food and liquid through feeding and hydration (nasal-gastric) tubes. Until a few years ago I opposed very strongly the withdrawal of nutrition and hydration from dying patients, on grounds that food and water are necessary to sustain all life, and that our primary duty, especially to the terminally ill, is to provide them with these most basic necessities.[46] Nevertheless, in recent years a

45 In addition to this ancient Christian hymn, the apostle Paul offers a profound meditation on the meaning of death in his letter to the Romans, chs. 6-8.
46 For a similar opinion, see Gilbert Meilaender, "On Removing Food and Water: Against the Stream," in Th. Shannon, *Bioethics* (3rd. ed., 1987), pp. 215-222. To his mind, withholding or withdrawing food and hydration comes perilously close to "aiming to kill." On the other

number of scientific articles, published by both nurses and physicians, have led me to reconsider the question. Nurses have long noticed how frequently dying patients tear out naso-gastric tubes and I-V lines. Previously when this happened, the medical team assumed that the patient was suffering from acute mental or emotional stress. Therefore they quickly replaced the tubes and often strapped down the patient's arms and hands to assure that the tubes would remain in place.

Recently, however, it has been determined that in terminal cases—where the patient is clearly, quickly and irreversibly approaching death—dehydration and the withholding of food has a definitely beneficial effect. Dehydration, in particular, allows for a rapid increase in the production of "keytones." These are chemical substances in the brain that act as a natural analgesic. Similarly, dehydration and malnutrition in terminally ill patients causes "azotemia," in which elevated waste nitrogen products in the blood act as a natural sedative, thereby decreasing the sensation of pain. In the words of one researcher,

> "The technological imperative to have patients die in electrolyte balance and well-hydrated is a grave disservice. It serves only to ward off the sedative effect of the azotemia. The result not only increases pain perception, but also adds to the mental agony of the patient who is kept alert enough to appreciate the minute-by-minute hopelessness of his or her situation."[47]

Moreover, it has been shown that continued hydration also increases the level of pain and discomfort experienced by the terminally ill also by complicating various renal, pulmonary and gastrointestinal functions.[48]

Withholding food and water from a dying patient permits the shutdown of cellular activity throughout the body and normally allows the patient to slip quietly into a coma and die. It seems appropriate, then, that we add use of hydration, nasal-gastric and gastrointestinal tubes to

hand, Jacquelyn Slomka, "What Do Apple Pie and Motherhood Have to Do With Feeding Tubes and Caring for the Patient?" in *Archives of Internal Medicine*, vol. 155 (26 June, 1995), 1258-1263, makes an important distinction between social and medical uses of food: "Nutrition and hydration should be viewed as food and drink, with primarily a *social* meaning. Artificial nutrition and hydration should be viewed as medical treatment, with primarily a *physiological* meaning" (1260).

47 F. R. Abrams, MD, "Withholding treatment when death is not imminent," *Geriatrics* vol. 42 (5 May 1987), 77-84, at 84.

48 Paul C. Rousseau, M.D., "How Fluid Deprivation Affects the Terminally Ill," *RN* (Jan. 1991), 73-76.

the list of *extraordinary* measures that can be morally refused by the terminally ill or their proxies.[49]

Numerous recent studies have supported this view, and it is confirmed
by the experience of nurses who treat dying patients.[50] As they make clear,
however, allowing dehydration requires that the medical team pay close
attention to the condition of the patient's mucous membranes. These can
be carefully and continuously hydrated by means of ice chips or specially
prepared glycerine swabs. Such care is routine in hospices, and can be assured at home as well, with little inconvenience to the caregivers.

Note, however, that careful monitoring of dying patients is essential,
especially when they are comatose or otherwise unable to make known
their level of distress. Some hydration of the body, for example, may have
to be continued in order to ensure the proper circulation and absorption
of morphine and other medications, and to avoid pain in the joints. And
given the pressures toward euthanasia in our society today, we need to add
what should be obvious: that any patient, terminally ill or not, should be
provided with adequate food and water if they are conscious and request

49 See R. McCormick, "Nutrition-Hydration: The New Euthanasia?," in *The Critical Calling:
    Reflections on Moral Dilemmas Since Vatican II* (Washington, DC: Georgetown University Press,
    1989), 369-388; and T. A. Shannon, J. J. Wolter, "The PVS Patient and the Forgoing/Withdrawing of Medical Nutrition and Hydration," in *Theological Studies* 49/4 (1988), 623-647. Compare
    the remarks of S. H. Wanzer and team, "The Physician's Responsibility Toward Hopelessly Ill
    Patients," *The New England Journal of Medicine*, vol. 310, no. 15 (12 April, 1984), 955-959, at
    958: "*Patients in a persistent vegetative state.* In this state the neocortex is largely and irreversibly
    destroyed, although some brain-stem functions persist. When this neurologic condition has been
    established with a high degree of medical certainty and has been carefully documented, it is morally
    justifiable to withhold antibiotics and artificial nutrition and hydration, as well as other forms of
    life-sustaining treatment, allowing the patient to die. This obviously requires careful efforts to
    obtain knowledge of the patient's prior wishes and the understanding and agreement of the family."
    As we stressed in the previous section, the only justification for removing nutrition and hydration
    from a PVS patient is irreversible destruction of the neocortex or higher brain. Short of that determination, normal palliative care, including food and liquid, is ethically mandatory.
50 See esp. the "Pastoral Letter on the Care of the Sick and Dying from the Roman Catholic Bishops
    of Maryland" (released 14 October, 1993 by the Maryland Catholic Conference and kindly
    supplied to me by Sr. Sharon Burns, Ph.D, Chaplain of the Stella Maris Hospice, Towson,
    MD); and the articles by Joyce V. Zerwekh, "The Dehydration Question" in *Nursing83* (Jan.),
    47-51; Joanne Lynn and James Childress, "Must Patients Always Be Given Food and Water?"
    in *The Hastings Center Report*, vol. 13, no. 5 (October 1983), 17-21; F. R. Abrams, "Withholding Treatment When Death Is Not Imminent," *Geriatrics* vol. 42 (5 May, 1987), 77-84;
    and Porter Storey, "Artificial Feeding and Hydration in Advanced Illness," in K. W. Wildes, F.
    Abel and J. C. Harvey (eds.), *Birth, Suffering and Death. Catholic Perspectives at the Edges of Life*
    (Boston: Kluwer Academic Publishers, 1992), 67-75.

it, even if they had previously signed a Living Will that rejected any and all life-sustaining measures.

Such basic respect for patient autonomy is rapidly waning, not only in Holland (PAS without informed consent) but also in the United States. For example, the media focused some years ago on the case of a brain-damaged Michigan man whose wife received court-sanctioned permission to have his feeding tube removed, thereby guaranteeing that he would starve to death. He was neither comatose nor terminally ill, and he clearly expressed the desire to live. This case illustrates how important it is for all decisions to remove hydration and feeding tubes to be made under the strictest controls, in light of the patient's actual physical condition, and only in cases of imminent death where such a procedure can be shown to be of significant medical benefit to the patient.

The greatest hesitation in removing a nasal-gastric tube is due to the fear that the patient will suffer from starvation and dehydration. As researcher Jacquelyn Slomka has pointed out, however: "The assumption that dehydration and/or starvation causes a painful death is unfounded based on numerous case reports, data from hospice caregivers, and a recent empiric study. The developing consensus is that (a) food and fluids not desired by dying patients do not add to the comfort of these patients; (b) artificial nutrition and hydration in terminally ill patients may increase pain, edema, respiratory congestion (and the need for suctioning), nausea, and vomiting; and (c) discomfort associated with dehydration results from thirst, which can be controlled with frequent mouth care, oral ice chips, and sips of fluids"[51] A conscious patient can make such discomfort known. In comatose or PVS patients, however, it must be clearly determined that neurological damage has rendered the person brain-dead, i.e., that trauma or illness has permanently destroyed the cortex and cerebral hemispheres, before any consideration can be given to withdrawing nutrition and hydration.

Withholding or withdrawing hydration and feeding tubes, in other words, can be considered a moral option only when the patient is 1) according to the best medical judgment, *irreversibly* comatose—and he or she has expressed, through a Living Will or Durable Power of Attorney, a clear

---

51 *Art. cit.*, 1262; see her bibliographical references that offer medical support for this opinion.

and uncoerced desire to forgo such procedures; or 2) when the patient is conscious yet clearly in the last stages of the dying process, and requests repeatedly (or otherwise indicates the desire) that food and liquid be withheld. This latter case does not constitute active euthanasia or suicide. It merely accepts the reality of impending death and allows the disease (illness, bodily trauma or whatever) to take its natural course there where medical care is unable to restore health.

Another point, alluded to earlier, needs to be made regarding "extraordinary" measures. *Antibiotics* are administered so routinely that they can hardly be considered anything but "ordinary." Yet their use has deprived terminally ill patients of a relatively simple and painless death by pneumonia. This long respected "friend of the dying patient" no longer performs its vital function, and the terminally ill person is left to die by some other means: means that can only be treated by extraordinary procedures. Adequate pain management is obligatory. This does not mean, however, that antibiotics need be administered if they will merely extend the biological life span while increasing the pain and discomfort of the dying patient. Given this consideration, use of antibiotics in terminal care—together with any other procedure that merely *prolongs the dying process*—should be classed under the rubric of "extraordinary measures" that can be morally refused or withheld.

The research lying behind these protocols has very significant implications for the way we care for the terminally ill. It suggests that the appropriate place for the dying patient is not the cold, busy, technologically sophisticated environment of the hospital. It is, rather, in the home or in a hospice, where the patient can benefit from appropriate pain medication, personal care and, above all, the loving and prayerful presence of family and friends.

The question we need to discuss as Orthodox Christians, who are concerned with the sacredness of life from its beginning to its end, is this: *How can we as Christian people once again take control of the way we die?* This raises as well a number of corollary questions. How can we as the Church develop appropriate hospice programs that will guarantee for the terminally ill adequate pain management, together with an environment of peace, love and prayer? And what steps can we take to enable the terminally ill to die at home, again with appropriate medical care and with as much interaction with loved ones as possible? How, in other words, can we recover, for ourselves and for those facing the end of their earthly existence, the conviction that death is not "terminal," but that it is to be embraced as a longed-for beginning, a dying and awakening into the joy of eternal life?

Christian Diakonia and the Dying Patient

There comes a point in end-of-life treatment where aggressive therapy should give way to pain management and a concern for the patient's overall comfort. Here various *hospice programs* come into play, developed both through the churches and through various social agencies.

A three-tiered hospice system has been created in this country, operating out of hospitals, in private homes, and in resident facilities which are usually open only to the terminally ill. As with hospital and home-care programs, these in-house facilities have proven highly effective in offering the compassionate, personal care and medical attention that can most adequately ease the dying process and provide a truly "good death," even to those who suffer potentially painful and debilitating illnesses. A sense of abandonment and loss of control over their lives is the gravest affliction experienced by most dying patients. The various forms of hospice care, if well administered, can relieve patients' anxiety by providing trained personnel to accompany them in their final journey and offer the emotional and spiritual support they crave.

Orthodox hospice programs could provide an essential liturgical and sacramental setting, in which patient and priest together can seek healing through God's forgiving grace, even as the body nears death. Services of this kind should be ranked as high priorities among the many pastoral tasks the church is called to assume. A monastic community can be an ideal setting in which to end one's earthly existence. But most communities are not equipped to offer the degree of care and comfort dying persons need. A new form of philanthropic organization, even a new expression of Christian vocation, seems required today, if the church is to provide a genuine alternative to physician-assisted suicide. True "aid-in-dying" could be furnished by specially trained Christian lay persons or medical professionals who find themselves called to a vocation of service to the terminally ill.

There is a great deal of discussion within the Orthodox Church today about renewing the deaconate as a vocation of charitable *diakonia*. The suggestion has also been made that we create—or rather, rediscover and reactivate—the vocations of "deaconess," "virgin," and "widow." What better way to utilize the extraordinary yet sadly neglected gifts and capacities of Orthodox women, than to offer them the officially recognized and blessed opportunity to minister directly to those who are dying? While an "order of Sisters of Mercy," for example, would sound foreign to Orthodox ears, if it is carefully distinguished from the traditional monastic vocation and established as a pastoral ministry in its own right, such an order could provide the worthiest of services while enabling its members to undertake a genuinely Christian ministry "in the world." And of course such a ministry need not be restricted to women, but could be open to anyone who wants to care for the sick and dying in a framework of nurture and prayer.

On a more modest level, our parishes could sponsor selected members of the community to be trained in hospice work, home-health-care, hospital visitation and the like. It is a well-known fact that as patients approach the terminal stage of life, doctors and other care providers tend to withdraw from them, leaving them with a desperate sense of abandonment. Care for the terminally ill is basically a *spiritual* task—one that relies on appropriate medication, but acknowledges and accepts the inability of most medical teams to minister pastorally, spiritually, to those who no longer respond to their attempts to heal. *It is the Church's task to provide the loving care and nurture required to reconcile dying patients with God, family and friends, and to journey with them to the threshold of life beyond death.* For our parishioners to assume this vital aspect of the church's ministry, however, they need a proper framework, with appropriate training and adequate funding. As difficult and utopian as this proposal might sound, experience has shown that a parish mobilized around an authentic *diakonia* can provide the material support that service requires. And service of this kind offers its own reward by rejuvenating parish life through a renewed and living experience with the gospel of love.

These few suggestions are proposed simply as initial steps, to counter the pressure now growing in American society for a "final solution" to the problem of the terminally ill. The church must reject active euthanasia.

But it can reasonably do so only by demonstrating through its actions and overall witness that there is indeed a better way.

With regard to Oregon's Measure 16 and the inevitable sequels it will spawn, we must affirm that physician-assisted suicide, euphemistically referred to as "aid-in-dying," is morally abhorrent and contrary to the will of God. To license doctors to kill would undermine the medical profession and the need for patients to trust implicitly that their physician is there to heal; it would sanction suicide as an acceptable "way out" in virtually any circumstances; and it would create a system of basic inequality between those who can afford full medical coverage and thus life-prolonging care, and those who can not. The real victims of legislation akin to Measure 16 will be the poor, the abandoned, the mentally ill, and generally the marginalized members of our society. If ever the slippery slope posed an intolerable risk to personal and social welfare, it does so in the case of physician-assisted suicide.

This being the case, we need to justify our rejection of the practice by offering feasible and positive alternatives for the care of dying persons. As with the crisis of abortion, we cannot reject the solution of expediency unless we are willing to assume spiritual and material responsibility for the persons involved.

Above all, through the preaching and teaching of the Church we must convey the conviction that there is a greater value than sustained physical existence in a terminal state. The life freely bestowed by God must one day be freely and willingly surrendered to him, in order that he remain Lord over both the living and the dead. Our task is to find ever more compassionate and pastorally sound ways to accompany the dying toward the final step—that they alone can take—of surrendering their life and eternal destiny into God's open and loving hands.

Rather than dread death as the frustrating conclusion to our human aspirations and intentions, we must learn to embrace it as a truly "Blessed Pascha," a painful but necessary step in a pilgrimage without end. The divine challenge to "choose life!" means that we preserve, protect, nurture, and cherish earthly life by any and all means, and in all circumstances and conditions. Yet it also means that when death does come, we receive it, in faith and hope, as a blessed transition to life beyond.

At the close of one of his Edifying Discourses, the Danish existentialist theologian Søren Kierkegaard spoke of life's final step in words that appropriately describe the ultimate leap of faith: "So we may understand that the same God who by his hand led us through the world, now withdraws it, and opens his embrace to receive the longing soul."[52] For most people, the dying process involves at some point the sense that God has indeed withdrawn his hand, and the resulting sense of abandonment can lead them to spiritual shipwreck and despair. In such moments, suicide—especially if it is physician-assisted—can seem both a reasonable and compassionate "way out."

To preserve them from this final and most tragic temptation, we need to accompany dying persons with compassion, love, and unshakable hope. And by our words and gestures, we need to convey to them the ultimate truth about death: that God's own deepest longing is precisely to open his embrace and to receive his dying child in a place of eternal rest, where sickness, sorrow and suffering are no more, but only the joy of life everlasting.[53]

52 "The Expectation of Faith," *Edifying Discourses I* (Swenson, tr.) (Minneapolis: Augsburg, 1943), 33.

53 In this chapter I have only briefly mentioned the matter of Living Wills and other advance directives. In 1993 a task force drafted an excellent example of a Living Will adapted to the theological and pastoral perspective of the Orthodox Church. Entitled "A Living Will and a Christian Death," it represents the concerted reflection of an Orthodox anthropologist, medical doctors, and an Athonite monk. The final summary sections have been printed as a brochure, available through the St. John of Kronstadt Press Bookservice, Rt. 1, Box 205, Liberty, TN 37095; and inquiries may be addressed to M. L. Sill, Rt. 2 Box 2343, Wayne, WV 25570.

6

Summary: Bioethics and the
Sacred Gift of Life

> *"It is impossible to live without life,
> and there is no life except by
> participation in God. This parti-
> cipation consists in beholding God
> and rejoicing in His goodness."*
>
> —St. Irenaeus

> *"Adam lost the earthly paradise and
> sought it weeping. But the Lord
> through His love on the cross gave
> Adam another paradise, fairer than
> the old—a paradise in heaven where
> shines the Light of the Holy Trinity.
> What shall we render unto the Lord
> for His love to us?"*
>
> —St. Silouan

The field of "bioethics" arose in response to modern technology: the prodigious development in recent years of various medical tools and procedures aimed at creating and sustaining the *bios*, that is, human life considered especially in its physical or biological aspect. This new science, dating from the end of the 1960s, focuses particularly on three main areas: 1) the beginning of human life (including methods of artificial procreation, abortion, and *in utero* surgery); 2) various means for preserving and sustaining life (including dialysis machines and ventilators, drug and gene therapies, and vital organ transplants); and 3) the end of life (including pain management for terminally ill patients, withdrawing or withholding of food and hydration, and euthanasia). Other related areas of concern include patient autonomy, distributive justice in a world of limited resources, and informed consent. In countries such as the United States, where health care is considered to be a service for those who can pay rather than a right guaranteed equally to all citizens, there are the additional issues of health delivery systems, including so-called "managed care" and the financing of "catastrophic illness." When health care is subjected to the laws of the market place, injustices are inevitable. These, too, are increasingly the focus of attention of specialists in the area of bioethics.

The primary question that concerns Christian ethicists or moral theologians today is evident: Which moral and spiritual values do we need to respect and protect in the wake of these recent technological developments and social pressures, given the fact that neither Scripture nor patristic tradition deals explicitly with them? That question is especially difficult to answer in a pluralistic world, where in the minds of our contemporaries all values are relativized and basic or "absolute" principles no longer exist. Ours is a world in which human life is often considered—and treated—as a mere product that we can *create* on demand and *eliminate* for reasons of convenience, as with elective abortions and euthanasia without informed consent.

If we are to remain faithful to the Orthodox vision, the only possible reply to the question concerning moral and spiritual values to be protected in this technological age must be thoroughly grounded in biblical and patristic anthropology: the vision of the human person, created in the Image of God and called to grow toward actualization of the divine Likeness. In Pauline language, we are called to a life of authentic "freedom": a freedom lived in God and for God, by the indwelling presence and sanctifying power of the Holy Spirit.

Accordingly, bioethics is a science which by its very nature is *theological*. The ultimate meaning of human existence is to be found in the quest for *theosis* or deification: eternal communion with the Three Persons of the Holy Trinity. It is this communion that determines our relationships with other persons as well as with God himself. As a theological discipline, bioethics reflects on the intrinsic values of human life, as it does on the means by which biomedical technology can properly serve life's ultimate end: our participation as human *persons* in the *personal* life of the triune God. From this perspective, bioethics is conceived as a function of the discipline of Christian moral theology. Its primary concern is to discern and to actualize, within the Church and the world at large, the conditions necessary for the individual Christian to realize and fulfill his or her life according to the familiar petition of our Litany of Supplication: "a Christian ending to our life, painless, blameless and peaceful…"

The moral and spiritual values we need to respect and to protect in all of our reflection in the area of bioethics include the following: 1) *the sacred character of human life*, which is to be acknowledged and preserved from conception to the grave and beyond; 2) *the sacrificial love of God* as the origin and basis of every human relationship (for example, between the physician and the patient, or between the organ donor and the organ recipient); and 3) *the call to holiness and to theosis*: participation in divine life, which alone provides ultimate meaning to human existence and serves as its ultimate end.

It is profoundly Orthodox values of this kind—the sacredness or sanctity of human life, the sacrificial love of God, and the deification of the human person—that will determine our attitude toward procedures and protocols such as abortion on demand, *in vitro* fertilization, genetic engineering (including the cloning of human embryos), psychotropic drug therapy, and euthanasia.

To the degree that the medical team strives to remain faithful to the Gospel, it will recall that every medical decision is taken within an *ecclesial* framework. This means that every decision concerning the life or death of a person also involves the lives of all those who are united to the patient in the communion of the Body of Christ. It means that medical treatment is an aspect of the *priestly ministry* common to every member of the Church. The question the physician must answer is therefore the question every member of the ecclesial body must deal with: How can we exercise an authentic *synergy* or cooperation between man and God, such that our choices and decisions concerning life and death conform thoroughly and faithfully to the divine will? How should we act so that the love of God is the true foundation on which all of our relationships are built, particularly our relations with those who are suffering from disease and disability? In liturgical language, how can we take responsible action toward another person in such a way as to fulfill the basic priestly role incumbent on each of us, to "offer ourselves and each other, and all our life, to Christ our God"? How can we make biomedical decisions that will fully respect the fundamental analogy that exists between the offering of the person and the offering of the Holy Eucharist: "Thine own of Thine own, we offer unto Thee, on behalf of all and for all"?

These are just a few of the basic questions we have attempted to address, in order to preserve an essentially theological perspective toward the issues raised in connection with biomedical therapies and their related technologies. The danger facing all those who involve themselves with bioethics today is that the field itself is at risk of being taken over by interests that are sociological and economic rather than theological and spiritual. In a world of limited resources and increasing medical demands, all too often the choice to treat one patient over another is made on grounds of convenience and experimental usefulness. Orthodox medical ethics, however, is teleological rather than utilitarian; it serves the divine *economia* rather than the interests of human progress or productivity. Therefore it necessarily focuses on the individual *as a person*, created in the image of God and endowed with transcendent value: a person who, by his or her very nature is an "ecclesial being," characterized by "otherness" and "communion," as by the dialectic between freedom and responsibility. To reduce the person to a purely physical or material object is to deny the transcendent aspect of the human creature and to betray the very vocation of medicine, which, like the eucharist itself, exists for the healing of both body and soul.

Let us move on at this point to a brief summary of some of the major areas that we have focused on in the previous chapters. What are the most important problems posed by the science of biomedicine that necessitate the serious and concerted reflection of those concerned with the ethical or moral consequences of that science?

Bioethics, once again, considers especially, but not only, problems that arise at the beginning and at the end of human life. A course outline in bioethics will ordinarily begin with a question that is both philosophical and medical: "At what moment does human life begin?" (at conception? at implantation? at birth?). And the course will conclude by considering the problem of euthanasia: the so-called "right to die," together with the increasingly widespread practice of physician-assisted suicide.

Closely linked to the question of procreation is that of human sexuality in general. We have stressed the Orthodox conviction that gender distinction and complementarity are basic aspects of human nature and characterize the human person in his or her quest for participation in divine life. This means that every expression of genital sexuality has its proper place only within the context of a monogamous, heterosexual, blessed conjugal union. Against the cheapening of human life and relationships reflected and encouraged by so much of the media and entertainment industry today, we need constantly to affirm *the ultimate sacredness and dignity of the human person.* The intimacy of sexual relations is such that its expression outside the framework of the covenantal bond of marriage leads inevitably to sinful exploitation of other persons and to a certain level of abuse with regard to one's own dignity as a bearer of the image of God. This is especially true with adultery, where the covenantal bond that makes of husband and wife "one flesh" for their sanctification and mutual salvation is violated to the core.

From a Christian perspective, marriage is a divinely established, sacramental relationship that serves three basic purposes: to deepen the bond of love, devotion and faithfulness between spouses; to enable them, through procreation, to participate in God's own creative work; and by an ongoing ascetic effort that involves repentance, forgiveness and mutual intercession, to enable the couple to live and to labor for each other's salvation. It is this profoundly *sacramental* aspect of marriage that makes of it an essentially covenantal relationship, whose purpose, above all, is to lead husband and wife into an eternal union with one another. That union transcends the limits of earthly existence and finds its fulfillment in *eternal communion* with the glorified Christ, the true Bridegroom, in the Kingdom of God.

In the United States today, the most difficult and divisive bioethical issue is certainly that of abortion. Other societies are equally torn by the problem but have not yet come to acknowledge its gravity: the immense social and spiritual tragedy that consists in willfully destroying millions of unborn children every year. It is well known that Orthodoxy, ever since apostolic times, has vehemently opposed elective or "convenience" abortions. From the moment at which fertilization or "syngamy" is complete there exists a unique human being whom the Church recognizes as *personal,* a being in relationship with God and with other persons. Abortion, therefore, is tantamount to murder: the willful taking of a human life in violation of the interests of the victim.

There are, as we have noted, so-called "hard cases" that seem to many ethicists to offer grounds for accepting abortion under special circumstances: 1) serious danger to the life of the mother, 2) psychological stress produced by the pregnancy that threatens the mother's well-being, 3) pregnancy resulting from rape or incest, and 4) a diagnosis, provided by amniocentesis or chorion villus sampling, indicating that the child is afflicted with serious genetic "defects" or anomalies.

Traditionally, the only grounds on which the Church can accept abortion are a true and serious threat to the mother's life. In such increasingly rare instances, she should be given priority over the child she is carrying, simply because of the web of relationships and responsibilities that is hers, that the child does not yet enjoy. As tragic as rape and incest are, studies have shown that aborting the fetus usually does more psychological and physical harm to the mother than helping her to bring the child to term (and, if need be, to place the child for adoption). How, in our present climate of legalized abortion and a nearly absolute priority given to "rights" over responsibilities, is the Orthodox Church to defend the unborn against what has been rightly called the "abortion holocaust"? How are we to proclaim effectively the traditional conviction that personhood is bestowed by God from the time of conception, and is thus wholly independent of human calculations or convenience? How, in other words, are we as Orthodox Christians to enter the debate on the "status of the embryo" in such a way as to make the point that *procreation* is ultimately an act of *divine creation*, and that the conceptus from the very beginning bears the image of God and is called to assume the personal likeness of God through a life-long inner pilgrimage that leads to deification?

This conviction concerning the fully human, and indeed personal quality, of the embryo has profound implications for the matter of assisted reproduction and the use of various technologies in the procreative process. Among the most problematic of these are genetic screening and *in vitro* fertilization. The only purpose of genetic screening is to detect genetic anomalies—such as Down's syndrome, spina bifida, Tay Sachs disease, or the Lesch-Nyhan syndrome—with the aim of aborting undesirable fetuses, since at the present time it is not possible to correct these defects by genetic surgery. Yet with the rapid advances now being made in the field of gene therapy, some form of screening will soon become both mandatory and desirable, insofar as certain anomalies can be corrected *in utero*. What limits should be imposed on genetic screening?

How can we assess the *value* of the diagnosis provided by such screening as compared with the *danger* it represents both to the mother and to the child she is carrying?

As for *in vitro* fertilization, the primary objection to the procedure concerns so-called "extra embryos." Ordinarily several ova are fertilized in a petri dish, two or three are transferred to the woman's uterus, and the others are either discarded, frozen for future transfer, or used for experimentation. Because it holds the age-old conviction that personal human existence begins with conception, Orthodoxy cannot accept such a protocol. Most Orthodox ethicists, in fact, are reluctant to sanction the donation of extra embryos even in the interests of providing children to otherwise sterile couples. The legal complications produced by the existence of frozen embryos, together with cloning and other forms of manipulation, make it impossible for us to accept IVF where it leads to abuse of the germ cells or the newly created zygote. The recently developed procedure of Intra-Cytoplasmic Sperm Injection (ICSI), may offer a partial solution, insofar as it enables a single ovum to be fertilized by a single selected sperm, thereby eliminating the need for extra embryos. This does not prevent manipulation of human gametes and embryos, but it does offer a new possibility for couples to conceive without creating unwanted human life.

The question is: From an Orthodox perspective is it morally acceptable—that is, acceptable in the eyes of God—to create life outside the womb? The Roman Catholic Church has strongly condemned such procedures, citing both the invasiveness of the technique in the life of the couple and the danger of the slippery slope that leads to ever more manipulation.[1] Orthodoxy does not have a "natural law" approach to the matter as does the Roman Church. Nevertheless, we still need to reach some degree of consensus as to whether we can accept medical procedures that involve drugs to increase ovulation, laparoscopy to retrieve ova, masturbation to acquire the needed sperm, and manipulation of the gametes in a laboratory, to arrive at a less than twenty percent chance of a successful pregnancy. In addition, we need to ask whether the Church can countenance a procedure that is so expensive that only the wealthy can have

---

1 Expressed especially in *Donum Vitae*, the "Instruction on Respect for Human Life in its Origin and on the Dignity of Procreation," published by the Congregation for the Doctrine of the Faith on 22 February, 1987.

access to it. These are issues that call for both serious reflection and carefully weighed decisions.

This leads us to the matter of the bio-possibilities and biohazards of genetic engineering in general. On the one hand, production of medicines, drugs, hormones and proteins by means of what the French aptly term "le génie génétique" holds out extraordinary possibilities for new medical treatments of formerly incurable diseases. The human genome project is providing us daily with knowledge of our genetic heritage, and it promises to furnish new therapies that will decrease the mortality rate among children while increasing the quality of life of those who in an earlier age would have borne debilitating mental or physical handicaps. Nevertheless, the most important question in this regard concerns not our physical or mental condition, but rather our degree of spiritual health and well-being. Manipulating DNA with the aim of "improving" the human species will lead us inevitably down the slope toward Ramsey's "fabricated man": the human person created according to human criteria—that is, human desires and perceived needs—rather than according to the image of God.

Who, after all, will determine what criteria are to be applied in producing genetically engineered human beings? And what will those criteria be? Without doubt, utility and intelligence will take precedence over sanctity and wisdom. Traits such as an aggressive temperament, an analytic mind, and physical strength will certainly be more prized in today's highly competitive Western societies than Jesus' own values as articulated in the Beatitudes: values such as poverty of spirit, humility, pursuit of justice, and self-sacrifice out of love for another person.

There appears to be an increasing level of anxiety among Christian medical specialists as the genome project moves ahead. Once the human genotype is fully mapped out and the manifold functions of the DNA molecule are known, scientists will hold the power to manipulate genetic material at will. This will lead not only to the creation of chimeras (already human genetic material is being introduced into other organisms), but it could potentially lead to a resurgence of the eugenics movement that proved so disastrous during the first half of the 20th century. Scientific eugenics, founded around 1890 by Francis Galton, had two chief aims: to prevent undesirables such as the mentally retarded and physically handicapped from reproducing, and to "improve" the human race through genetic selection. The question now, as then, remains: Precisely who, using what criteria, is going to determine those who constitute the socially undesirable, and to what "final solution" will they be subjected in order that the human race be "improved"?

The extraordinary recent successes in the area of cloning demand special attention from the Church and from Christian bioethicists. The birth of the famous ewe "Dolly" elicited the question: "Today the sheep, tomorrow the shepherd?" (answered tentatively but ominously in the affirmative by the birth of the human gene-bearing sheep Polly). Dolly was the first mammal to be cloned using an adult cell (although, as we have noted, the project scientists themselves have raised the possibility that the cell in question was in fact embryonic). Previously it was only possible to clone an embryonic cell, one selected prior to the onset of cellular differentiation. This and other new technological possibilities open the way toward human cloning, including creation of anthropoids: sub-human creatures programmed to act as slaves, with perfect efficiency and unquestioning obedience. In reply to a request made by the White House in April of 1998, the Orthodox Church in America sent to President Clinton a declaration that categorically condemns all scientific experimentation that would lead toward the cloning of human beings.[2] Although such experimentation has

---

2 The text of the statement is as follows:

"The recent cloning of a sheep from a single adult cell opens the way to the cloning of other species, including human beings. Although no one can prevent scientific research and experimentation from proceeding in this direction, the question arises as to whether the United States government should ban or regulate this activity and provide it with public funding.

The worldwide body of Orthodox Churches adhere strictly to the view that human life is sacred: that each human being is created as a unique person "in the image of God." Accordingly, the great majority of Orthodox ethicists will insist that all forms of eugenics, involving the manipulation of human genetic material for nontherapeutic purposes, are morally repugnant and detrimental to human life and welfare.

Various cloning techniques using animals have been developed over the past ten years, promising enhancement of human life through the creation of new drugs, proteins and other useful products. Such endeavors deserve public support and funding. The prospect of human cloning, however, raises the specter of the "slippery slope" in the most direct and ominous way. In a "fallen" world, where rights outweigh responsibilities, cloning techniques using human cells will inevitably lead to abuse: the commercialization of "prime" DNA, production of children for the purpose of providing "spare parts," and movement toward creation of a "superior" class of human beings. Moreover, scientists at present are unable to determine if a selected cell contains mutations or other defects that could produce crippling deformities or mental retardation in the cloned child.

In light of these factors, the Orthodox Church in America urges emphatically that a government ban be imposed on all forms of experimentation to produce human clones and that government funding for such activity be denied. A moratorium on this activity is urgently needed."

gone on for many years using embryonic cells, the possibility of cloning adult cells—if indeed the procedure can be duplicated and applied to humans—vastly increases the likelihood that we will soon be producing "made-to-order" babies. Consequently, the Church must speak out, even if its declarations serve no other purpose than to limit the use of federal funds for this kind of manipulative abuse.

Genetic engineering should be encouraged and supported by public monies insofar as it can increase the quality and quantity of edible plants and animals, and provide appropriate therapies for human medical care. In the area of food production, this could even include the cloning of livestock, already well under way in the wake of the "Dolly" phenomenon. (Although it should be noted that many Orthodox find such manipulation of animal life to be abhorrent and ethically inadmissible.) What is totally unacceptable is the manipulation of human gametes with a view to augmenting or improving certain traits, just as it is morally unacceptable to create children for the purpose of providing "spare parts" for organ transplantation. This judgment holds in spite of the fact that fetal brain cells, for example, can significantly attenuate the symptoms of Parkinson's disease by increasing levels of the neurotransmitter dopamine. Or that fetal organs can be transplanted without triggering a rejection response.

Despite the medical advantages of fetal tissue and the hope fetal transplants hold out to some patients, there remains a moral truth that we must respect: However noble the end may be, it cannot justify immoral means. This is a fundamental principle of Christian ethics, affirmed by the apostle Paul himself: *we may not do evil that good may come* (Romans 3:8). Human cloning is abhorrent and unacceptable because of the abuse that will inevitably follow from it, as is the stockpiling of fetal parts because of abuse inherent in it. By insisting on this point, we do not at all wish to hamper scientific progress or impede appropriate medical care. Our concern is simply to render unto God that which is God's, beginning with human life. To recall once more St. Paul's words to the Corinthians: "You are not your own; you were bought with a price. Therefore glorify God in your body!" (1 Cor 6:19f). Such a command is impossible to respect insofar as we give in to the temptation to fashion ourselves after our own image and to reconstitute ourselves with the organs of other people, particularly the nonconsenting unborn.

With regard to treatment of the terminally ill, a question raised today with special urgency is that of *pain management*, particularly in cases of cancer and other illnesses where physical and mental suffering can become unbearable, even "dehumanizing." If euthanasia, in the form of physician-assisted suicide, preoccupies the media as well as medical ethicists today, it is because too little attention has been given to the proper and reasonable use of opiates such as morphine, often because of the unfounded and unreasonable fear that the patient will become addicted to them. We should recall that the St. Christopher hospices in England have for many years provided terminally ill cancer patients with the so-called Brompton cocktail that has proven to be highly effective in allowing patients to experience an end to their life that is indeed "painless, blameless and peaceful." Patients provided with such medication tend to require lower doses than do others who are connected to a morphine drip, because they themselves are in control of the process of pain management.[3]

Serious attention paid to the problem of pain management would go a long way toward halting the frenetic rush toward legalizing physician-assisted suicide. Serious abuses arising from the Dutch experiment with euthanasia have been well publicized. They should make us aware of the extraordinarily powerful attraction the so-called "right to die" exercises on the minds of those who feel themselves living in a world bereft of transcendent meaning. Yet, as studies have shown, those who seek medical assistance to end their lives dread not so much death as the *dying process*. The prospect of spending weeks, months or years attached to a ventilator, fed intravenously, and slowly expiring in a hospital ward is demeaning and depressing. The Church needs to put its moral weight behind alternatives—beginning with hospice programs—that offer consolation and hope rather than the frustration and despair which lead to suicide.

A related ethical matter we have stressed concerns the feeding and hydration of terminally ill patients. In recent years we have witnessed a sig-

---

3   The 2 January, 1998, issue of the journal *Science* announced tests of a compound related to nicotine that acts as a more powerful analgesic than opiates, including morphine, but without the negative side effects or a significant risk of addiction. Termed ABT-594 (for Abbott Laboratories, which is developing the so-called "nicotine analog"), the compound represents a potential breakthrough that would provide physicians with a highly safe and effective means to control pain, while avoiding the toxicity and addictive properties of today's commonly used drugs. Unlike various forms of cloning, this is the kind of research the churches and other religious bodies can and should encourage.

nificant change of attitude in this regard. Since food and water are essential to sustain a living organism, it used to be taken for granted that they were mandatory in any treatment protocol. It was considered immoral and unthinkable to deprive dying patients of food and water because it was assumed that they would suffer the agonies of starvation and dehydration. When members of the medical team observed terminally ill patients tearing out naso-gastric tubes and I-V lines, they quickly replaced them, supposing that the patient was mentally unstable or was simply reacting to the irritation they caused. Today we recognize that this gesture is more often due to an intuition, common to dying patients, that continued feeding and hydration in the final stages of life (that is, with only hours or at most days to live) does more harm than good. For the patient in a terminal state, the absence of food and water allows the organism to produce natural analgesics (enkephalins, endorphins and similar neurohormones) and to increase azotemia, which also has an analgesic effect. This permits the cellular system to shut down progressively, allowing the patient to die with a minimum of physical pain.

In certain cases, then, it is medically appropriate to increase the dosage of opiates, such as morphine, thereby rendering bearable otherwise intractable pain. In unquestionably terminal cases this is morally acceptable treatment even there where the procedure threatens to slow or shut down the respiratory system. Similarly, in certain cases (determined by at least two physicians) it is appropriate at the terminal stage of life to withhold or to withdraw feeding and hydration tubes (provided that the body's mucous membranes are kept moistened by ice chips or glycerine swabs). These actions do not, as it may appear, violate the first principle of the Hippocratic Oath, *primum non nocere*, "first of all, do no harm." This is because, according to the "principle of double effect," accepted by Orthodox as well as Roman Catholic ethicists, 1) one acts for the good of the patient; 2) the benefits that result are proportionally greater than the negative consequences (in that dying more quickly but in peace is preferable to a prolonged dying process marked by unbearable pain); and 3) the intention of the act is not to kill the patient but to reduce as much as possible his mental and physical suffering.

This said, however, we must insist on the fact that from an Orthodox perspective there is a fundamental difference between killing and allowing to die. Whereas allowing the patient to die merely accepts the limits of human existence and of modern biotechnology, and permits the illness to pursue its course until the end, the act of killing, including so-called "mercy killing" or euthanasia, usurps from God power and authority that belong to him alone. No matter what form it takes, euthanasia is morally unacceptable because God is Master of both life and death. Therefore, to inflict death intentionally, whatever the motivation, is to commit murder.

This conviction has important implications for the determination of death, as it does for those cases in which extraordinary means are used to maintain a patient's physical existence. Organ transplant teams are understandably preoccupied by the chronic shortage of available organs. This has led to pressure to declare anencephalic newborns to be technically dead, in order that their organs might be harvested. And it has created in the popular mind the specter of the transplant team hovering over the body of a terminally ill patient, ready to remove vital organs before the patient is actually dead. Still more troubling are initiatives to declare patients in deep coma or persistent vegetative state to be legally dead, even though they can be maintained, often for many years, by life-support technology. Given our limited resources and the technological capacity to transplant vital organs successfully, should such patients' lives be ended by withdrawing or withholding life support? And if so, should they then be considered candidates for organ harvesting?

A prior question, however, is whether it is morally acceptable to harvest and transplant organs in the first place. From the point of view of Orthodox, and especially patristic tradition, the matter could be argued either way. On the one hand, we insist on the "sanctity of life," the inherently sacred quality of human existence, created in the image of God. This leads some theologians to hold that organ transplants should be prohibited because they violate the human body and reduce the dying person to a potential reservoir of "spare parts." Since an Orthodox medical ethic will value the life and integrity of the patient above all else, it is immoral to use anencephalic infants or dying adults as sources for harvesting organs.

On the other hand, it could be argued that the greatest act of love the dying patient can make consists in offering his or her vital organs to others, in order that their life might be prolonged or improved. St. John Chrysostom's homilies on wealth and poverty, for example, might be interpreted as follows: All that "belongs" to us, including our personal existence, is a gift from God and in reality belongs to God; we are called to assume stewardship over our body in the name of Christ, and to exercise unconditional love toward our neighbor (the "sacrament of the brother"); therefore, we are morally obligated to offer to others vital organs that we ourselves can no longer use.

However we are to decide this issue, there are some basic guidelines that we need to respect. In recent years the criterion for determining death has shifted from cardio-respiratory cessation to so-called "brain death." This latter, however, is ambiguous. Does the irreversible cessation of upper (hemispheric) brain functioning constitute death? Or should death be declared only where *brain-stem* activity has ceased? As we have pointed out, brain-stem death means the onset of putrefaction. It signifies the "death of the whole organism" rather than merely "death of the organism as a whole." Therefore, once brain-stem death has occurred, it is too late to harvest organs. Using brain-stem criteria to determine death, we are left with the gruesome fact that vital organs can only be harvested from patients who are technically still alive.

In all of these cases—anencephaly and terminal illness, as well as PVS and deep coma—we must remember one crucial factor. *Human personhood is determined not by medical diagnosis, but by divine Providence.* An anencephalic child, considered "useless" and perhaps not fully human from a strictly social perspective, is nevertheless a *person* in the eyes of God. The same is true with the irresponsive PVS patient, or the trauma victim whose life can only be sustained on a ventilator. In making judgments regarding life and death, that truth remains fundamental. Neither illness nor death deprives the human creature of "personhood" in the eyes of God.

Nevertheless, given the reality of limited medical and economic resources, together with the fact of our mortality, *it is irresponsible and lacking in stewardship to prolong the dying process* through technological wizardry. There is a time to live and a time to die. Once the body has entered the terminal state (and anencephalics are by definition terminal patients) then reasonable and faithful treatment will consist of pain management, providing comfort, and allowing the "peaceful separation of soul and body" that we pray for in our prayers for the departing. Medical heroics ("dysthanasia") all too often represents a kind of bio-idolatry, a "vitalism" that seeks to preserve mere biological existence, irrespective of the patient's wishes or the cost to society.

The determination of what constitutes useless or futile treatment, as distinct from valiant efforts to preserve and improve the quality of the patient's life where possible, is one that must be made *in each individual case.* The Church's biblical and patristic tradition will not give us specific answers as to when and how life support should be maintained or discontinued. It will, however, insist on the *infinite value of the human person.* In so doing, it will provide us with the basic guideline for all medical decisions: unqualified respect for the patient as a bearer of the divine Image. This means that such decisions must have as their final aim to surrender the person into the loving and merciful hands of God, with the unwavering conviction that God, and God alone, should determine the limits of life and death.

It is in light of this kind of reflection that the great majority of Orthodox theologians reject categorically all forms of medically assisted suicide, just as they reject any action whose aim is to end a person's life, even there where the ill patient is enduring what seems to be unbearable suffering. The answer to such situations is not the tragic death known by the euphemism "euthanasia." It is rather to create measures that will effectively diminish the suffering, so that the terminally ill patient can die with a maximum of consciousness and a minimum of pain.

At the end stage of life, it is essential that dying persons be able to prepare for death in such a way as to preserve certain fundamental values and goals. They need to preserve to the fullest extent possible a conscious and personal relationship with God and with other people, they need to be able to confess and receive Holy Communion one last time, and they need to know that they are accompanied by the presence and prayer of those who love them and can surrender them gently and peacefully into the hands of God.

The offspring of modern medical technology, the field of bioethics focuses especially on biological and medical issues of philosophical and theological import, in order to bring to those issues insights and judgments that are both pertinent and just. The value of those moral judgments will depend wholly on the presuppositions that undergird them. Even among Orthodox ethicists, however, shared presuppositions often lead to differing conclusions—regarding, for example, contraception, procreative technologies, organ transplants, or experimentation on germ-line cells. In these areas there exist within Orthodoxy today widely divergent opinions as to what truly conforms to the "mind of the Church." Nevertheless, it is essential that we pursue our dialogue in order to arrive at appropriate solutions, even if it means agreeing to disagree on certain basic issues.

Dialogue among ourselves, however, is not sufficient. In the highly pluralistic, relativizing world in which we live—a world that is basically hostile to Christian values—it is of the utmost importance that we, as Orthodox Christians, join forces with others who call upon the name of Jesus Christ, to reflect together and to pray together, in order to discern the will of God for a world awash in moral confusion and unenlightened self-interest. And among ourselves as Orthodox theologians, medical specialists and concerned laity, it is equally important that we devote ourselves to the basic priestly task that consists in offering to God the problems and moral dilemmas of bioethics, together with the persons whose lives are touched by them. Our most basic responsibility, today and in the foreseeable future, is to submit to the Author of Life the multitude of difficult questions concerning life and death, with the hope and prayer that every ethical decision we make will serve his purpose and his eternal glory.

Appendix 1

This summary statement on abortion was written by the author several years ago as a brochure for distribution in Orthodox parishes and elsewhere. It was published by the Department of Religious Education, Orthodox Church in America, and is available through the DRE, P.O. Box 675, Syosset, NY 11791.

Orthodoxy and Abortion

Abortion: The Church's Stance

Every human being is created by God, bears the image of God, and receives the gift of life in order to glorify God and to enjoy eternal communion with Him. Christian teaching, therefore, insists upon the *sacredness* of human life from its inception.

The question at the heart of the abortion debate is: What precisely is the moment of life's inception? When does human life begin? This is the crucial question, since in American society the willful taking of a human life is still condemned as murder. Those who favor abortion-on-demand ("pro-choice") are not philosophically "pro-murder." Rather, they deny that the fetus is truly human.

The Orthodox Church has always taught that human life begins at conception, when a sperm unites with an ovum to produce a genetically unique, living being. In denouncing abortion in his own day, St. Basil the Great declared, "She who purposely destroys the fetus shall suffer the punishment of murder...and we pay no attention to the distinction as to whether the fetus was formed or unformed" (Canons 2 and 8). The patristic consensus holds that the soul is created at conception. We express this truth liturgically by celebrating feasts of the conception of St. John the Baptist (Sept. 24), of the Holy Mother of God (Dec. 8), and of our Lord himself (Annunciation, March 25).

259

Orthodoxy concludes, therefore, that abortion induced at any stage of pregnancy is a form of homicide; and it brings guilt upon the one who performs the act as much as it does upon the mother herself.

Exceptions and "Hard Cases"

Given this stance, can the Church ever admit exceptions? In those increasingly rare cases where a medical choice must be made between the life of the mother and that of her unborn child, it is morally permissible to favor the mother. This is not because she is a full "person" whereas the fetus is merely "potential life," for both are equally human. It is rather because of the mother's place and responsibility within the family, where her nurturing and loving presence directly affects the lives of her husband and other children.

Nevertheless, a mother who willingly surrenders her own life in favor of her infant performs the profoundest act of Christian charity. "Greater love has no one than this," Jesus declares, "than that he lay down his life for his friend" (Jn 15:13). Any such decision, however, must be made in light of the needs and wishes of other family members, since the family as a whole constitutes a covenantal body that reflects the love between Christ and His Body, the Church (Eph 5). It is advisable, therefore, that the couple, together with their spiritual advisor, openly and frankly discuss such an eventuality during the early stages of the pregnancy.

The twin traumas of rape and incest are often invoked as justifiable grounds for abortion. Both acts are by their very nature brutal and dehumanizing. Pregnancies so induced, however, are extremely rare. Whenever a woman does become the victim of rape or incest, she should seek immediate medical treatment to prevent conception if at all possible. The science of embryology has determined that fertilization, the union of the nucleus of the sperm with the nucleus of the ovum, takes at least thirty-six hours to complete. This leaves a "window" of well over a day for such intervention to occur, without the risk of aborting a *conceptus*, recognized by the Church as a human "person" as well as a human "individual."

From a very young age children should be sensitively yet frankly taught about the place and function of sexuality within the conjugal relationship. They should also be taught that sexual violence occurs, both within and outside the family, and that they need feel no shame if they become its victim. Rather they should seek whatever medical, spiritual and psychological treatment may be needed to heal the wounds of the trauma as well as to avoid conception.

If pregnancy does occur as a result of rape or incest, then the child should be brought to term and, if the mother is unable to accept responsibility for it, the baby should be given up for adoption. This is a "hard teaching," to be sure, especially in our society where abortion has become an accepted and legally sanctioned form of birth control. It is a tragic fact that faithful Christian women, too traumatized by rape to seek medical attention, have committed suicide because a well-meaning pastor or family member has pressured them to bear the conceived child. The "sanctity of life" principle applies as much to the mother as to the child in such cases, and in the rare instance where the trauma is so severe that it constitutes a real danger to the mother's life, abortion after implantation (which occurs within six to eight days after conception) may be the lesser of two evils. The concept of "trauma," however, must never be extended to cover cases which involve merely the mother's discomfort, embarrassment, anxiety, financial limitations, career plans, etc. Nor may it be morally invoked in cases where the mother becomes pregnant as a result of freely engaging in sexual intercourse.

Does the Church condone abortion in cases where the child is determined by genetic screening (amniocentesis, chorionic villus sampling, etc.) to be genetically defective, destined to live with a severe, life-long handicap? Given the inherent sacredness of every human life, the answer can only be that it does not and can not. In some cases, as with Down's Syndrome, it is the parents or other care-givers who feel the handicap, not the child. In others, such as severe cases of spina bifida, medical technology can provide significant relief to the patient, enabling him to lead a relatively pain-free and creative existence. In the rare instances of highly debilitating and incurable diseases, such as the Lesch-Nyhan syndrome or cystic fibrosis, the dilemma seems more acute since unrelieved physical and mental suffering can accompany the illness, and prolonged treatment can impose an intolerable financial burden upon the family. There is no more moral justification for aborting such children, however, than for killing a "defective" newborn who can survive with proper medical attention and loving parental care. Given the origin of life at conception, abortion is as reprehensible as infanticide. The tragedy of our age is that the latter is becoming as acceptable in the popular mind as the former. If we can destroy the unborn, why should we not do away as well with the unwanted newly born? The question may seem repugnant; yet it is being asked in ever more strident tones today, even by would-be Christian ethicists.

An Orthodox Response

Contrary to claims made by pro-abortion activists, pregnancy does not involve just the woman and her own body. Pregnancy is a *relationship* created between the mother and the unique, personal being who lives and grows within her. Whether she acknowledges it or not, her own life belongs to God and is wholly under his dominion. The same is perforce true of her unborn child.

Orthodox Christians in the United States live in a society in which six percent of young women have had at least one abortion by the time they reach the age of 15, and the rate is increasing. Teenage pregnancy is not the only reason for abortion, but it is a major one. The Church must teach young and old alike the meaning of sexuality and the need for sexual responsibility. It must do all possible to convince Christian young people that overt sexual activity has its proper place only within the context of a sanctified, heterosexual conjugal union. And it must stress as well the full and equal moral, spiritual and financial responsibility of the father in any instance where a child is conceived. Such instruction cannot be left to the schools or other organizations within our society, since these have proven more often than not to undermine Christian ethical values. The uncontrolled spread of AIDS today is in large part due to the popular option for so-called "safe sex" over authentic moral principle.

But it is not enough for us as Christian people simply to state the Church's traditional position on the matter of abortion. Every effort must be made to provide for unwanted or abused children, who cannot or should not be raised within their family of origin. This means providing financial support where necessary, both for the mother and the child, and working for legislation that will responsibly ease adoption procedures throughout the country. It means, in short, that we cannot reasonably condemn abortion unless we are willing to assume responsibility for the welfare of unwanted children who are brought to term, irrespective of their health, mental capacity, or racial background.

Speaking of the depth and breadth of Christian responsibility within the Church and within God's world, St. Paul provided an image that applies as well to our responsibility towards those who would seek abortion and those who would be victims of it: *"We, though many, are one body in Christ, and individually members one of another"* (Rom 12:5).

If we refuse to apply this image to the issue of abortion, we betray not only the unborn but the Author of Life himself. And conversely, to offer adequate material support and loving care to "one of the least of these" is to offer reverence and service to him as well.

Further Reading:

— Fr. Stanley S. Harakas, *Contemporary Moral Issues Facing the Orthodox Christian*, (Minneapolis: Light & Life Publishing) 1983, Part III, "Sex and Family Issues."

— Fr. John Kowalcyzk, *An Orthodox View on Abortion*, (Minneapolis: Light & Life Publishing) 1979.

The Tenth All-American Council of the Orthodox Church in America produced the following affirmation, distributed throughout the parishes on Sanctity of Life Sunday, Jan. 18, 1998.

Synodal Affirmation On Abortion

Abortion is an act of murder for which those involved, voluntarily and involuntarily, will answer to God.

Those finding themselves confronted with tragic circumstances where the lives of mothers and their unborn children are threatened, and where painful decisions of life and death have to be made—such as those involving rape, incest, and sickness—are to be counselled to take responsible action before God, Who is both merciful and just, to Whom they will give account for their actions.

Women and men, including family members and friends of pregnant women considering abortions, are to be encouraged to resist this evil act, and be assisted in bearing and raising their children in healthy physical and spiritual conditions.

Women who have had recourse to abortion, men who have fathered aborted children, and others involved in cases of abortion, are to be provided with pastoral care which includes recognition of the gravity of the act and assurance of the mercy of God upon those who repent of their sins.

Orthodox Christians are to contribute to legislative processes according to their knowledge, competence, ability and influence, so that laws may be enacted and enforced which protect and defend the lives of unborn children while being sensitive to the complexities and tragedies of life in contemporary society.

Appendix 2

Reflections on the Problem of Suicide

"A suicide kills two people,
Maggie, that's what it's for!"

—Arthur Miller
After the Fall, Act III

"Suicide" refers to the taking of one's life through a free exercise of will. It implies an intentional and voluntary act of self-destruction, free from both external and internal constraints.

Suicide, therefore, must be clearly distinguished from such acts as "voluntary passive euthanasia," where the terminally ill patient or their proxy refuses life-support measures (a decision that does not conflict *a priori* with Christian responsibility in the face of impending death; a point made in chapter 5 of this book, one that has been repeatedly affirmed by Orthodox as well as non-Orthodox ethicists). It must also be clearly stated that the death of Jesus and of zealous martyrs such as St. Ignatius does not constitute suicide either, since they were actually executed by external authorities. This remains true despite Jesus' affirmation, "No one takes my life; I lay it down of myself [i.e., of my own free will]" (Jn 10:18).

From the works of the ancient Greeks, through David Hume's *Essay on Suicide*, philosophical writings have defended a perceived human right to commit suicide under certain circumstances: protracted unbearable pain, situations of dishonor, the completion of a life's work, a signal from the gods that one's time has come, etc. Plato's *Phaedo*, with some ambivalence, argues the case for suicide (cf. esp. 62C), while there is no ambivalence at all in the arguments presented for it by Cynics, Stoics and even some Epicureans. Cicero expresses the widely held conviction that the god(s) must signal the moment, or provide a "valid reason" (*causam iustam*), for committing the act.

265

Then, says Cicero, "with certainty your true wise man will joyfully pass forthwith from the darkness here into the light beyond" (Tusc. disp. I.74). The consensus in antiquity held that suicide committed under proper circumstances would lead directly to immortality.[1]

Until recently, the case for suicide was generally limited to writings such as *The Myth of Sisyphus* by the French existentialist Albert Camus, who declared that suicide constitutes "the only truly serious philosophical problem." Increasingly in our day, however, ethicists and exegetes are posing questions as to its legitimacy and desirability, particularly in light of advances in biomedical technology that have transferred the "final sting" from death to the dying process.

These scholars point out that condemnation of suicide as an irredeemable sin dates only from the time of St. Augustine, and that Scripture nowhere explicitly condemns the act. There are five cases of suicide recorded in the Old Testament: Abimelech (Jg 9:54); Saul and his arms-bearer (1 Sam 31:4f; 1 Chr 10:4f); Ahithophel (2 Sam 17:23); and Zimri (1 Kg 16:18). The New Testament knows only the case of Judas (Mt 27:3-5), whose suicide constituted a sign of repentance and remorse. Intertestamental Judaism records several suicides that represent acts of courage or honor (cf. 2 Macc 14:37-46; and Josephus' praise of Eleazar and the Jews at Masada who resorted to suicide in order to escape capture by the Romans, *Jewish War* VII.320ff). In no case is the act *per se* condemned; rather it appears as a noble alternative to dishonor or humiliation. St. Augustine developed his polemic against the taking of one's life in the context of a denunciation of the pseudo-martyrdom practiced by certain Donatists, which was, he argued, merely a form of suicide.[2] From this time on, Western theologians increasingly depicted suicide as self-murder, until it virtually replaced "blasphemy against the Holy Spirit" as the one unforgivable sin.

A similar attitude toward suicide developed in the East, particularly under the influence of the Alexandrian Patriarch Timothy I (381-85). In his "Canonical Answer 14" he declares that unless it can be clearly determined that the suicide victim was "truly out of his mind" when he took his life,

1   See A.J. Droge, "*Mori Lucrum*: Paul and Ancient Theories of Suicide," *Novum Testamentum* XXX/3 (1988), 263-286.
2   J. Bels, "La mort volontaire dans l'oeuvre de S. Augustin," *Revue de l'histoire des religions* 187 (1975), 147-180.

"no offering ought to be made in his behalf."[3] This clearly presupposes an existing practice and attitude that firmly opposes serving either a burial or a memorial service in cases of "rational suicide." It is on this authority that the Nomocanon 178 utters a similar prohibition. The Velikii Trebnik appeals to this same authority: "If anyone takes his own life, sing nothing over him nor remember him except if he were insane" (rubrics for the memorial service), as does Bulgakov,[4] who notes the agreement of a number of patriarchal directorates. N. D. Patrinicos[5] expresses the present-day Orthodox consensus, that no funeral service, church burial or memorial services may be held for those who "as a result of their own volition have cut themselves off from the communion of the Church." It is noteworthy, nonetheless, that until the late fourth century, Christian witnesses are either silent on the issue or regard it in a positive light, insofar as it might be assimilated to martyrdom.[6]

What are the theological grounds for the Orthodox Church's rejection of suicide as a moral option? Comments on the issue focus regularly on two fundamental themes: the creation of human persons in the image and likeness of God (Gen 1:26); and the conviction that life is a gift from

---

3 It should be noted, however, that Timothy's answer is aimed at protecting the priest, who might be led to serve a burial or memorial service at the urging of relatives and friends of the deceased who insist upon his insanity. The Answer concludes: "It is incumbent, therefore, upon the Clergyman in any case to investigate the matter accurately, in order to avoid incurring judgment," meaning judgment upon himself. *The Rudder (Pedalion)*, Chicago: Orthodox Christian Educational Society, 1957, p. 898. A note in the *Pedalion* alludes to a precedent in the person of "the Presbyter of a certain monastery of St. Pachomius [who] ordered that two nuns who had committed suicide should not be accorded memorial services."

4 "A person who has consciously committed suicide is denied Christian burial" (rubrics for the burial service). See S. V. Bulgakov, *Nastol'naia Kniga dlia Sviashchenko-Tserkovno-Sluzhitelei* (*"Desk Book for Clergy"*; Karkhov, 1900).

5 *A Dictionary of Greek Orthodoxy*, NY: Greek Orthodox Archdiocese of North and South America, 1984, p. 346.

6 A. J. Droge, *art. cit.*, has recently defended the view that St. Paul was favorably disposed toward suicide, considering it a legitimate means for dying and "being with Christ." His argument is based on the Apostle's statement in Phil 1:21-23, "for me to live is Christ and to die is gain," and particularly on his "lusting after death" (*tēn epithymian echōn eis to analusai*). This, he holds, is confirmed by 2 Cor 5:1-8, as well as by such affirmations as Gal 2:20; 2 Cor 4:8-11; and Rom 8:38f. See as well his more popular presentation, "Did Paul Commit Suicide?", *Bible Review* V/6, Dec. 1989, 14-21. At best, Droge has demonstrated that Paul longed to die in order to deepen and fulfill his communion with the risen Christ. In my opinion, his argument for Paul's "suicide" is weak and unsubstantiated, presupposing as it does that the Apostle had adopted a "Socratic" attitude toward the act (the Phaedo, as interpreted by the Stoic philosopher Epictetus). See also A. J. Droge and J. D. Taylor, *A Noble Death. Suicide and Martyrdom Among Christians and Jews in Antiquity* (San Francisco: Harper, 1992), the most thorough study to date from a biblical and patristic perspective.

God, originating in him and standing under his dominion. As a gift, human existence calls forth responsibility in the form of "stewardship." Our life belongs not to us in the first instance but to God our Creator, to whom we are called to offer ourselves as a "sacrifice of praise." Because he is Lord of life and death, of the living and the dead, this self-offering must be total, embracing every aspect of our earthly existence from conception to decay.

If we owe both life and death to God in his role as Creator, we do so all the more because of his self-sacrificing activity as Redeemer. The gift that we can offer of ourselves to him is simply our response to his infinitely greater gift to us in the person of Jesus Christ. "Thine own of Thine own" involves first ourselves, as bearers of the divine image, and only then does it involve the Holy Gifts; just as we invoke the descent of the Spirit first upon ourselves, and only then upon the Bread and Wine, that both we and the eucharistic offering might be transformed into the Body of Christ. Accordingly, the chief focus, the primary object of divine love and concern, is upon the *person*, understood as an indivisible psychosomatic entity, a being whose material aspect participates essentially in the healing, saving "way" of sanctification and deification. Our biological existence, then, serves in some fashion as a "type" (*typos*) of life in the Kingdom of God. It images our eternal life, which preserves our somatic as well as our spiritual identity (1 Cor 15:44).

Destruction of that psychosomatic whole through suicide is condemned by many voices within Orthodoxy as an irreversible and therefore unforgivable act of rebellion against God as both Creator and Redeemer. In Bulgakov's terms, it defiles both self and God, representing "a complete lack of faith" in divine providence. As such, it is the ultimate expression of blasphemy. Bulgakov even refers to one who takes his life as "a spiritual descendant of Judas the Betrayer, rejecting God and rejected by God."

However we may assess Bulgakov's conclusion that someone who takes his or her own life is "rejected by God," it is clear that his overall view represents the prevailing attitude toward suicide within the Orthodox Church. The very term is emotionally laden, to the point that any questioning of that attitude is likely to call forth charges ranging from moral insensitivity to heresy.

Yet it is precisely because of the emotional charge that has been invested in the word "suicide" that so much confusion has arisen concerning the Church's proper attitude towards the act itself. For it is no secret that today, just as in fourth-century Alexandria, the normative penalty for "rational suicide"—denial of burial or memorial services—is often suspended, particularly where the deceased is a beloved member of the family or church community. We seem to sense that something is not quite right about that refusal, even though we (rightly) remain convinced of the immorality of suicide as such. Consequently, we either fall back on "tradition" and unreflectingly and unbendingly refuse to bury the victims as a matter of principle; or we look, with a certain desperation, for some convincing sign of their insanity.

The dilemma posed by suicide obliges us to raise certain questions about the one universally accepted justification for burying persons who have taken their own life: the matter of insanity. What in fact constitutes "insanity," and how are we to arrive at the kind of determination in any given instance of suicide that will enable us to make a just, right and proper decision regarding burial? With regard to the concept "insanity," it must be pointed out that it is vague and misleading, rather like the terms "mad" and "crazy." It is not a proper diagnostic term and therefore is not even considered in the standard *DSM-IV*.[7]

Ethicists and psychologists have long argued over whether or not there is really such a thing as "rational suicide."[8] Is a person who takes his own life ever in full possession of his rational faculties? Can he ever be said to be fully "sane"? The Orthodox, and until recently the Roman Catholic, tradition has historically answered this question in the affirmative. In fact, most discussions of the matter seem to presuppose that the person who commits suicide does so as a free agent and that the act itself results from a free exercise of will. If that will is in any way diminished, it is seen as being due to "moral weakness," "sin," a "lack of faith," or (again, Bulgakov's words) "despair" and "blasphemy."

---

7   *Diagnostic and Statistical Manual of Mental Disorders*, 4th. ed., pub. by the American Psychiatric Association, Washington, DC, 1994.
8   For a useful contribution to the debate, that concludes that rational suicide does exist, see S. Hauerwas, "Rational Suicide and Reasons for Living," *On Moral Medicine* (S. E. Lammers & A. Verhey, eds.), (Grand Rapids: Eerdmans, 1987), 460-466.

In the light of recent discoveries in the disciplines of human psychology and neuroscience, this judgment needs to be reconsidered. This does not mean that "rational suicide" does not exist and carry with it the full weight of moral responsibility. It does mean, however, that *far more cases of suicide than have heretofore been recognized involve "insanity" or its neurological equivalent.* That is, most suicidal acts proceed less from "sin" or "moral weakness" than from factors beyond the control of the victim, such as "recurrent major depression" (MDR) and "post-traumatic stress disorder" (PTSD). These conditions have received inordinate publicity in the past few years, and many diagnoses have been made too rapidly and too lightly. Nevertheless, the conditions definitely exist, are widespread, and amount to serious and debilitating illnesses.

Recent studies have demonstrated a statistically significant correlation between suicide and the impairment of neurotransmitters.[9] And it is a well-known fact that diseases such as Parkinson's and similar neurological disorders affecting the basal ganglia result in a depletion of dopamine and consequent depression, often marked by a mood downswing of such intensity that the patient succumbs to what amounts to a suicidal "drive" or "impulse."[10]

Simple chemical imbalances within the body (e.g., those involved in premenstrual syndrome or PMS) can have similar effects, as can thyroid dysfunction. In the process of grief there are clinically established stages through which the patient passes on the way to "release." From initial denial, through feelings of "sadness" and "craziness," one moves toward anger and then hope. The stage of "hope," however, is normally characterized by mood swings that sink to depression or "despair," in which the susceptibility to suicide is greatly increased.

The relatively new field of "family systems therapy" has shown that in households where at least one adult is actively alcoholic—particularly if

9   John J. Mann, "Post Mortem Neurochemical Correlates of Suicide," a lecture given in the Dept. of Neurology, Cornell University Medical College, NY, Jan. 9, 1986. See the appended quotations.
10   On 23 March, 1998, the Associated Press announced that two Swedish physicians, reporting in the *British Medical Journal*, have discovered a significant correlation between use of calcium channel blocker drugs (used in cases of high blood pressure and angina) and suicide. Despite the extraordinary advances made recently in knowledge of the functioning of brain chemistry, medical researchers admit they are investigating the tip of the iceberg.

the alcoholism is accompanied by verbal, physical or sexual abuse—children often grow up suffering from PTSD, and manifest the same symptoms of confusion, lack of self-esteem, guilt and rage that characterized so many veterans of the Vietnam war. Unable to express their anger outwardly toward the offending adult, they tend to "bury" or "stuff" it, turning it in upon themselves in a pathology of self-destruction. Post-traumatic stress disorder is an alarmingly widespread fact of our social life, occasioned as much by dysfunctional family systems (drugs, alcoholism, sexual abuse) as by the trauma of war.[11]

This list could easily be extended. I offer it not to deny that rational suicide exists, nor to weaken the Church's strong and proper moral stance against suicidal acts. I do so, rather, as grounds for an appeal: that we reconsider the criteria upon which we make judgments in cases of suicide, to take into account the psychological and neurochemical factors that might lie behind the choice for self-destruction. It is no longer sufficient to ask concerning a suicide victim, "Was the person insane?" The question has no real meaning for us today, given the advances that have occurred recently in the field of medical science. Rational suicide does indeed exist. Often the motivating factor is uncontrolled anger that leads a person to "kill two people": oneself (physically) and the other (emotionally) who is the object of one's hostility. In such cases, the person acts on the basis of his or her own sin and rebellion against God and self, and they bear full moral responsibility for taking their own life and grievously wounding the lives of others. But with our present knowledge of the mechanism of suicide, we must be aware of and pastorally sensitive to the fact that often such persons are victims of pathologies over which they have little or no control, and for which they can not and should not be held responsible.

This implies, however, that we should "presume innocence" until responsibility for the act can be established beyond doubt. Our present practice (as in Patriarch Timothy's Answer 14) is to presume that suicide is a product of the will acting in freedom. In many if not most cases, as clinical evidence irrefutably demonstrates, this is not true. The will is impaired by sin; but it is also impaired by disease and various forms of abuse that mark a person from childhood to the grave. Christian charity will

11 See *DSM-IV*, 424-429.

recognize this fact in the light of modern medical research, and it will make its judgments accordingly.

Another element in the debate over suicide, considered briefly in chapter five of this book, needs to be mentioned here as well. The question is posed today whether we should accept suicide in cases of terminal illness or even there where the "will to live" has for some reason been diminished. Should we, in other words, affirm choices such as Elizabeth Bouvia's or Janet Adkins'? In the former instance, Bouvia, a handicapped woman severely afflicted with cerebral palsy, wanted the courts to mandate that the hospital allow her to starve herself to death yet continue to offer palliative care. In the latter, Mrs. Adkins, afflicted with early stage Alzheimer's Disease, took her own life using Dr. Jack Kevorkian's "death machine." Both committed what would normally be considered a rational suicide, although Bouvia manifested certain symptoms of clinical depression. Should the Church condone such acts?

The answer can only be "no," whether the suicide victim acted "rationally" or under the constraints of mental or physical illness. There is great pressure in our country today from well-meaning but misguided groups such as the Hemlock Society, that would "institutionalize" suicide as a humane way to end life with peace and dignity. The only "dignity" that accrues to human existence, however, lies in the gift of divine life that fills and sustains it. Since God is indeed "closer to us than our own hearts," he alone has the power, the authority and the love capable of bestowing genuine "dignity," ultimate meaning and value, upon both our life and our death. Our death thus belongs to him as fully as does our biological and spiritual life.

There is an essential *social* dimension to our existence that also militates against accepting suicide as a legitimate means to end our life. We belong to God, and we belong to one another in the Body of Christ. While one might accept suicide in principle for those outside the Church, to do so would doubtlessly lead down the "slippery slope" to intolerable abuse. The Church, in other words, must say "no" to acts of self-destruction.

But does it follow that those who succumb to this most terrible of temptations should not receive proper liturgical burial within the Church, if they were communicating members during their lifetime? My conviction is that the ambiguities surrounding suicide, the complexities of the issue itself, together with the uncertainties that inevitably remain regarding the psychological (and neurochemical) state of the victim, at the very least justify the principle: when in doubt, grant a church burial and memorial services. Would such a practice, grounded in love for the deceased and for the often guilt-ridden survivors, really offend God?

A final word in this regard by the eminent Protestant ethicist Stanley Hauerwas seems relevant: "Suicide is not first a judgment about the agent, but a reminder that we have failed to embody as a community the commitment not to abandon one another." [12] Suicide is a tragedy, yet it involves each of us as members of the one Body. And to some degree, its responsibility falls upon us all.

Since our understanding of the vast variety and complexity of causes that can lead one to self-destruction is still at an elementary level, to refuse a suicide victim proper ecclesial burial is to exercise a judgment upon the person that God alone can properly render. Shouldn't our response to such an act be rather to "weep with those who weep," both the deceased and his or her loved-ones (who often suffer a crushing burden of both guilt and grief), while we surrender ourselves and the departed brother or sister to the mercy of God?

This appeal that we reexamine the motivations and impulses behind suicide, once again, is not made with the intention of weakening the Church's strong stance against willful acts of self-destruction. It is made rather with the hope of strengthening her still stronger commitment to love, compassion and pastoral responsibility.

In conclusion: Modern medical research has produced conclusive evidence that many factors—genetic inheritance, child abuse, clinical depression, a "broken home," as well as hormonal imbalance or depletion of certain neurotransmitters—can actually create a self-destructive impulse over which the victim (perhaps the term "patient" is more appropriate) has little or no control. In light of this evidence, we need to rethink our approach both to those who commit suicide and to those who suffer most from their death. Perhaps the time has come to produce a liturgical service that would allow burial, but where the tragic and fallen condition that led to the act is fully acknowledged: something analogous to the penitential marriage service.

12 *Art. cit.*, 403.

The following includes a few sample quotations from relevant scientific studies on the etiology of suicide drawn from J. J. Mann and M. Stanley, *Psychopathology of Suicidal Behavior*, Annals of the New York Academy of Sciences, vol 487, 1986. They demonstrate that in the majority of cases there are psychosocial and neuropsychological correlates of suicide which lead to the kind of cognitive distortion usually associated with clinical depression. Suicide, in other words, is more often a medical problem than a (uniquely) spiritual one.

— Once assumed to result primarily from depressive disorders, suicide "is now regarded as the end point of some combination of genetic, psychobiological, psychosocial, and drug-related factors." (Mann-Stanley, Preface, ix)

— Influences in a child's social environment can create "vulnerability to suicidal behavior." In 91% of sample cases of suicide and attempted suicide, the homes examined were rated either unstable or chaotic. A major factor is deteriorating personal relationships in the family, leading to fear of imminent rejection. Consequent depression, complicated by drugs and alcohol, often leads to impulsive suicide attempts. (K. S. Adam, "Early Family Influences on Suicidal Behavior," in Mann-Stanley, 63-71. See also H. Henseler, "The Psychology of Suicide," in *Concilium* 179 (3/1985), 21-28. Henseler recalls that the sociologist E. Durkheim, in 1897, was the first influential researcher to suggest that most suicides are not the product of a free will.)

— Repeated interpersonal losses play "a significant precipitating role in both attempted and completed suicide." This is particularly true when several such losses occur within a matter of a few months. Depression—due to or coupled with a lack of social supports (family, friends) and especially early loss of one or both parents—"appears to represent a predisposing psychosocial risk factor for suicidal behavior in adulthood..." (C. K. Cross and R. M. A. Hirschfeld, "Psychosocial Factors and Suicidal Behavior," Mann-Stanley, 77-86.)

— Suicide runs in families. While psychological factors are significant, recent studies have confirmed "beyond a doubt that there are genetic factors in suicide" that can lie behind family histories of self-destructive behavior. (A. Roy, "Genetics of Suicide," Mann-Stanley, 97, 101).

— Abnormal neurochemical activity, especially low levels of serotonin, has been shown to create pathological depression and lead to suicide. The chemical 5-HIAA (5-hydroxyindoleacetic acid, a neurochemical related to serotonin) correlates with impulsiveness, aggressiveness and suicide attempts. (J. J. Mann et al., "Postmortem Monoamine Receptor and Enzyme Studies in Suicide," Mann-Stanley, 114ff. See as well the following study by Stanley, Mann and Cohen, "Serotonin and Serotonergic Receptors in Suicide," 122ff.)

— The widely used antidepressant Prozac and other SSRIs (selective serotonin re-uptake inhibitors) seem to work by maintaining normal levels of serotonin in the brain. Families and pastors of persons with suicidal tendencies should inquire of a physician as to whether SSRI treatment would be appropriate for persons who appear to be potentially self-destructive.

An especially interesting group of studies has been made recently on the "unconscious" factors that lead to suicidal behavior. See A. A. Leenaars and D. Lester (eds.), *Suicide and the Unconscious* (London: Jason Aronson, Inc., 1996), Parts II ("Theoretical Perspectives on Suicide and the Unconscious") and III ("Studies of the Unconscious and Suicide"). Of particular interest is the article by Herbert Hendin, "The Psychodynamics of Suicide," 13-31, which considers the importance of depression, anxiety and panic disorders as sources of suicidal ideation.

To return to the definition given at the beginning of this appendix: the term "suicide" should be restricted to "the taking of one's life through a free exercise of will." It signifies a *rational* act and carries the full weight of moral responsibility. Acts of self-destruction that are not verifiably rational—for which there is evidence of a neuropsychological, genetic or environmental etiology—do not bear that same weight of personal responsibility. Whether it is "physician-assisted" or performed with complete autonomy, the act of taking one's own life under such "non-rational" circumstances is a tragic one that calls for understanding and forgiveness on the part of the family and the community (the parish, the network of friends and other relationships).

The Church's responsibility in such cases is to welcome both the deceased and those most wounded by this tragic death, and to offer them to the loving mercy of God. Pastoral care will focus on healing for the bereaved, avoiding any judgment or condemnation. Only God can understand the complex factors that lead to suicide, whether it appears "rational" to us or not. Our role is to surrender the victim into God's gracious care, while we bear witness to the truth that the saving love of Christ is stronger even than self-inflicted death.

Appendix 3

An Orthodox Perspective on Cremation

"Cremation" refers to the disposal of a dead body by reducing it to ashes through a process of burning.

Historically, cremation was widely practiced throughout the ancient Near East, except by Jews and Egyptians. Among the ancient Hebrews, bodies were burned as an extension of the death penalty: e.g., in cases of sexual "depravity" (Lev 20:14 and 21:9—the punishment of death by fire rather than cremation as such), and the collective purging from Israel's midst of Achan and his family (Jos 7:25). Yet it appears that partial cremation was also practiced in some circumstances in order that the remaining bones might be transferred to a proper place of burial (1 Sam 31:12f; Amos 6:9f). So-called "secondary burial"—disinterment for purposes of transferring bones to a family ossuary—was in any case widely practiced (2 Sam 21:12-14; cf. Gen 25:8; 35:29; Num 20:23). In certain cases (e.g., Saul), partial cremation seems to have been an accepted practice in order to facilitate such a transfer immediately after death, prior to inhumation. The likely state of bodily decay may also have contributed to the decision to submit Saul's remains to limited burning. The intention, however, was not to reduce the body to ashes, but to facilitate transfer of the bones for proper burial.

The dread of exhumation and non-burial expressed in Jer 8:1f and 25:33 (cf. Rev 11:9) confirms the importance for an Israelite of being "gathered to the fathers." Such a "gathering" presupposes that even where partial cremation was practiced, some bodily remains were preserved. This has significance for the later Christian cult of relics.

If indeed the ancient Israelites practiced occasional cremation to permit the transfer of bones, the practice is condemned by the Mishna and does not appear during the intertestamental period. This may be due to the growing belief among Jews in a personal existence after physical death that would suggest burial as proper preparation.[1]

Cremation was widely practiced throughout the Roman Empire until the fifth century when, under Christian influence, it was finally abolished. Early Christians insisted upon burial rather than cremation because of the entombment and bodily resurrection of Jesus. Special veneration for Jesus' intact physical body was demonstrated by the large quantity of expensive myrrh and aloes provided by Joseph of Arimathea, and the concern of the Myrrhbearing Women to complete the burial rites in strict accord with Jewish custom. The catacombs bear witness to the care early Christians took in recovering and preserving the bodies of their martyrs. By the mid-second century, such preservation served the interests of a growing cult of relics (cf. The Martyrdom of Polycarp).

Patristic tradition seems generally to condemn cremation as a dishonoring of the dead (esp. Tertullian), probably in light of Gen 3:19 ("You are dust, and to dust you shall return"). This phrase occurs in the Orthodox burial service and is often cited as a proof-text for accepting inhumation as the only acceptable Christian practice.

In the mid-19th century (1844, 1846) the Roman Catholic Church felt obliged to condemn cremation that had reappeared under secular influence. The penalties then enacted were rescinded, however, by instruction of the Holy Office on July 5, 1963, and modern Catholic service books include an office to be prayed at the crematorium. By the 1960s, certain Catholic ethicists were speaking in favor of cremation as a means of countering American funeral customs that demonstrate an exaggerated concern to preserve the body from corruption.[2]

1 Other biblical sources generally opposing cremation are given by J.J. Davis, *What About Cremation? A Christian Perspective* (Winona Lake, IN: BMH Books, 1989), esp. ch. 4. This is a well-balanced treatment of the issue by a noted Evangelical biblical scholar, archaeologist, and ardent bass fisherman.

2 See H. Richard Rutherford, "Honoring the Dead: Catholics and Cremation," in *Worship* 64/6 (1990), 482-494. He observes: "...from the perspective of [Catholic] liturgical law, cremation is simply a technologically accelerated process of physical decomposition." With a growing number of Roman Catholics today, Rutherford gives no consideration to the question of inhumation in the interests of preserving possible relics. Protestant Christians, who tend to reject the very notion of relics, generally see cremation as a reasonable alternative to abuses of the "American way of death," including embalmment, expensive caskets, and other mortuary costs. See William E. Phipps, "The Consuming Fire for Corpses," in *The Christian Century* (4 March, 1981), 221f.

Modern secular arguments in favor of cremation include economic and ecological considerations. Incineration of a body is much less costly than the usual (American) funeral, which averages from $4,000-$6000. Then again, coffins are largely nonbiodegradable, while cremation disinfects and disposes of bodies that otherwise might transmit disease or be the source of epidemics. Nevertheless, since embalming is not legally required and simple coffins are available, the economic argument is moot. And today adequate precautions can be taken in cases of disease to prevent its spread via a dead body. A widespread epidemic may so overburden health care facilities and mortuaries that cremation is deemed necessary. Yet even in such cases Orthodox bishops have refused to sanction cremation.[3]

A further argument in favor of cremation concerns the instinctive horror some people feel at the thought of being buried in the earth. This is a psychological problem, however, rather than a theological or spiritual one. In fact, if the actual process of cremating a dead body were more widely known by the general public (incineration of the soft tissue, crushing of the bone fragments, frequent mixing of one person's "cremains" with another's, together with errors and neglect in modern columbaria), cremation might not seem as simple, dignified and antiseptic as it is usually thought to be.

Neither the canonical nor the dogmatic tradition of the Orthodox Churches prohibits cremation. There are, however, "definite opinions against it," to the point that certain local rulings oppose it "on penalty of the departed Orthodox being deprived of the funeral and burial rites."[4] The question is whether such penalties are consistent with the Or-

---

3   See the article by Fr. George Papaioannou, "Cremation vs. Burial Rites," *Orthodox Observer* (7 December, 1988), p. 5. He notes that in the summer of 1987 a heat wave killed more than a thousand people in Athens. The city mayor requested the Archbishop "to reconsider his opposition on the cremation of the dead, for special hazardous situations. The Church of Greece refused the request."

4   N. D. Patrinacos, *A Dictionary of Greek Orthodoxy*, 104. The prohibition of cremation by Metropolitan Nicholas of the Carpatho-Russian Archdiocese (*The Church Messenger*, 22 September, 1996) is particularly severe in this regard: "[C]remation of the body...is contrary to our faith and to holy tradition. A church funeral is to be denied to any believer who has been or will be cremated, having had full knowledge of the church's teaching and having made a deliberate decision to proceed with cremation regardless. Requiem services afterwards are forbidden to such individuals because the person in question has already abandoned hope in the Lord, who will come one day to raise the soul and body from death." Given the disgust many

thodox position regarding the human body and the proper means for laying it to rest. The matter can only be addressed on theological grounds, by reviewing key biblical and patristic attitudes toward the body and physical death. Some of the elements of such a review may be noted as follows.

Support for burial as opposed to cremation may be found in Christ's own burial in view of bodily resurrection, as well as in the raising of Lazarus. Jewish belief held that after a body had been dead four days, irreversible decomposition had set in. By raising his friend at this moment, Jesus demonstrates his lordship over death and corruption. Such a demonstration could not have been made, of course, had Lazarus been cremated. The fact that he was raised bodily from a tomb further foreshadows both Jesus' own resurrection and the general resurrection of the dead (Jn 5:28f).

But while this serves as an eloquent prophecy of bodily resurrection, it does not, as is often maintained, constitute an argument one way or the other concerning cremation, since nothing indicates that divine power would be limited by the actual physical condition of the body to be raised. Accordingly, Orthodoxy has never held that a person whose body is consumed in a house or automobile fire, or is even vaporized by a nuclear bomb, is for that reason incapable of being resurrected. The same, *a fortiori*, must be affirmed of martyrs burned at the stake.

First Corinthians 15:42-50 is often invoked as an argument against cremation. The passage, however, refers to the raising of a spiritual body (*sôma pneumatikon*) as opposed to a physical body (*sôma psychikon*), and therefore it is irrelevant to the debate over cremation or burial. St. John Chrysostom's remarks indicate that the physical condition of a dead body has no bearing on its transformation into a spiritual body capable of inheriting eternal life: "Let us despise death...for indeed it will translate us to a far better life. 'But the body decays,' [you say]. Why, on this account most especially we ought to rejoice, because death decays, and mortality perishes, not the substance of the body" (Hom XXXIV.4 on Matthew; here "substance" is equivalent to St. Paul's "spiritual" body). And again:

Orthodox (and other Christians) feel today toward abuses connected with usual American funeral practices, it is not clear that all those who opt for cremation do so having "abandoned hope in the Lord." But Metropolitan Nicholas expresses a universally held view among Orthodox Christians concerning the "importance of the bodily dimension of the human person," a view that is fully consistent with Church Tradition.

"By sowing here [1 Cor 15:42] (St. Paul) means not our generation in the womb, but the burial in the earth of our dead bodies, their dissolution, their ashes" (Hom XLI.5 on 1 Corinthians).

"Ashes" in this context does not refer to cremation as such, but it does show how little value the physical body possesses compared to its reality as a raised "spiritual body." In this regard, St. Ignatius' remarks are relevant. Writing to the Romans, he implores them not to interfere with his martyrdom, but to allow his physical body to be completely devoured by beasts in the arena: "Suffer me to be eaten by the beasts, through whom I can attain to God...entice the wild beasts that they may become my tomb, and leave no trace of my body [*mēthen katalipôsi tôn sômatos mou*], that when I fall asleep I be not burdensome to any" (Rom 4.1-2). From these patristic readings, it is clear that one's physical body can be completely destroyed, as a result of burial in the earth or by some other means, without in any way jeopardizing one's salvation.

The strongest arguments against cremation are Christ's own burial and the place of relics within Orthodox piety.

St. Paul uses the expression "co-buried" (*synthaptô*) with Christ to describe Christian baptism (Rom 6:4; Col 2:12). Baptism marks the true death and rebirth of the believer; yet "resurrection" is to be achieved only in the eschaton. Buried with Christ through the Church's ritual, we await bodily resurrection and participation with him in his own glory. Therefore it is important theologically to preserve continuity between the living physical body and its condition after death. Once again, however, this importance is relative: salvation is in no way jeopardized there where the body is reduced to ashes or otherwise destroyed (as in the case of St. Ignatius; yet relics of the great Antiochian martyr have been preserved).

The sacredness of the human body is manifested most strikingly by the incorrupt relics of the saints. In Fr. Harakas' words, "These saints were so sanctified and transfigured by the Holy Spirit dwelling within them that their bodies also bear the marks of holiness and serve as a source of sanctification and healing power for believers even today."[5] Thereby they witness as well to the truth that every Christian is called to be—in body as in soul—a "temple" of the Holy Spirit (1 Cor 6:19f).

5 *Contemporary Moral Issues,* 183.

For theological and pastoral reasons, then, inhumation of the intact physical body should be regarded as normative and desirable for Orthodox Christians. Nevertheless, laws in some countries and states (Japan, Louisiana) require cremation in certain regions, and such laws should be respected. Cremation may also be mandated by civil authorities in times of epidemics. When for some (relatively) acceptable reason cremation is required, the ashes should be interred rather than scattered, in order to permit visitations at the burial site and the celebration of memorial services.

A final consideration in favor of cremation should be mentioned. Population density in urban areas increasingly reduces the land available for interment. As Prof. John Erickson observed in our discussion of this issue, we may soon find ourselves obliged to consider cremation as a means for keeping the deceased of a local community close to the place of worship, thereby facilitating visitation and memorial services, and fostering a sense of abiding communion with those who have passed on before us.

Nevertheless, Orthodoxy and Christian tradition in general have strongly opposed cremation, insisting that the proper way to dispose of the dead is through inhumation. As we have stressed throughout this book, Orthodox anthropology is holistic. It conceives of the human person as a unity of soul and body, the spiritual and material. From a biblical perspective, the very concept of "body" includes flesh, mind and spirit. The physical body, therefore, is to be honored and protected, so that in those rare but important instances where the person attains genuine sanctity, the body in the form of sacred relics might be preserved and venerated.

Quotations

Introduction:

—St. Irenaeus of Lyons, *Adv. Haer.* IV.20.7.

—Abba Joseph of Panephysis, in *The Sayings of the Desert Fathers. The Alphabetical Collection.* Tr. by Benedicta Ward, SLG (London & Oxford: Mowbrays, 1975), 88.

—St. John Climacus, *The Ladder of Divine Ascent.* Tr. Archimandrite Lazarus Moore (Willits, CA: Eastern-Orthodox Books, 1973), 266.

Chapter 1:

—St. Basil the Great, *Treatise on the Holy Spirit* 16, quoted in O. Clément, *The Roots of Christian Mysticism* (London: New City, 1993), 64.

—Bishop Kallistos Ware, "In the Image and Likeness: the Uniqueness of the Human Person," in *Personhood. Orthodox Christianity and the Connection Between Body, Mind, and Soul,* ed. John Chirban (Westport, CT & London: Bergin & Garvey, 1996), 11.

Chapter 2:

—St. John Chrysostom, *Homily on Eph.* 5:22-33; *On Marriage and Family Life* (NY: St Vladimir's Seminary Press, 1986), 52, 57, 61.

—Simone Weil, quoted in W. H. Auden, "A Certain World."

Chapter 3:

—St. Irenaeus, *Adv. Haer.* IV.38.3.

—St. Gregory Nazianzen, *Theological Oration* 45.

—St. Gregory of Nyssa, *On the Soul and the Resurrection* 9.

Chapter 4:

—C. S. Lewis, *The Abolition of Man* (London: Geoffrey Bles, 1967), 41.

Chapter 5:

—Prayer for the terminally ill, *Orthodox Euchologion*, quoted in Stanley Harakas, *Living the Faith. The Praxis of Eastern Orthodox Ethics* (Minneapolis, MN: Light & Life Publishing, 1992), 129.

—Peter Kreeft, *Love is Stronger than Death* (San Francisco, CA: Ignatius Press, 1992), 67.

Summary:

—St. Irenaeus of Lyons, *Adv. Haer.* IV.20.5.

—St. Silouan, "Adam's Lament," in Archimandrite Sophrony, *Saint Silouan the Athonite* (Essex, England: Monastery of St. John the Baptist, 1991), 456.

Appendix 2:

—Arthur Miller, *After the Fall*, Act III.

Index